From Pigskin to Saddle Leather:
The Films of
Johnny Mack Brown
by
John A. Rutherford

The World of Yesterday
Waynesville, North Carolina
1996

ISBN: 0-936505-13-3

Library of Congress Catalog Card Number: 96-61207

Published by
The World of Yesterday
Route 3, Box 263-H
Waynesville, NC 28786-9551
Phone (704) 648-5647

First Printing 1996 9 8 7 6 5 4 3 2

Manufactured in the United States of America

Dedication

This book is dedicated to all those great "B" Western people, both in front and behind the camera, who gave us kids so much pleasure during our formative years.

Also, I wish to express my appreciation to my wife who was uncritical and put up with a "B" Western fan who never outgrew his childhood.

OTHER BOOKS BY JOHN A. RUTHERFORD

Cowboy Shooting Stars with Richard B. Smith III

More Cowboy Shooting Stars with Richard B. Smith III

Acknowledgments

Photos used in a book like this are always hard to round up. But this book seemed to be a lot harder than usual. White Hats need to be handed out to several people for going into their private collections and helping us: TOM MCLAUGHLIN, BOBBY COPELAND, JIM STRINGHAM, MERRILL McCORD, JOHN M. BRETH, ED BILLINGS, JOHN ARNOLD, NORMAN FOSTER for the picture of the Birthplace of Johnny Mack Brown used on the back cover and to RAY PENCE at Jerry Ohlinger's Movie Material Store, GAYLA at Film Favorites, and lastly RON and LINDA DOWNEY at World of Yesterday. You are all good guys with White Hats.

Johnny Mack Brown and his trusty steed from a scene in **The Oregon Trail** (Universal, 1939). (Courtesy of Jerry Ohlinger's Movie Material Store.)

CONTENTS

A publicity photo of Johnny Mack Brown from early in his career. (WOY Collection.)

1 • Football Hero

A gentleman on screen and off, Johnny Mack Brown was truly the cowboy from Alabama. Noted for his soft southern drawl, his flashing good looks and outstanding athletic ability, he was an obvious choice to become an enduring western film star during the heyday of the "B" cowboy film. Indeed, his entrance into the movies was almost a movie screenplay in itself.

Johnny Mack Brown was born in Dolthan, Alabama on September 1, 1904. He was one of nine children from a most respected old family of Alabama. His grandfather had been the first settler in the area. With a six foot build and being naturally athletic, Johnny became a highly capable football player while in high school.

In 1923, when he enrolled at the University of Alabama, Johnny tried out for the football team and easily made the squad. During his first game for the University he caught one of the longest passes on record against Georgia Tech. In a game with Kentucky he ran 100 yards to score the winning touchdown. And, as if both college and football were not enough to keep him busy, Johnny found time to work part time in a local shoe store and to participate in collegiate dramatics. (Parrish, James Robert. *Great Western Stars*. New York: Ace Books, 1976, pp. 29-38.)

Johnny was selected as the captain of the 1925 University of Alabama football team. Then on New Year's Day in 1926 he attained national fame for his catch of the longest pass yet thrown in a Rose Bowl Game. It was 65 yards and allowed Alabama to defeat the University of Washington 20-19. (*Ibid.*) His fellow football teammates gave Johnny Mack Brown the nickname, "Dum Dum," perhaps reflecting his explosive (like a "Dum dum" bullet) running power when he had the pigskin.

According to The New York Times story on January 2, 1926, "Johnny Mack Brown led the attack as the southerners hustled the ball across the purple line thrice in rapid succession..." (Sports, p. 16.) The newspaper article went on to say that in the third period of the game Johnny Mack caught a pass from quarterback Huburt of 65 yards and a touchdown. This set a new record for football, both in the nation and the world. Not done yet, Johnny made another touchdown and knocked down a last desperate pass by the University of Washington team. It truly was Johnny's day in the Rose Bowl game of 1926.

Johnny Mack's collegiate football career thus ended on a glorious note. For his exploits in the Rose Bowl Game, he was named the game's outstanding player. Previously, he had already been named All Southern Conference Halfback for both 1924 and 1925. In addition to his great catches, Johnny was also well known for his end around plays on the outstanding undefeated

1926: Johnny was football Captain for the University of Alabama before M-G-M signed him up.

Mack Brown of Alabama (1925 titlist) is trailed by referee Walter Ec... ...go, 1905) and stalked by Herman Brix of Washington in the Rose B...

Johnny Mack Brown of Alabama and Herman Brix (later Bruce Bennett and a movie star also) of Washington in a exciting moment from the 1926 Rose Bowl game. (Photo courtesy of Tom McLaughlin.)

Alabama team of 1925 which was coached by Wallace Wade. (Mendall, Ronald L. and Phares, Timothy B. *Who's Who In Football*. New York: Arlington House, 1974, pp. 48-49.)

In 1957 Johnny Mack Brown was inducted into the National Football Foundation Hall of Fame. He was the only western film star to achieve such additional fame. At his induction he commented: "... because we were the first southern team to participate, we were supposed to be kind of lazy down South, full of hookworms and all. Nevertheless, we came out here and beat one of the finest teams in the country, making it a kind of historical event in southern football. We didn't play just for Alabama, but for the whole South." (Obituary, The New York Times, November 16, 1974, 34:1.)

Paralleling the film careers of other former pigskin performers such as John Wayne and Charles Starrett, Johnny Mack found his entrance into motion pictures as an actor rather easy. Accounts

differ slightly as to how he first became interested in a film acting career. Based upon the account in his obituary in The New York Times, his first contact with the film industry came about in Alabama. According to the story, a film crew was on location in Birmingham for the filming of **Men of Steel**, a motion picture starring Victor McLaglen. The crew and cast attended an Alabama football game and were introduced to the players following the game. George Fawcett, a character actor, remembered Johnny Mack Brown well from his exploits in the Rose Bowl Game the year before and encouraged Johnny to look him up if he came to Hollywood.

Later, in 1927, when Johnny returned to California as an Alabama football assistant coach during the school's second straight Rose Bowl Game appearance, he contacted Mr. Fawcett. The actor, in turn, introduced Johnny to the famous film director, Erich Von Stroheim, who

10

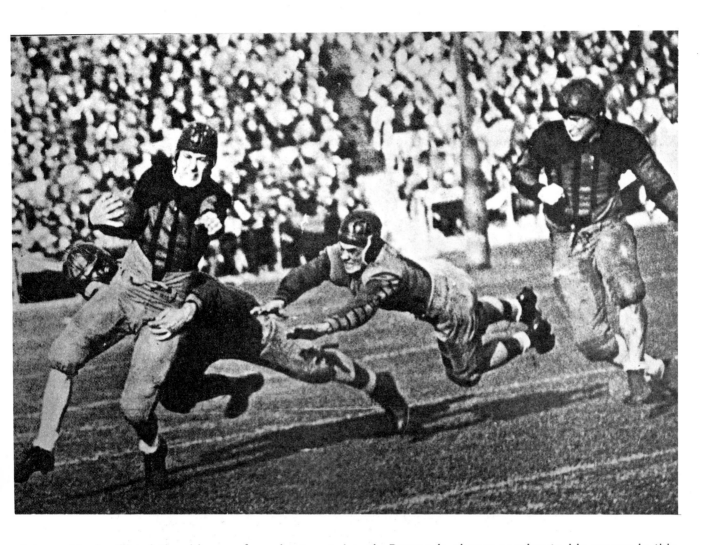

Johnny Mack still twisting his way for a long run; Lovely Barnes is shown coming to his rescue in this scene from the 1926 Rose Bowl game. (This Xerox is Courtesy of Tom McLaughlin.)

supposedly "... cupped Brown's face in his hands, gazed into his eyes and said, 'You could be an actor.'" (*Op. cit.*)

Parrish gives a slightly different account in his book. It was at the 1927 Rose Bowl Game that Johnny first talked with George Fawcett, "who had earlier advised him to take a screen test." Johnny had apparently ignored this recommendation then, but now wished to have the test. With Mr. Fawcett's help, he was given the screen test and then placed under contract to Metro-Goldwyn-Mayer Studio. (*Op. cit.*, p. 29.)

Both stories complement each other and likely both are true, at least in part. Regardless, it was the sort of story that Hollywood studio publicists dream of. Johnny Mack Brown was on his way in the movies.

Meanwhile, Johnny's personal life had continued. Johnny had married his college sweetheart, the former Cornelia "Connie" Foster, after the big Rose Bowl victory in 1926. She was the daughter of a prominent Tuscaloosa judge. Over the years their marriage was to produce four children: Jane; John Lachlan; Cynthia and Sally. By the age of 23 Johnny was beginning his family as well as his film career, both of which were to be long lasting.

11

The Boys in Hollywood

COACH WADE talking to the team in a practice preceding the game.

JOHNNY MACK BROWN telling Clements, Campbell, and Singington all about the camera at the M-G-M Studios.

A page from The 1931 Corolla the yearbook of the University of Alabama. Fred Singington, in the upper right picture, is still living in Birmingham. He played major league baseball for a few years in the late 30s. (This Xerox is Courtesy of Tom McLaughlin.)

2 • Early Days in the Movies

When Johnny began his film career, the silent film era was coming to its end. However, visual appearance was still what filmmakers were most interested in when discovering new star material. Johnny's handsome face and clean cut personality, along with his superb physical stature, made him a natural for the juvenile leading man type. His sports background and athletic ability caused him to be cast initially in films about sports and youth. His first picture at M-G-M was a baseball film, starring William Haines, entitled **Slide, Kelly, Slide** (1927).

However, Johnny's first real leading role in pictures was in **The Fair Co-Ed** (M-G-M, 1927) in which he played a youthful basketball coach. His co-star was Marion Davies who portrayed a "flapper" basketball star of the girl's team. She has to win Johnny away from the college "vamp". For his performance in this film Johnny received fine notices as shown by this review: "Johnny Mack Brown serves this picture well as the wonderfully fortunate coach." (*The New York Times Film Reviews* New York: Arno Press, 1971, pp. 394.)

In 1928 Johnny moved up into major films as he co-starred with Greta Garbo in a drama about a great actress in the Sarah Bernhart mold, **The Devine Woman** (M-G-M, 1928). He played a young admirer of the great actress. That same year he was loaned out to Fox for several small budget productions, playing opposite Madge Bellamy. In **Soft Living** (Fox, 1928) Johnny played a young newlywed with problems. Again he received good reviews for his performance: "Mr. Brown is eminently satisfying as the good looking man who wants to marry for life." (Mordaunt Hall, *The New York Times Film Reviews*, p. 439.) In **The Play Girl** (Fox, 1928) he played a character who was vamped by golddigger Madge Bellamy. He also received a good review for his work in this film. (Mordaunt Hall, *The New York Times Film Reviews, Op. cit.*, p. 439.)

Back at M-G-M, Johnny was cast opposite a young Joan Crawford in yet another picture about the wild young people of the roaring twenties, **Our Dancing Daughters** (M-G-M, 1928). In the film Johnny played a young heir to a multi-million fortune who does not marry the wild living girl played by Joan Crawford. The hard drinking flapper then tries to lure Johnny away from his trusting wife.

Next, he was co-starred with Norma Shearer in **A Lady of Chance** (M-G-M, 1928). In this film Shearer is a crooked lady who falls for Johnny while trying to swindle a fortune away from him. However, it turns out that our hero is not really rich at all, but just a young inventor who lives with his mother. Johnny is hard at work on a formula for a revolutionary new cement mix. After being caught for her fraudulent activity, Norma refuses to involve Johnny in her blackmail racket and is sent up to the reformatory. But Johnny hunts her down and secures a parole for her. An interesting sidelight to this film is Johnny singing a song. Remember, the film is silent. Does this make Johnny one of the first singing cowboys? Tom Mix had done the same thing in his film, **Riders of the Purple Sage** (Fox, 1925).

He followed this film with another role opposite Greta Garbo in **A Woman of Affairs** (M-G-M, 1928). Johnny played the unfortunate husband of a famous star. Because of her reckless living, Johnny's character commits embezzlement and ultimately dies by his own hand, jumping from a hotel window. John Gilbert was also a co-star in this film.

In 1929 Johnny appeared in films for several other studios, notably United Artists, Fox, Columbia and RKO. He supported Paul Muni in **The Valiant** (Fox), a melodrama about a ruthless killer. Back at M-G-M, Johnny once again was cast in support of Greta Garbo as a young man driven to suicide by a woman. His last film that year was **Jazz Heaven** (RKO), a musical with sound. In the picture Johnny portrayed a young man from the South who is flat broke, owning nothing but a melody and a bum piano. Sally

Wallace Beery as Sheriff Pat Garrett and Johnny Mack Brown as Billy the Kid talk on the set of **Billy the Kid** (MGM, 1930). This film launched Brown's western movie career. (Courtesy of Bobby Copeland).

O'Neill played the girl singer who lived in the same rooming house. They join forces and become musical successes in radio broadcasting.

In this way Johnny made the transition from silent to sound pictures. Although his speaking voice was strong enough for sound films, his distinctive southern drawl was to prove a handicap in his rise to stardom. Movie producers were looking for voices with stage diction rather than regional dialects for the new medium of talking pictures. However, Johnny had now made 18 pictures, including several starring roles, during his first three years in films, so his future in sound films was not in jeopardy. Soon he would make his first western film, an omen of things to come.

Johnny began 1930 in a melodrama at Universal, entitled **Undertow**, co-starring with Mary Nolen. He played a lighthouse keeper who goes blind and whose wife is unfaithful to him. He was now rather typecast as the tragic young man whom women would mistreat. However, in this film he regains his sight and saves the day.

Then M-G-M cast him in a western film, albeit a modern one, **Montana Moon** (1930), opposite Joan Crawford again. She played a wild Manhatten girl who flees her strict but wealthy father to a swanky dude ranch in Montana. There she meets Johnny, a ranch cowhand, and lures him into wedding her. But she finds life on the ranch too slow for her taste and when city slicker Ricardo Cortez shows up on the ranch, she flirts so shamelessly with him that Johnny gets riled up and puts his foot down. Angry at Johnny, Joan leaves him to return to New York. But Johnny, masquerading as a Mexican bandit, stops her train and steals her back. The result, of course, is a happy ending. It was a small western film beginning, but a beginning just the same.

The western film was regaining its popularity with sound films now that the technical problems with outdoor films had begun to be solved. **In Old Arizona** (Fox, 1929) had earned Warner Baxter an Oscar as best film actor and **The Virginian** (Paramount, 1929) with Gary Cooper had been a

Frank Hagney talks to Sheriff Pat Garrett (Wallace Beery) as Billy the Kid (Johnny Mack Brown) looks concerned in this scene from **Billy the Kid** (MGM, 1930). (WOY Collection.)

top money maker so M-G-M had decided to enter the lucrative outdoor film market too. For its initial entry it chose to make **Billy the Kid** (1930), the story of the legendary youthful gunman of the Southwest.

Johnny was cast as the famed outlaw gunfighter and Wallace Beery as his friendly antagonist, Pat Garrett. As with most of its projects, M-G-M went first class. King Vidor, fresh from his successful **The Virginian**, was chosen to direct the film. William S. Hart, the veteran silent western film star, was employed as technical advisor. It was Hart himself who coached Johnny on how to draw his six-guns and mount a horse. The film was shot on location in Lincoln County, New Mexico, where Billy the Kid had lived and died. Johnny used the Kid's own guns, borrowed from Hart, in the film. Thus, it was not surprising that the picture was faithful to the look of the old West or that it "... recaptured some of the grimness of **Hell's Hinges, White Oak** or **Tumbleweeds**." (All Hart films.) (Adams, Les and Rainey, Buck.

Shoot-Em-Ups. New York: Arlington House, 1978, pp. 43-44.)

To cap it all, the film was shot in an experimental 70mm wide screen size to capitalize on the panoramic scenes in the picture. However, this limited its showing in many small town theaters across the country where the western films were the most popular. But M-G-M was giving Johnny the big build-up to make him its top action star.

Yet not everyone was happy with Johnny Mack being cast as the lead. King Vidor, the director, opposed his casting, stating that Johnny looked more like a varsity athlete than a ruthless young outlaw. (Eames, James. *The M-G-M Story.* New York: Crown Publishers, Inc., 1977, p. 70.)

However, both Johnny and Wallace Beery gave excellent performances in the film and found highly receptive audiences wherever the picture could be shown. Johnny Mack Brown had made his indelible mark as a western film star although he was about to falter in other aspects of his motion picture career.

A publicity photo for **Billy the Kid** (MGM, 1930) showing Johnny waiting patiently to enter the stage door where filming is going on to "shoot" a scene for this production. (WOY Collection.)

Following **Billy the Kid**, Johnny was cast as the wagon master in a historical epic, entitled **The Big Meadow** (M-G-M, 1931). It was the story of pioneers who trekked from Virginia to Kentucky in 1776. The picture was based upon the Edna Maddox Roberts historical novel of the same name. Like most filmed historical dramas, it was not exactly a roaring success at the box office, but it allowed Johnny to continue to show his potential in outdoor action films.

Johnny worked again with Wallace Beery in a gangster film, entitled **The Secret Six** (M-G-M, 1931). In the film they were joined by another young M-G-M hopeful, a male actor named Clark Gable. Both young men played reporters. As the studio was developing its young actors for bigger things, Johnny was in competition with Gable for stardom. His southern drawl was beginning to limit his potential at the studio for some types of films. However, he continued to get good reviews for his performances: "Brown (is) better than in sometime," commented The New York Times.

(Wednesday, May 6, 1931, p. 23.) Yet it was Gable whom M-G-M decided to make their top star rather than Johnny. When his contract with M-G-M ran out, the studio did not pick up his option.

In the next few years Johnny Mack Brown would move about among the smaller studios, taking roles wherever he could get them. The great depression was in full swing and an actor not under contract to a major studio found the going rough.

As he moved from studio to studio, Johnny appeared in lesser films. In **The Last Flight** (First National, 1931), a film about World War I airmen returning from the war, starring Richard Barthelmess, Johnny played a young former airman who dies from the foolish act of throwing a flying tackle at a fighting bull. In a low budget action film for Monogram, **Flames** (1931), he portrayed a playboy about town with tailored clothes and a fancy roadster who learns about real life as a fireman.

16

Johnny Mack Brown and Noah Beery, Jr. in a climatic scene from **Fighting with Kit Carson** (Mascot, 1933). (Courtesy of Jim Stringham.)

Then he made another western film, **Lasca of the Rio Grande** (Universal, 1931), starring Leo Carillo. Johnny was the Texas Ranger for whom a dancing girl sacrifices her life to save him during a cattle stampede. Previously he had let her go free after she had killed a man. Slowly Johnny was becoming more and more identified with western films. He followed **Lasca** with another western picture at Paramount, **The Vanishing Frontier** (1932). Johnny was cast as the debonair bandit chief of Spanish origin in old California. In the film he opposes the cruel Mexican military, but falls in love with the daughter of his arch enemy and carries her off to his bandit lair where he entertains her by playing the piano. Although the film gave Johnny a demanding role with a different dialect, that of a Spanish Robin Hood, the plot of the film was so unbelievable that the film was not successful. (Hardy, Phil. *The Western*. New York: William Morrow and Co., Inc., 1983, p. 40.) Even the usually supportive trade journal, <u>Variety</u>, was derisive toward the film,

commenting: "There are times when Brown, both in voice and mannerisms, does a perfect Maurice Chevalier. The whole thing is so exaggerated it doesn't register, even as a fable." (Tuesday, September 20, 1932, p. 15.)

In a second Paramount film, **70,000 Witnesses** (1932), Johnny was cast as a football player who was murdered by the villainous team doctor. His football renown frequently had resulted in Johnny's being cast in sports films.

But now that he was no longer a rising young M-G-M star, Johnny's career was definitely at a low ebb. The great depression was having its effect upon Hollywood with filming in a decline and work hard to find. Johnny found himself taking roles at "poverty row" studios just to have work. Such films as **Malay Nights** (1932), made for Mayfair, were about all he could find. Again, <u>Variety</u> was not favorable in its review: "No particular appeal and a safe booking only where there is nothing else." (Tuesday, February 7, 1933, p. 13.)

17

Noah Beery, Jr., Johnny Mack Brown, Helen Gibson, Betsy King Ross, and Noah Beery, Sr. in a scene from **Fighting with Kit Carson** (Mascot, 1933). (WOY Collection.)

That same year Johnny made a western serial at Mascot Pictures, **Fighting With Kit Carson**. He had sunk far from mighty M-G-M, but little did he know that he was entering a new phase of his film career. More about that later. Throughout 1933 and 1934 Johnny would be busy making low budget pictures or taking small parts in bigger films in order to hold on to his fading film future.

At Universal in 1933 he appeared in support of Robert Young in yet another football film, **Saturday's Millions**. At First National he played one of the several handsome young workers that rich girl Ruth Chatterton arranged to have brought to her mansion to be seduced by her in **Female** (1933). According to Variety, Johnny's role had him give "in like a creampuff under a steamroller." (Tuesday, November 7, 1933, p. 10.) What a comedown for our former football hero and future cowboy star!

In **Son of a Sailor** (First National, 1933), a Joe E. Brown comedy about life aboard an aircraft carrier, Johnny played the love interest to the young heroine, Jean Muir. Then, teamed with Charles Starrett, another young budding "B" western film star, Johnny played a young ship's officer in the ZaSu Pitts comedy, **Three on a Honeymoon** (Fox, 1934). His love interest was Sally Eilers who played a spoiled rich girl. In **Cross Streets** (Invincible, 1934) Johnny portrayed a surgeon who becomes a hobo after being disillusioned about the practice of medicine. Twelve years later as a bum he is called upon to perform surgery and saves a life. But then, after his gallant comeback, he is killed by a jealous husband.

That same year he returned to Paramount and was cast as the second lead to Mae West in **Belle of the Nineties**. He played the handsome, well-to-do-young man with whom Mae dallied for a while until she tired of him. In these years Johnny Mack Brown's film career was full of ups and downs. At times it appeared that he was about through. But around the corner another phase of his movie career was about to begin that would last for many years.

3 • Early "B" Westerns

Since 1930 Johnny Mack Brown had shown that he could perform well in western films. Thus, during his hard times it was natural for him to move into a series of "B" western films. In 1935 Johnny hooked up with a "poverty row" film company, Supreme Pictures, headed by A.W. Hackel, although the latter half of these films were distributed through Republic, a newly formed film company with which Hackel had become associated. Bob Steele was already making a western series for Supreme when Johnny became its other western star.

The Supreme films and those released by Republic were fine examples of "B" western pictures. In addition to Hackel's production values, they sported such directors as Robert N. Bradbury (Bob Steele's father), Sam Newfield, S. Roy Luby and Albert Ray. Johnny's leading ladies included Lois January and the beauteous Iris Meredith among others. The supporting casts sounded like a roll call of "B" western character actors: William Farnum; George Hayes; Earl Dwire; Charles King; Forrest Taylor; Ted Adams; Horace Murphy; Jack Rockwell; Karl Hackett; Edward Cassidy; Warner Richmond; Dick Curtis; Dick Alexander; Slim Whitaker; Bud Osborne; Budd Buster; Steve Clark; Jim Corey; Dick Alexander; John Merton; Ernie Adams; Frank Ellis; Frank LaRue; Syd Saylor; Earle Hodgins; Bob Kortman and Al St. John. Villains, old codgers, sheriffs, henchmen, and ranchers were all there.

Johnny's first Supreme western picture was **Branded a Coward** (1935). The story was interesting enough but, according to Don Miller, was "badly let down by Nobel's poor cinematography and Snell's weak development of an interesting story." (*Hollywood Corral*. New York: Popular Library, 1976, pp. 49-50.) In a flashback the audience learns that Johnny had seen his parents killed in a gun battle when he was a little boy. As a result he now becomes panic stricken when faced with gunfire. He has to overcome this psychological problem as he takes on the villain who is revealed to be his own brother at the end of the picture. Syd Saylor with the stammer and bobbing Adam's apple was the comic relief for the picture. It was an unusual, but not particularly satisfying beginning to Johnny's career as a "B" western film series hero.

Bur his next oater was a dandy, maybe one of his best films overall. **Between Men** (Supreme, 1935) tells the story of a son searching for his father who was forced to flee as an outlaw years before. The father, played by William Farnum, believes his son was killed in the incident that turned him into an outlaw. The script was by Robert N. Bradbury which Don Miller believes might have been intended originally as a vehicle for his own actor son, Bob Steele. (*Hollywood Corral*, p. 49.) Although made on the usually slim budget of an independent "B" and with attendant short cuts such as weak camera work at times, the filmed story presented its involved plot in a straight forward manner. The acting of Farnum, Johnny Mack and Earl Dwire, who played the villain, was superior. Seen today, more than 50 years since it was made, the film holds up well and is head and shoulders above most other oaters of its period.

The third film in the series, **The Courageous Avenger** (Supreme, 1935), was somewhat slower in action and less of an epic tale. Johnny played a special agent sent to capture a band of outlaws who raid ore shipments from mines. It is also a vengeance tale as the bandits have killed Johnny's girl's brother who was also his best friend.

The bandits use silver bullets which they make from a hidden desert silver mine. They force men they find wandering in the desert to work their mine while they rob shipments from the other mines. Johnny tracks down the outlaw band, saves the kidnapped heroine from them and reveals a mine foreman to be in cahoots with the raiders. Warner Richmond played the bandit leader and Ed Cassidy the crooked foreman.

Johnny Mack Brown, Mary Pickford and Charles Farrell at a party put on by The Thalians (a Hollywood social organization) at the Cocoanut Grove of the Ambassador Hotel in November 1932. (WOY Collection.)

In **Valley of the Lawless** (Supreme, 1936), directed by Bradbury, Johnny was given the support of George Hayes. Hayes played a non-comedic, dramatic role as Johnny searches for lost gold from a doomed wagon train which has been hidden for years. After whipping an outlaw leader in a fair fight, he is nicknamed "Tiger" by the bandit chieftain. Then he has to compete with the heroine and her youthful brother in locating the lost treasure.

Desert Phantom (Supreme, 1936) was a good western picture with both Charles King and Karl Hackett as the nasties who are attempting to fleece the heroine, Sheila Manners, out of her ranch. Johnny played the mysterious stranger who goes to work for the girl and protects both the ranch and the girl from the marauders. This picture was a remake of Harry Carey's **The Night Rider** (Artclass, 1932).

Johnny played an undercover secret service agent, masquerading as a highwayman in **Rogue of the Range** (Supreme, 1936). This film sports two heroines for Johnny, a girl on a gospel wagon whom he saves from a runaway team and a saloon gal for whom he falls, all while trapping an outlaw gang and their leader.

In **Everyman's Law** (Supreme, 1936) Johnny was a disguised ranger who pretends to join an outlaw gang. As the "Dog Town Kid", he and his fellow rangers hire themselves out to a rancher who is attempting to rid his range of homesteaders. However, Johnny and his confederates turn on the rancher and help the homesteaders, routing the crooked cattlemen. Horace Murphy was the sheriff in this one.

The Crooked Trail (Supreme, 1936) was a most unusual "B" western film that featured a superb villainous role for John Merton along with an exceedingly strong plot. Johnny played a well known gunfighter who comes upon two unconscious men in the desert just as he is heading for the gold fields. He saves them and

20

Mrs. Johnny Mack Brown and her son John Lachlan Brown in April 1937. Some newspaper editor in the past has put crop marks on the photo. (WOY Collection.)

one becomes his partner in a mining claim. Then Johnny falls for a girl and marries her. Merton, jealous of the new bride's influence upon Johnny, tricks her into running off with him in order to get back at Johnny. When Johnny pursues them, Merton shoots the girl and flees with Johnny hot on his heels. After a lengthy chase and fierce fist fight, Johnny prevails. He returns to his wounded wife to learn that she had been faithful to him all the while. It was an unusually complicated plot for a "B" western film with an excellent character role for Merton who carried it off well.

Undercover Man (Republic, 1936) had Johnny as a Wells Fargo agent who rescues a girl and saves the gold in a stage holdup. He then sets out to trap the leader of the outlaw gang, the local saloon owner.

In **Lawless Land** (Republic, 1936) Johnny was a Texas Ranger who rides into town, solves several murders and gets the girl, Louise Stanley. Ted Adams supplied the villainy and Horace Murphy the comedy.

Bar Z Badmen (Republic, 1937) had Johnny play a dual role in this film. He was the hero who arrives at a cabin in the woods only to find his twin brother dieing of a gunshot wound, received at the hands of fellow badmen. Johnny takes his dead brother's place in order to bring the gang to justice in the end.

Gambling Terror (Republic, 1937) provided Johnny with an excellent role himself in a "B" western picture. He played a gunfighting gambler who comes to town to set up a casino in the local saloon. There he finds an extortion gang has been terrorizing the local townspeople. After refusing to knuckle under to the toughs, Johnny takes a hand as a local lawman to end the reign of terror of the gang. Then he pretends to get in with the leader of the gang until he can secure enough evidence to arrest them. In the end he not only does in the outlaws and gets the girl but he also changes from the "gambling terror" into the

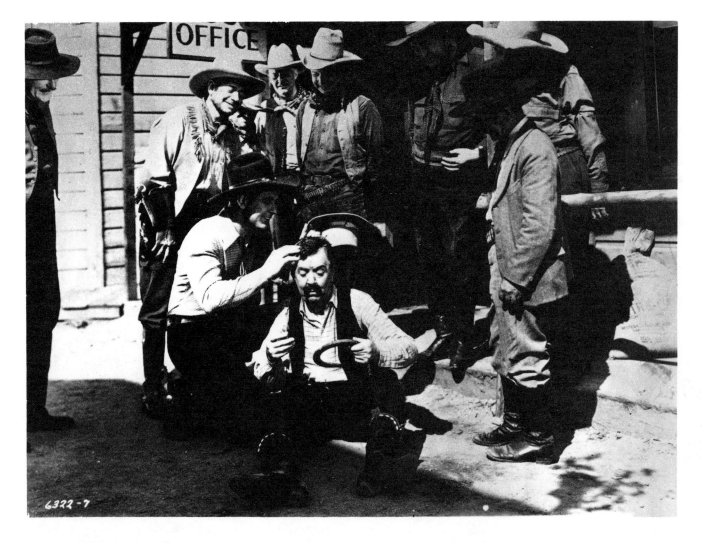

Johnny Mack Brown examines Horace Murphy's head in this scene from **Lawless Land** (Republic, 1936). (WOY Collection.)

local hero.

Trail of Vengeance (Republic, 1937) had Johnny playing another of his by now well known gunfighter roles. He rides into a range war to find out what has happened to his brother. His reputation causes both sides to try to secure his services. However, he has to face an equally adept gunman in the person of Warner Richmond, the chief villain.

In **Guns in the Dark** (Republic, 1937) Johnny played a character who is tricked into thinking he has accidentally killed his best friend in a saloon gunfight. He then discards his guns and goes to another town to forget. There he runs into a gang of rustlers who are engaged in a range war with a girl rancher and her riders. When the real killer of his friend turns up as the brains behind the gang and makes off with the girl, Johnny goes after her. Without guns he has to use both his fists and wits to rescue her. When the Mexican police nab the outlaw gang, Johnny is about to be arrested for the shooting of his friend south of the border. Then he is exonerated, revealing the bandit leader as the real killer. Syd Saylor provided the laughs as well as the surprise ending.

A Lawman Is Born (Republic, 1937) had Johnny as a wild young man who comes to town where a local marshal and his wife decide to help him reform. When the marshal is shot down, Johnny takes his place to clean up cattle thieves and land grabbers. Iris Meredith played the heroine and Warner Richmond a worthy villain. Variety's review of the film was quite positive: "A first class western, much better acted than most." (Wednesday, July 7, 1937, p. 13.)

Johnny wound up his series for Hackel and Republic with **Boothill Brigade** (Republic, 1937). This oater was about a range war between ranchers and squatters. Johnny played a rancher who defends the nesters and riles his girl, the daughter of another rancher. But he rights himself with her as he corrals the behind-the-scenes

Johnny Mack Brown and Captain Leroy Monsky (All-American guard on the right with his eye bandaged) welcome the Crimson Tide in December 1937 when they played in Pasadena. (WOY Collection.)

manipulator of the trouble. Dick Curtis supplied the brawn as the chief henchman with whom Johnny trades blows. Variety was even more enthusiastic about this film, calling it "one of the better acted sage sagas." (Wednesday, September 29, 1937, p. 15.) Johnny was singled out for his performance also: "Johnny Mack Brown is one of the most acceptable action stars in the Hollywood badlands. Dialogue throughout is way above the hackneyed." (*Ibid.*) Republic did not seem to realize what it had in Johnny Mack Brown and soon he would go on to better things.

The Hackel-Republic series had firmly established Johnny Mack Brown as a "B" western film star of the first order. The films had generally been considerable above average in story and extremely well acted and produced. Johnny was now headed for the top of the line in oaters at Universal.

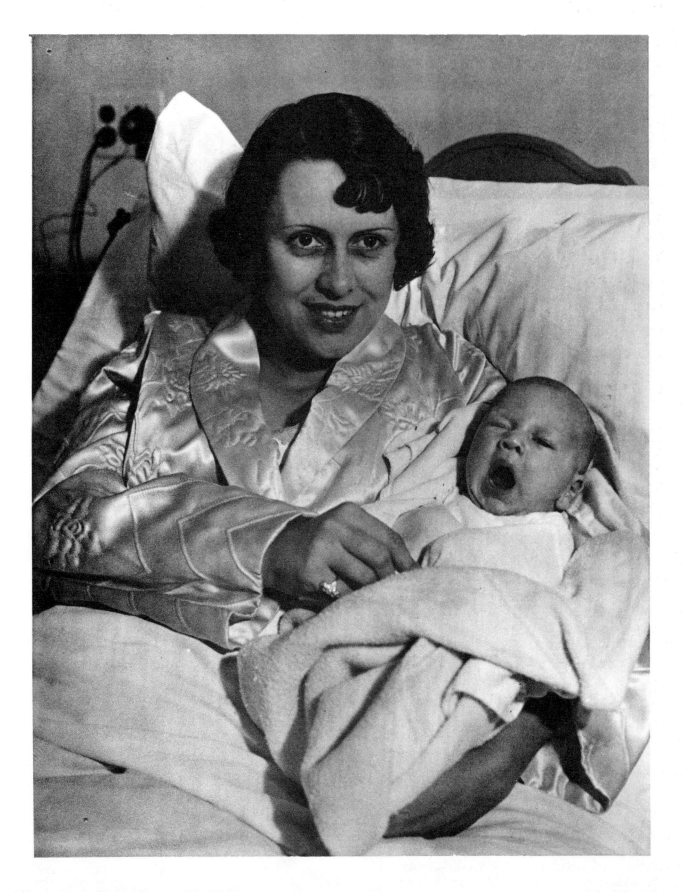

Mrs. Johnny Mack Brown (the former Cornelia Foster, daughter of Judge Henry B. Foster) holding her week old son, John Lachlan Brown. September 27, 1933. He will be welcomed by his four-year-old sister, Jane Harriet. (WOY Collection.)

4 • King of the Western Serials

In 1933 before he had begun his "B" western series with Supreme, Johnny Mack Brown had starred in his first western serial, **Fighting With Kit Carson** (Mascot). It had been his first "B" western role, actually predating his "B" western features by more than a year.

Johnny portrayed the rugged frontiersman, Kit Carson, in the serial. In the initial chapter he is leading a government gold train across the prairie when it is suddenly attacked by a band of outlaws known as the Mystery Riders. With the assistance of Nokomas, his young Indian friend as played by Noah Beery, Jr., and the U.S. cavalry he later rounds up the outlaw gang.

Johnny then returns to a nearby trading post where his young female sidekick, as played by Betsy King Ross, is keeping watch on the suspected leader of the raiders, as played by the senior Noah Beery. When confronted, Beery escapes. Johnny follows his trail with troopers disguised as Mystery Riders. He hopes to locate Beery and the secret hiding place of the outlaws where they keep their loot.

But the wiley Beery spots a badge on one of the disguised troopers and leads them into an explosive trap. After narrowly escaping being killed in the explosion, Johnny learns of the real location of the bandit hideout from Betsy. It is under the villain's barn. Then Johnny leads his men to the cache, trapping the outlaw chieftain and his gang and recovering the gold. This 12 chapter serial helped launch Johnny Mack Brown into his "B" western film career. (Weiss, Ken and Goodgold, Ed. *To Be Continued...* New York: Crown Publishers, 1972, p.37.)

In 1935 Johnny moved to the larger production facilities at Universal for his second "B" western serial, **The Rustlers of Red Dog**. This was another epic frontier story in which Johnny helps protect the settlers from Indians and renegade whites.

As a former peace officer, Johnny and his pals,

Laramie, an old frontiersman played by Raymond Hatton, and Deacon, a gambler of sorts as played by Walter Miller, are requested by the civic leaders of Red Dog to stay on as lawmen and clean up the town. But the trio sign on with a wagon train heading west. The wagon train with which the heroine is traveling is infested with renegades intent upon stealing the gold aboard one of the wagons. They are led by a tough outlaw chief, Rocky, played by Harry Woods.

When the wagon train is attacked by Indians, the outlaws unite with the settlers to fight off the savage marauders. During the attack, a cavalry escort arrives to lead the wagons to a nearby fort. But after they reach the fort, the Indians attack again and the gang of outlaws use the battle as cover to make off with the wagon containing the gold. Destroying the gates of the fort in their flight, the outlaws make it possible for the Indians to take the fort and capture its defenders.

But Johnny finds that he has a friend among the Indians. A young chief whom he had previously befriended gives him his freedom. However, his sidekicks are to be burned at the stake and the girl, Mary, to become a squaw. But just as his friends are about to be burned alive, cavalry reinforcements arrive and Johnny stampedes the Indians' horses. He then releases his friends, frees Mary and they all escape during the confusion.

Meanwhile, Rocky, the bandit leader, and his men have discovered that the stolen gold is enclosed in a heavy safe which they cannot open. They take it to a cave where they can blast it open with explosives. However, Johnny and his friends come upon the outlaw cave and stealthily make off with the gold wagon. They return the wagon to the wagon train and travel with it to Nugget, the town where Mary lives.

The gold is hidden in Mary's brother's house and Johnny is made town marshal. He and his sidekicks then set out to capture Rocky and his gang. But while they are gone, Rocky has an old

The villains, Charles Stevens and a player, are sneaking up on Kentucky (Johnny Mack Brown) in this scene from **Wild West Days** (Universal, 1937). (WOY Collection.)

prospector come into town and start a fake gold rush. When the excited townspeople leave the town unguarded, the outlaws raid the town for the gold.

Out on the trail, Johnny and his pals rescue a stagecoach from an Indian attack. The old prospector who started the goldrush is among those saved and in gratitude he tells them of Rocky's plans. The trio race back to town on the stage. By the time they arrive, Rocky's men have located the gold, looted the stores and bank, and are preparing to leave. They allow the stagecoach to enter town in order to use it to carry off their booty. But when Rocky opens the stagecoach door, he finds himself covered by twin sixguns. Johnny forces him to have his men surrender, but Rocky attempts to escape. In a final gun duel, Johnny plugs Rocky. The serial ends with Johnny and Mary planning to wed. (Weiss and Goodgold, *Op. cit.*, pp. 73-74.)

In addition to making a fine action western serial that was to serve as a forerunner to several

more Universal chapterplays, Johnny had introduced his striking, black frontier buckskin costume with fringed sleeves, which established an enduring image in the minds of his many fans. Today, one of the things best remembered about him is that outfit.

Johnny Mack Brown's next western serial offering was **Wild West Days** (Universal, 1937). This time his sidekicks were Frank Yaconelli as Mike and the usually villainous Bob Kortman as Trigger. Johnny played a character called Kentucky, a frontiersman who goes to the aid of a brother and sister to help save their mine.

Playing a scheming newspaperman, Russell Simpson plots to steal the mine away from its owners. He has the brother framed for murder and attempts to have him lynched. Although Johnny rescues the brother and sets him free, a renegade Indian, played by Chief Thundercloud, recaptures him and Johnny has to rescue him a second time.

Then the crooked newsman fakes a gold strike (Where have we seen this before?) as a ruse to

A villain (Roy Barcroft) is about to get a surprise from Tex Houston (Johnny Mack Brown) in this scene from **Flaming Frontiers** (Universal, 1938). (Courtesy of Jim Stringham.)

locate the secret mine. But as the crazed townspeople head out of town, Johnny reveals the hoax and captures the outlaw confederates of Simpson.

However, renegade Indian allies of the crooks attack Johnny and his men. Only the arrival of reinforcements saves them from the redskins. In the closing chapter Johnny goes after the outlaw leader, Simpson, who has been brought out into the open, finally. When he draws his gun, Johnny knocks him unconscious and jails him along with his gang. The trigger trio then depart for further adventures, leaving a wistful heroine behind them. (Weiss and Goodgold, *Op. cit.*, p. 117.)

By now Johnny's black garb has become his standard serial outfit and further established his western film personna. He followed his earlier success in western serials with **Flaming Frontiers** (Universal, 1938), set during the Pony Express days. He played Tex Houston, a famous Indian scout, who gets involved in the famous mail service as he discovers a dead Pony Express rider, killed on the trail by Indians.

When he brings in the slain rider's mail, he comes upon a young woman and her dad being threatened by a ruffian who is trying to get the girl to marry him in order to acquire her brother's California gold mine. He helps the girl and her father escape the unwelcome advances of the schemer by means of a wagon train headed west, but the scalawag follows them.

On the trail Indians attack the wagon train and the father is killed, but the girl is rescued by none other than Buffalo Bill himself, as played by John Rutherford.

Upon reaching California, the girl's brother is framed by another villain, Charles Middleton. But a rival gang of thieves under the direction of the unwelcome suitor, help the brother break jail in order to force the mine's location from him. Johnny has come west too and he rescues the brother just as Indians attack the town.

In successive chapters Johnny and the brother escape death from explosives and flaming death and manage also to save the sister from a wagon crash. Eventually Johnny clears the brother of the murder charge and brings both the villains and the henchmen to justice in a climactic gun battle.

Jeff (Johnny Mack Brown) finds Margaret (Louise Stanley) by the overturned wagon and lifts her tenderly in his arms in this scene form **The Oregon Trail** (Universal, 1939). (Courtesy of Jim Stringham.)

Johnny and the sister settle down together at the end. (Weiss and Goodgold, *Op. cit.*, p. 127.)

The Oregon Trail (Universal, 1939) was Johnny's final western serial. In this frontier epic Johnny played a frontier scout whose job it was to stop the raids on the wagon trains crossing the plains to Oregon.

With his sidekick, "Deadwood," as played by Fuzzy Knight, he joins a wagon train headed for Oregon. When it is attacked by Indians, he saves its people from massacre. As the journey progresses, Johnny suspects the wagon master of being responsible for the misfortunes of the wagon train. Soon this renegade leader incites the Indians to attack the wagons again. But this time Colonel Custer, as played by Roy Barcroft who is usually a villain, arrives with cavalry to save the settlers.

Later, the crooked wagon master attempts to burn the wagon train in a prairie fire but once again Johnny saves the train by leading the wagons to safety. Then he captures the outlaw leader and jails him.

However, the chief villain of this serial is a fur syndicate manager who fears that his crooked wagon master henchman will reveal his part in planning the Indian raids. He then arranges for the captured henchman to escape. Johnny gives chase and overtakes the fleeing crook on a runaway stagecoach, upon which they fight. When the stage goes over a cliff, the renegade perishes, but Johnny manages to survive the fall into a raging river and swims ashore.

The wagon train reaches Oregon finally where the scheming fur trader attempts to force the new settlers to pay him for their land claims, using a bogus land grant as his right. But Johnny exposes him as a fraud and arrests him, allowing the settlers to begin building a new state in the Union. (Weiss and Goodgold, *Op. cit.*, p. 146.)

Woven in with his early "B" western film series at Supreme and Republic, these western serials helped Johnny Mack Brown to become deeply entrenched as a favorite western star. The supportive casts, special effects and general production values at Universal had all combined with Johnny's natural talent for action films to make him foremost in popularity with western film fans.

5 • Universal Westerns: Top of the Line

Johnny Mack Brown's first feature release for Universal was **Desperate Trails** (1939) which co-starred him with the resident studio singing cowboy, Bob Baker, who was on the way out as a western star at this time. Brown was brought to the studio western film series to provide more believable action than the singing cowboy had. He not only did this but also took over the series rapidly. A slugfest between Johnny and a rustler came across particularly well in the film. The Hollywood Reporter reviewer praised Johnny Mack for his performance, saying: "Johnny Mack Brown appears a sure bet as a spurs-and-chaps star. He is bound to increase in popularity with the western mob and his current series with Universal, if **Desperate Trails** is any tip, won't go begging for time." (August 12, 1939).

In addition, Fuzzy Knight, the resident comic sidekick at Universal, came in for his share of the accolades in the film: "Fuzzy Knight is an ideal western type and although he accounts for many of the laughs in this release, one of the best comedy scenes is one in which the break-away wagons, buggies, carts, etc. figure when a vigilantes party is broken up." (*Ibid.*)

The next oater in the series was also a good western film entry. **Oklahoma Frontier** (Universal, 1939) contained a "B" western version of the Oklahoma landrush. A band of unscrupulous outlaws plot to stake out the best locations for themselves before the race actually begins. Johnny played a former U.S. Marshal who comes to the aid of honest land seekers and foils the plans of the schemers. Bob Baker played the brother of the heroine and was killed off early in the film. Fuzzy Knight was his usual outspoken self as "Windy Dan". The film was also graced by the presence of the beautiful Anne Gwynne as the sister with whom Johnny falls in love.

Chip of the Flying U (Universal, 1939) continued the trio of Brown, Baker and Knight in a modern western story that had bank robbers and foreign agents dealing in explosives. In addition

to the traditional payroll theft, shooting of the bank president and chase scene, there were modern elements of a siege of a cabin chock full of munitions and secret agents with explosive results. The film was somewhat similar to the Republic Gene Autry films of the same period. It was not one of the best for Johnny Mack and company.

West of Carson City (Universal, 1940) was a more traditional western story of a goldrush boomtown into which crooked gamblers come to bilk the miners of their gold. Johnny played a cattleman who realizes that the local judge and his daughter need help in cleaning up the town. With the aid of his two pals, Nevada as played by Baker, and Banjo, played by Knight, he proceeds to do just this. Baker does get to perform in tough fist fights in this film along with Johnny. Peggy Moran, another Universal beauty, was the heroine.

In **Riders of Pasco Basin** (Universal, 1940) Johnny was a rancher leading cattlemen in upsetting the plans of sharpies who are taking money for the supposed purpose of building a dam for land irrigation. Baker and Fuzzy were along for the ride.

Johnny got to play a dual role again in **Bad Man from Red Butte** (Universal, 1940). As twin brothers they were typically one good and one bad. When he comes to town to lay out a new stagecoach route, Johnny is mistaken for his outlaw brother. Together with Baker as a local attorney and Fuzzy as a hair tonic drummer, they clean up the town, bringing the saloon keeper-mortgage holder villain and his gang to justice. Anne Gwynne played the lovely heroine. This film marked the end of Bob Baker's part in the series. Hereafter, Johnny Mack and Fuzzy would ride alone, at least until Tex Ritter joined them in 1942.

Son of Roaring Dan (Universal, 1940) was notable for the entry of a new type of character into the Brown western film series at Universal. Nell O'Day was introduced in this film. She was a

Chip Bennett (Johnny Mack Brown) talks to Margaret Whitmore (Doris Weston) in this scene from **Chip of the Flying U** Universal, 1939). (Courtesy of Jerry Ohlinger's Movie Material Store.)

small, youthful girl who could ride like the blazes. Although too youthful appearing to be a serious love interest for the more mature Johnny Mack Brown, she often would play a perky sidekick whose riding scenes especially enlivened the series. Generally, a more mature heroine was included in the cast to provide the romantic touch. But it was Nell O'Day whose riding frequently stole the feminine interest in the films.

Son of Roaring Dan had the old play of the long lost son returning after being away many years. Johnny had to pretend to be the lost son as he tracks down the murderers of his real father. In the end he nabs the killers and gets the older gal, Jeanne Kelly.

Ragtime Cowboy Joe (Universal, 1940) provided the musical, comic sidekick, Fuzzy Knight, with a showcase role in the series. In addition to rendering the title song of the feature, Fuzzy also played the befuddled cowboy of the title. Johnny played a range detective who chases down a murderous gang of rustlers and land grabbers. In the process Johnny has to choose between the two heroines, one of whom this time is Nell O'Day. The other girl is Marilyn Merrick. Johnny goes for the more mature gal, of course. Dick Curtis provided excellent villainy with Roy Barcroft to back him up.

Law and Order (Universal, 1940) may well be the best film of the series if not the best of all of Johnny Mack Brown's "B" western films. It was a "B" remake of the "A" western film of the same name, starring Walter Huston and Harry Carey from 1932. Written by W.R. Burnett, it was the story of Wyatt Earp and Doc Holliday and the shootout at the O.K. Corral, but with different names. Johnny played the ex-marshal who has come to town to settle down and retire from gunslinging. But when he sees how wild the town is, he accepts the job of local marshal and cleans up the town. James Craig was excellent as ill-fated gambler sidekick who takes chips in the hand

Johnny Mack Brown holds a saloon full of men at bay in this scene from **Son of Roaring Dan** (Universal, 1939). (Courtesy of Jerry Ohlinger's Movie Material Store.)

dealt to Johnny. Fuzzy was the other sidekick who aids Johnny.

In the film Nell O'Day is the youthful heroine rather than a female foil to an older gal. She and her brother, Jimmy Dodd, are threatened by the villainous Daggett clan who have run the town before Johnny's arrival. Filled with action, the film builds to the climactic gun battle at the end. It is by all standards a fine horse opera.

Johnny followed this excellent picture with a frontier story about the Pony Express, **Pony Post** (Universal, 1940). It told the story of the formation of the famous mail service and the difficulties encountered in getting the mail through during the early days of the West. Johnny redonned his popular black buckskin outfit from his serial days which was about the best thing in this weaker entry of the series. Too much footage was wasted in showing the Pony Express riders going and coming at the expense of the plot. Also the obvious use of so many outtakes in the film detracted

from the story. Much of the old footage was plainly taken from the earlier serials to save money on the production. Even Nell O'Day's exciting riding scenes, a fine cast and the inclusion of Jimmy Wakely's musical trio did not help this picture. As a final slam, even Fuzzy's humor was panned by The Hollywood Reporter reviewer who summed up the film with the critical comment: "Nobody expects a cactus meller to have an original plot — in fact the traditional one is preferable. But such yarns should be crammed with action and headlong pace. This one ain't." (December 11, 1940).

However, a number of good action films followed this one in the series. In **Boss of Bullion City** (Universal, 1941) Johnny Mack and Fuzzy were called upon to thwart the actions of a crooked sheriff. An interesting sidelight is that Maria Montez, soon to be Universal's queen of technicolor costume action dramas, was featured as the heroine. In **Bury Me Not on the Lone Prairie** (Universal, 1941) Johnny played a mining

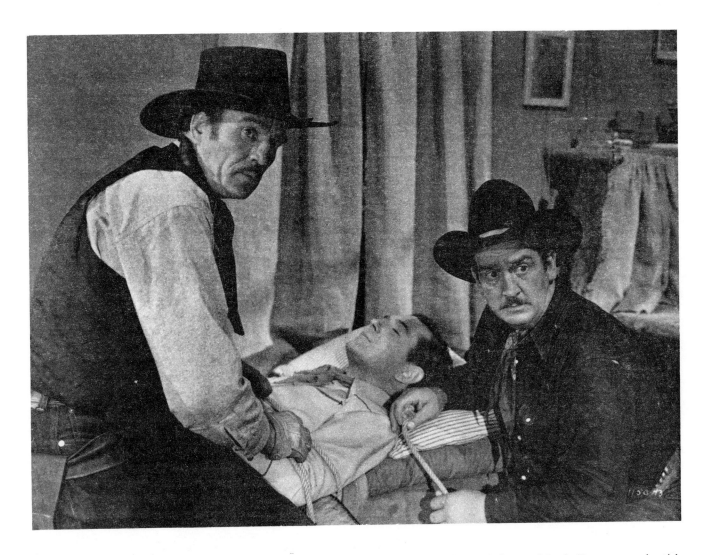

Two villains (the one on the right is Charles King) tie an unconscious Johnny Mack Brown up in this scene from **Law of the Range** (Universal, 1941). (Courtesy of Jerry Ohlinger's Movie Material Store.)

engineer who rounds up a gang of claim jumpers and avenges the murder of his brother.

Next came a top flight story in the series, **Law of the Range** (Universal, 1941). It was a remake of the Buck Jones classic "B" western, **The Ivory Handled Gun** (Universal, 1935). **Law of the Range** had all of the ingredients missing from **Pony Post**: plenty of action, clear characterization and an unbroken storyline. In addition, the conflict was better motivated than in many such films.

The story was a combination of a second generation feud and a war between cattlemen and sheepmen. The usual two female leads also added to the plot. One daughter of a rancher, with whom the hero's family has long been feuding, believes Johnny guilty of her father's slaying. The other daughter thinks him innocent. Johnny has to end the feud with his fast gun nemesis, the Wolverine Kid, while at the same time settling the range war peacefully. In addition to a positive reaction to the

picture overall, The Hollywood Reporter reviewer gave Johnny plaudits for his performance in the film, noting: "Johnny Mack Brown brings an unusual degree of acting skill and authority to the role of the deadshot hero." (July 8, 1941).

In the next entry of the series, **Rawhide Rangers** (Universal, 1941) Nell O'Day got to warble a song, "A Cowboy Is Happy," an unusual function for the high riding, action queen. The story was the familiar one about the rich western businessman who secretly leads the outlaws as they terrorize other ranchers. A twist in the plot was that he attempts to set up a protection racket at the same time. Johnny played the ex-ranger who comes to town to avenge the murder of his brother. Fuzzy was along with his usual brand of musical comedy.

Man from Montana (Universal, 1941) was one of the lesser films of the series. The story was rather stale, about homesteaders moving in on the ranchers' range. Naturally, the outlaws play the

Johnny Mack Brown is getting ready to punch out a bad guy in this scene from **Rawhide Rangers** (Universal, 1941). (Courtesy of Jerry Ohlinger's Movie Material Store.)

ranchers against the homesteaders for their own gain. Johnny played the local sheriff who has to solve murders on both sides in order to keep the peace. The two heroines were O'Day and Jeanne Kelly.

Like Gene Autry and the Three Mesquiteers at Republic, Johnny had to venture south of the border in his films to keep pace. In **The Masked Rider** (Universal, 1941) Johnny and his sidekick, Patches as played by Fuzzy, were seeking jobs at a South American mine where a masked rider and his gang have been robbing silver shipments and killing the guards. The duo unmask the bandit, save the silver shipment and win a senorita, Virginia Carroll, for Johnny. Nell O'Day was featured as the other girl and Fuzzy had more of a role than usual in this one. Grant Withers and Roy Barcroft supplied the evil deeds.

Arizona Cyclone (Universal, 1941) was a freight lines story with plenty of action and the usual supporting players. Johnny had to frustrate the villainy of a rival freight line boss who resorts to murder to obtain the stagecoach franchise.

Stagecoach Buckaroos (Universal, 1942) was also about a stagecoach line. In this one a gang of highwaymen harass Nell O'Day's father's line until Johnny and Fuzzy come along to stop them. Fuzzy gets to wear women's clothes as a part of a ruse to trap the robbers. He also sings one song with Nell O'Day, entitled "Just Too Darn Bashful".

Fighting Bill Fargo (Universal, 1942) had Johnny returning home from prison after serving time on a trumped up charge. He had come home to run his family newspaper. A crooked election results in a murder which is photographed in the act. A climactic gun battle routes the heavies and saves the town from their clutches. Nell O'Day played Johnny's sister while Jeanne Kelly was the love interest. The Eddie Dean Trio supplied the music.

In 1942 Johnny Mack Brown had a featured

A Lobby Card from 1942 picturing Fuzzy Knight, Jennifer Holt, Pals of the Golden West and Johnny Mack Brown. (WOY Collection.)

role in the Abbott and Costello comic western film, **Ride 'Em Cowboy** (Universal) along with Dick Foran, another Universal action star at the time. Johnny was the steady ranch foreman who lost the heroine to the singing rodeo cowboy, Foran. Anne Gwynne played the lady in question.

The Silver Bullet (Universal, 1942) was a revenge story. Brown's character carries a silver bullet memento from a professional killer who murdered his dad with a shot in the back five years before. He has been roaming the West ever since, seeking the man who can only be identified by a scar on his left arm. When Johnny comes to a town where a crooked politician has just killed his honest opponent, he decides to stay for a while. Johnny and Fuzzy do in the outlaws and nab the killer who turns out to be Johnny's long sought quarry in the death of his father. Jennifer Holt played the heroine and LeRoy Mason the villain. The final gunfight between Johnny Mack and Mason was a standout.

A final entry in Johnny Mack's solo series at the studio was **Boss of Hangtown Mesa** (Universal, 1942), the story of a telegraph line construction. Johnny was the sheriff who tracks down the culprits. It was not one of the top films of the series.

In 1942 Johnny Mack Brown was joined at Universal by another major western star, singing cowboy, Tex Ritter. Ritter had been successful in several western series since the late 1930's. He had begun his western film career at Grand National and then moved over to Monogram when Grand National closed down. Then he had signed with Columbia to co-star in a duo western series with Wild Bill Elliott. That series had been his most successful. Now Universal also wanted a duo team and Ritter was hired to co-star with Johnny Mack Brown. Fuzzy Knight stayed on for the humor while Nell O'Day departed the series.

Deep in the Heart of Texas (Universal, 1942) was the first of the duo oaters with Brown and

Jim Mallory (Johnny Mack Brown) helps his wounded father Colonel Mallory (William Farnum) in this scene from **Deep in the Heart of Texas** (Universal, 1942). (WOY Collection.)

Ritter. It was a fine Western. The story was concerned with a group of insurrectionist Texans who attempt to set up a separate government in order to grab land off the inhabitants. Johnny played the returning son of the governor of the new state. The father is merely a pawn in the hands of the real criminals. Tex played the Texas governor's agent sent to investigate the rebellion.

After an initial conflict between the two heroes, Johnny and Tex band together to bring this part of Texas back into the state government. Well cast, the film included William Farnum as the father, Jennifer Holt, the daughter of former star Jack Holt, as the heroine, Harry Woods as the chief henchman and the Jimmy Wakely trio for music. Fuzzy was even present as "Happy T. Snodgrass." An ensemble musical rendition of the title song provided a rousing finale, somewhat like a Roy Rogers film of the period.

Little Joe, The Wrangler (Universal, 1942) continued the fine series. This gold mining story had Johnny nabbed as an ore robber and a murderer in a frameup. Tex played the sheriff who faces ouster from his office because he believes Johnny is innocent and tries to help him. Once again, the climax has them team up to capture the real bandits in a wild and furious fist fight. Fuzzy played the deputy sheriff who invents strange contraptions such as the cowhide cactus protector. Jimmy Wakely and trio again provided the songs.

The Old Chisholm Trail (Universal, 1942) was the tale of the famous cattle trail. A villainous female rancher tries to make the cattle drovers pay for water along the trail which she has fenced off. Johnny and Tex have to get together to open the trail and rid the range of the crooked lady and her gang of cutthroats. Mady Correll played the bad woman while Jennifer Holt was the heroine.

Tenting Tonight on the Old Camp Ground (Universal, 1943), besides having one of the longest titles in "B" western pictures, was the oft repeated yarn about rival stagecoach lines

Johnny Mack Brown played a dual role in **Cheyenne Roundup** (Universal, 1943). Here he is the bad twin brother. (Courtesy of Jerry Ohlinger's Movie Material Store.)

competing for a government contract to deliver the mail. As Johnny attempts to build a roadbed for his line, his rival, together with the aid of a gang of toughs and dancehall hostess, Jennifer Holt, try to stop him by luring his men into a gambling dive. Tex comes to the aid of Johnny to help save the line and acquire the government contract.

As the studio completed the film series in 1943, Johnny Mack Brown signed a contract with Monogram Pictures to move over to the studio for a western series of his own. Tim McCoy had just left to return to military duty in World War II and Buck Jones had recently died as the result of a tragic fire at the Cocoanut Grove. Of the Rough Riders series stars only Raymond Hatton was left and Monogram did not want to lose the series altogether. Before Universal realized what had happened, the studio had lost its top western star. Johnny Mack Brown went to Monogram to make his first feature in a new series, **The Ghost Rider** (Monogram, 1943).

Meanwhile, three remaining Universal features were yet to be released. **Cheyenne Roundup** (Universal, 1943) had Johnny once again playing a dual role as twins, one good and one onery. The bad brother takes over a mining ghost town after having been run out of the country by Ritter. When Tex leads a posse to attack the outlaw gang in the ghost town, the bad brother is killed in the gunfight. The good brother arrives just in time to have his nefarious twin die in his arms. Ritter makes a deal with the good twin to masquerade as his dead brother and help clean up the rest of the gang, led by Harry Woods and Roy Barcroft.

Raiders of San Joaquin (Universal, 1943) told of the railroad building days. A gang of unscrupulous landgrabbers are stealing land from the ranchers under the guise of securing right-of-way for the railroad. Johnny played an undercover agent of the railroad who upsets their plans. Tex was the leader of the ranchers resisting the theft of their range. The Hollywood Reporter reviewer

Here Harry Wood, Roy Barcroft and Tex Ritter look on as Johnny Mack Brown and Jennifer Holt have a talk in this scene from **Cheyenne Roundup** (Universal, 1943). (WOY Collection.)

criticized the film on several points: "In this case the stuttering, bungling Knight isn't half as funny as he usually is, while also action is lacking to the point where frequently considerable slowness sets in." (May 25, 1943).

The last duo Western with Brown and Ritter was **The Lone Star Trail** (Universal, 1943). This retelling of the classic "Destry Rides Again" story has Johnny returning home after serving time for a framed up robbery. Paroled for good behavior, he pretends to be broken in spirit until he can get the goods on the quartet of crooks who sent him to jail.

Tex played an undercover marshal, following Johnny to recover the missing money he was supposed to have stolen. When Tex realizes that Johnny has been framed, he joins forces with Brown to nab the real culprits.

With Johnny Mack Brown leaving Universal so suddenly, the studio quickly moved Tex Ritter into the films as a solo star until Tex too left after

a few films in 1944.

Meanwhile, Johnny already had begun his long running "Nevada" Jack Mackenzie series at Monogram Pictures.

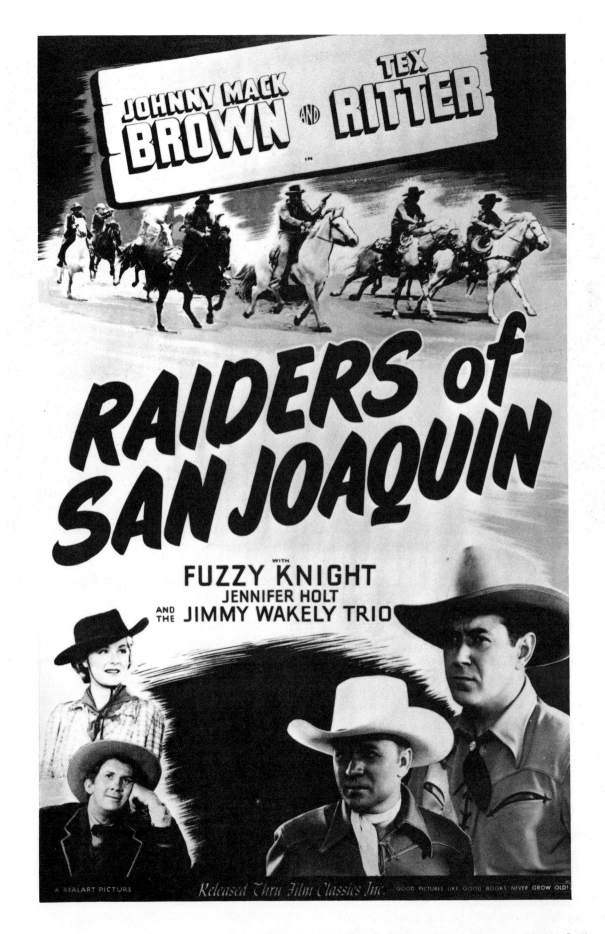

A one sheet picturing Jennifer Holt, Fuzzy Knight, Tex Ritter and Johnny Mack Brown. (WOY Collection.)

6 • Monogram: The Long Ride

Once Johnny had jumped the traces and gone with Monogram, he began his new series quickly. Although the series was a continuation of the "Rough Riders" series in a way since Raymond Hatton still played his Sandy Hopkins role, Johnny's Nevada Jack Mackenzie was a new character, replacing both the characters of Buck Jones and Tim McCoy. In the initial film, Nevada was on the owlhoot trail to hunt down the murderers of his father. Along the way he meets Marshal Sandy Hopkins from Texas who assists him in bringing in the killers. The villains were played by Harry Woods, Charles King, Bud Osborne and Edmund Cobb, a veritable army of veteran film outlaws. **The Ghost Rider** (Monogram, 1943) was a fine start for the new series, although Monogram could not provide the same quality of production values to a "B" western film series that Universal had.

After such a successful beginning with **The Ghost Rider**, Johnny followed up with **The Stranger from Pecos** (Monogram, 1943). In addition to Hatton, this entry featured Kirby Grant who was soon to become a western/action star in his own right at Universal, following in Johnny Mack Brown's footsteps, so to speak.

In this film Johnny has become a marshal himself. He has been sent to check up on a report of a land swindle. Property is being grabbed when mortgages cannot be paid. The local sheriff is in on the deal which includes both robbery and murder. Hatton has an excellent scene in a card game as he desperately tries to lose $3,000 back to a rancher from whom the money was stolen originally. The bandy little marshal has to throw away several top hands in order to lose the money. It was a fine touch by veteran director, Lambert Hillyer. The bad guys in the film were Roy Barcroft, Charles King and Ed Cobb.

By the end of the picture Nevada and Sandy had become a team of marshals who roam the West hunting down outlaws. The series was destined to last over a number of years.

Six-Gun Gospel (Monogram, 1943) was a showcase film for Raymond Hatton. In the film Hatton comes to town in one of his many disguises, that of an undertaker, but he is mistaken for the new parson due to arrive soon. He immediately impersonates the sky-pilot, playing the organ and singing to his new flock while Johnny Mack stands around, obviously amused by the whole affair. About the best he can do to cope with Hatton's blatant scene stealing is to demonstrate some of his fancy gun twirling tricks for which he was famous.

At the end, however, the dynamic duo bring the trio of bad guys (Roy Barcroft, Kenneth MacDonald, and Bud Osborne) to justice. Eddie Dew, who had been tried out as a western film hero and found lacking by both Republic and Universal, was featured in the film. Lambert Hillyer again was the director.

Outlaws of Stampede Pass (Monogram, 1943) had the two lawmen aided by a blacksmith's daughter as they try to find out who is behind the rustling of local cattle.

Continuing the excellent quality of the series beginning was **The Texas Kid** (Monogram, 1943). It was a notable film, due to the performance of Marshall Reed as the title character who is a secondary hero in the picture. Reed played a one time member of a highwayman band who now is trying to go straight. He manages to outwit his former cronies by bringing the stage and its load through in spite of being wounded. Johnny and Hatton round up the outlaws.

Raiders of the Border (Monogram, 1944) had marshals Brown and Hatton hunting down cattle rustlers. Hatton is disguised this time as an old codger who can hear only through an ear trumpet. The rustlers who exchange the cattle for illicit Mexican jewels are rounded up after a series of chases.

Partners of the Trail (Monogram, 1944) found the two marshals arriving in a small town only to find that local ranchers are being murdered. They uncover a plot to steal valuable gold claims on the

Johnny Mack Brown has taken something off the body in this scene from **Frontier Feud** (Monogram, 1946). (Courtesy of Jerry Ohlinger's Movie Material Store.)

ranchers' lands.

Law Men (Monogram, 1944) again featured Kirby Grant as a young man in trouble as Nevada and Sandy investigate a series of holdups. Johnny goes undercover, joining a gang while Hatton sets himself up as a businessman in town. Soon they have ferreted out the outlaw leader and arrested his gang.

Range Law (Monogram, 1944) showed the duo coming to the aid of a woman whose rancher friend has been falsely accused of cattle rustling by the real rustlers.

West of the Rio Grande (Monogram, 1944) had Hatton pose as a teacher and Johnny as a gunslinger. Together, they get the goods on a politician and his gang who are forcing the local citizens to give up their voting rights.

Land of the Outlaws (Monogram, 1944) had Johnny on the trail of a band of outlaws hijacking ore shipments with Hatton assisting him in the investigation.

Law of the Valley (Monogram, 1944) had outlaws after range land to control the local water supply since the railroad is planning to build a spur line through the valley.

Ghost Guns (Monogram, 1944) had a similar plot in that crooks try to control the valley because they know the railroad is coming through the area. Nevada and Sandy arrive to stop the killing of ranchers and the rustling of cattle. At the end of the picture director Hillyer had Johnny Mack again demonstrate his trick gun handling. Johnny carefully unholstered his six shooter, twisted, twirled and flipped the handgun end over end, finishing by tossing it over his shoulder and returning it to its sheath. As Don Miller said: "It was a great flash act and Brown repeated it once or twice in later films." (*Hollywood Corral*, p.228.)

By now the series films began to have a certain similarity to them. The two marshals would appear when things looked tough and, through

A Lobby Card from 1947 picturing Johnny Mack Brown and Raymond Hatton. (Courtesy of Jerry Ohlinger's Movie Material Store.)

investigation and quick action, the outlaws would come to the same end.

The series continued in the same pattern more or less throughout 1945, but with fewer of the films directed by the veteran, Lambert Hillyer. That year **Navajo Trail** (Monogram) was Johnny's first film. In it a fellow peace officer is killed and the two lawmen pals seek out the killer. Johnny poses as an outlaw to join the gang out to steal Indian horses.

Gunsmoke (Monogram, 1945) had Johnny and Hatton come upon a stagecoach where all the passengers have been murdered. In their investigation they discover a plot to steal an Indian gold mine.

The Hillyer directed films in the series were generally better than the others and one of the Hillyer films in 1945 deviated from the duo lawmen pattern considerably. **Flame of the West** (Monogram) was almost an "A" production, running 71 minutes and with a very mature story. In the picture Johnny played a frontier doctor who

is branded a coward by his sweetheart because he refuses to engage in gunplay with a band of tough hombres terrorizing the town. Douglas Dumbrille played the brave town marshal friend of Johnny's who is brutally murdered by the crooked gamblers in the town. After the killing of his friend, Johnny gets out twin Colts and cleans up the town single handed, proving his courage when the chips are down. It is a **Destry Rides Again** (Universal, 1939) type of plot without the humorous elements.

According to Don Miller: "Lambert Hillyer directed (it) with the same grace he had imbued in the Bill Hart silents..." (*Hollywood Corral*, p.228.) He also praised the film itself, saying: "The intense character studies build the narrative to a suspensefully strong climax. It was Brown's best western and anything coming after it would be anticlimactic. (*Ibid*.) Monogram had made a minor gem of a Western in its attempt to move into larger budget productions. However, the

Showering attention on Jeanette McDonald at a Hollywood reception are Cesar Romero and Johnny Mack Brown in September 1948. (WOY Collection.)

picture did not generate a move by Johnny Mack Brown into bigger pictures as Bill Elliott had made at Republic. The public wanted Johnny Mack Brown as an action cowboy in "B" Westerns rather than a frontier doctor. After this single effort to do something different, it was back to the tried and true formula with Johnny Mack and Hatton running down outlaws, although not as Nevada and Sandy always.

The Stranger from Santa Fe (Monogram, 1945) had lawman Johnny Mack impersonating a cowpoke drifting along. When he is forced to take part in a stage holdup, the gang frames him for murdering the guard. Then he has to clear himself and round up the gang.

In **The Lost Trail** (Monogram, 1946) Johnny and Hatton come to the aid of a girl whose stagecoach line is under attack by a gang of outlaws.

Our two heroes played two cowmen who arrive in a small town in Arizona just in time to stop the lynching of a rancher accused of murder in

Frontier Feud (Monogram, 1946).

Border Bandits (Monogram, 1946) brought to an end the roles of Nevada and Sandy in the Brown series as the two marshals aid a girl whose father has been robbed of valuable gems.

Drifting Along (Monogram, 1946) added something entirely new to Johnny Mack's role in "B" western pictures. A singing voice was dubbed into the sound track to create a new image of him as a singing cowboy, much like the earlier attempt with John Wayne in his Lone Star productions. Smith Ballew, a former western film singing cowboy for a short time, was credited as the voice warbling the title song for Johnny as well as singing several songs as himself in the film, including "Dusty Trails" and "You Can Bet Your Boots and Saddles."

The story had Johnny play an itinerant cowhand afoot who comes to the aid of a young woman as she resists an attempt to grab her ranch. In one fight scene Johnny flattens a whole flock of

Lynne Carver and Johnny Mack Brown in a scene from **Crossed Trails** (Monogram, 1948). (Courtesy of Jerry Ohlinger's Movie Material Store.)

heavies. But at the end of the picture with the bad guys corralled, he moves on as he came, singing the title song as the end credits appear. The heroine releases Rebel, his horse to be sure he comes back. However, the idea of a singing Johnny Mack Brown was not popular with his fans. Don Miller has commented: "It was not an inspired idea, nor was it a world beater." (*Hollywood Corral*, p. 228.)

The Haunted Mine (Monogram, 1946) returned Johnny to his more usual role of action cowboy. A band of crooks is trying to steal a mine from its lady owner. Johnny played a U.S. Marshal called in to find out who is murdering anyone interested in buying the property. The mystery angle is played up in this picture.

Another effort at making Johnny into a singing cowboy was made in **Under Arizona Skies** (Monogram, 1946) and had Johnny Mack and Hatton coming to the aid of a rancher whose land was sought by a renegade rancher and his gang.

Smith Ballew provided two songs along the way.

After the music in **Drifting Along** did not go over, the studio began to realize that Brown might become confused with their new singing cowboy, Jimmy Wakely, and the singing by the action cowboy was discontinued.

When the musical gambit did not go over well with Johnny's fans, the series quickly returned to a more acceptable format, although the Nevada and Sandy roles were gone for good now. In the following films Hatton more often played a leading character than a sidekick to Johnny Mack. Now Johnny would usually come to the aid of Hatton and some young woman in jeopardy. It was more or less standard fare. Johnny was beginning to show his age and had put on considerable girth, so now youthful supporting actors were used in the stories for romantic interest with the heroines. The star was more like a helpful uncle than a shy Romeo. Such youthful actors as Riley Hill or Marshal Reed usually got the girl as Johnny rode

Johnny discusses a land grabbing scheme with perennial badman, Jack Ingram, in **Law of the West** (Monogram, 1949). (Courtesy of Bobby Copeland.)

off into the sunset.

The Gentlemen from Texas (Monogram, 1946) had Johnny and Hatton as two lawmen who are called in to combat a crooked town boss. This film harkened back to the earlier pattern, but the others following did not.

Shadows on the Range (Monogram, 1946) was typical of the newer pattern. As Johnny rides along, a stagecoach is attacked and a rancher passenger murdered. Hatton played the rancher's foreman and John Merton the leader of the gang was trying to steal the ranch away from the young daughter of the slain cowman.

Johnny pretends to be an outlaw himself in order to penetrate the gang. Once he knows who the gang members are, he gets himself hired as the ranch ramrod. Then he creates dissension within the gang, splits it up and saves the girl's ranch for her before riding on.

Trigger Fingers (Monogram, 1946) had Johnny as a marshal who aids a youthful hothead.

When the kid shoots a crooked gambler, he is framed for murder by the man's gang.

Silver Range (Monogram, 1946) was the story of a cattleman, Johnny Mack, who comes to the assistance of a former lawman, Hatton, to locate a kidnap victim and the outlaws behind a smuggling ring.

Another rather offbeat entry in the series occurred in 1947. With Hillyer as the director, **Raiders of the South** (Monogram) told the story during the Civil War of a band of gorilla fighters who become common criminals. Johnny played a secret service agent who poses as an ex-Confederate in order to defeat a lawyer's scheme to build an empire through a land grab.

But Monogram's production values were not up to such an ambitious script and, despite good work by both Johnny Mack and the leading lady, Evelyn Brent, well known to "B" western fans for roles in several of the early Hopalong Cassidy films, the picture did not come off well. Still, it

Brown took a break from his Monogram series to appear in two "A" features with Rod Cameron, **Stampede** and **Short Grass** (Allied Artists, 1949 and 1950). (Courtesy of Bobby Copeland.)

was an interesting departure for a "B" western film series. Monogram has to be given credit for attempting to improve the series with more mature plot lines.

Johnny's films now followed the previously described plot pattern that had proved so successful throughout the years: undercover detection and plenty of action. **Valley of Fear** (Monogram, 1947) had Johnny play a cowpoke who returns home to find his uncle dead and himself accused of taking money the dead uncle supposedly had embezzled.

Trailing Danger (Monogram, 1947) told the story of an outlaw seeking revenge on a stageline superintendent who was responsible for sending him to jail. Johnny played the U.S. Marshal who stops him.

In **Land of the Lawless** (Monogram, 1947) Johnny Mack played a footloose rider who comes into a town, demonstrates his ability to fight and then is requested by the citizens to accept the job

of marshal. He agrees to take the job only if he can work undercover. Johnny gets in with the outlaws, headed by the female saloon keeper. Then, aided by Hatton, he gets the goods on her and her gambler cohort who have murdered a local gold mine owner for his claim. At the end of the film Johnny departs quickly without even accepting thanks from the good townfolk, almost in the Lone Ranger tradition.

In **The Law Comes to Gunsight** (Monogram, 1947) Johnny played a wandering cowpoke who meets a young fellow and rides home with him. There they find lawlessness running wild. Johnny becomes the local marshal and shuts down both gambling and guntoting in the town. When the crooked politicians attempt to have him killed, he turns the tables on them and rounds them up in jail. With the town now cleaned up, he departs, leaving Hatton behind as the new mayor.

Code of the Saddle (Monogram, 1947) had Johnny and his pal visit an old friend only to find

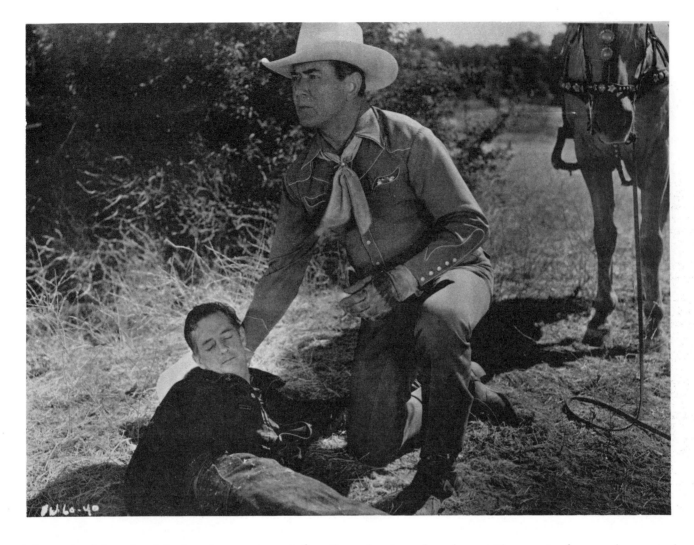

Johnny is determined to break up a gang of outlaws bent on keeping settlers out of a newly opened territory in **West of Wyoming** (Monogram, 1950). (Courtesy of Bobby Copeland.)

that he has been murdered. A neighboring rancher has been accused falsely of the killing. Johnny aids the slain man's daughter and the framed rancher in uncovering the real killer.

Flashing Guns (Monogram, 1947) was the story of Johnny fighting to save Hatton's heavily mortgaged ranch from a crooked banker in league with town gamblers. Robbery, marked decks, and forgery all figure in the swindle to deliver the silver rich ranch to the banker as Johnny intercedes and saves the ranch.

Prairie Express (Monogram, 1947) told of a respected citizen actually behind a gang trying to force a family off their ranch in order to buy it up cheaply before the railroad comes through.

Gun Talk (Monogram, 1947) had Johnny foiling an outlaw leader disguised as a barber whose gang is trying to seize Hatton's mine. Two heroines, Christine McIntyre as the saloon girl who aids Johnny in his fight with the outlaws and Geneva Gray as the eastern gal, enliven this story

by J. Benton Cheney, as does the direction by the old master, Lambert Hillyer. It was one of the better entries of the series.

Overland Trails (Monogram, 1948) was the story of a cowboy in love with a girl whose father is in league with outlaws. They grubstake prospectors and then kill them for their claims when the miners hit paydirt.

Crossed Trails (Monogram, 1948) found Johnny at the task of trying to prove that Hatton, the guardian of a young female ranch owner, was innocent of a murder frameup as the schemers attempt to grab the ranch for its water rights. With clever detective work, Johnny shows that Hatton was not present at the murder. Again, the competent Hillyer was at the directional helm.

Frontier Agent (Monogram, 1948) was the story of a land promoter trying to sabotage the completion of a telegraph line. Johnny played the trouble shooter for the parent company who comes to the aid of a rancher using his own

Johnny Mack Brown and Rod Cameron in a scene from **Short Grass** (Allied Artists, 1950). Some editor in the past has added crop marks. (WOY Collection.)

money to finance the line.

Triggerman (Monogram, 1948) gave Hatton an unusually good comic bit as he looks into a mirror at himself and it immediately cracks. Otherwise, this oater was pretty much a carbon copy of several other entries. It was the story of a Wells Fargo agent who goes to work undercover for a woman rancher. He uncovers a crooked real estate dealer after her place for the gold in it.

Back Trail (Monogram, 1948) had banker Ted Adams being blackmailed by saloon keeper Pierce Lyden for his past misdeeds. Johnny Mack played the local marshal. Several interesting scenes occur in this feature. Johnny whistles "Bury Me Not on the Lone Prairie" when outlaw Marshall Reed enters the saloon just prior to a showdown. During the fist fight Hatton holds a pair of henchmen at bay by making them lift beer barrels while Johnny pummels Reed and Lyden into submission. The fight, of course, was a put up job over Reed's belittling Johnny's preference for milk over

whiskey. Then at the end of the fight Hatton tells Lyden that he might become a pretty good man when he grows up. Snub Pollard had a bit part in the picture as a comical character named Goofy. In the end, naturally, villains Reed and Lyden are brought to justice.

In **The Fighting Ranger** (Monogram, 1948) it was Johnny Mack who discovers that his cousin has been framed for murder. He goes to investigate and finds out the plot is to get his cousin's ranch. Johnny hires on the spread as a cowhand to ferret out the real culprits.

During 1948 Monogram added a second comic sidekick to the series, Max Terhune of the Three Mesquiteers and Range Busters fame. In **The Sheriff of Medicine Bow** (Monogram, 1948) Hatton played a reformed bank robber whom Johnny had previously sent to prison. Hatton's daughter dislikes Johnny for his role in her father's jailing. Hatton holds no grudge, however, and tries to get his daughter to realize that Johnny

A Lobby Card from 1951 picturing Johnny Mack Brown, Lois Hall and Myron Healey. Notice the screenplay is by Myron Healey. (Courtesy of Jerry Ohlinger's Movie Material Store.)

is their friend.

Terhune played a ranch hand on Hatton's ranch. He and his dummy, Elmer, provide most of the comic relief while Hatton sticks to his character role. Max finds evidence of gold on the ranch just as it is about to be sold for back taxes. When Johnny helps get the taxes paid, a crooked assayer tells them the ore sample is worthless.

Then Hatton is accused of complicity in a fake bank robbery and Johnny is forced to jail Hatton for his own protection. Meanwhile, Johnny has the ore sample rechecked in another assay office and learns of the scheme by the bank president to bilk Hatton out of his gold rich ranch. Johnny outwits the outlaws and reveals the banker as the leader of the gang as he saves Hatton's ranch and his daughter from harm. Hillyer was the director again and the film, although slower in action than many, had a good story line.

By this time the Brown series had become very repetitious. According to Don Miller "The series had acquired a rubber-stamp quality now. Brown had been putting on weight since his early Universals, and it had now, seven years later, become quite noticeable. He had been out of the romantic running for the entire Monogram series... The Brown's were now undistinguishable." (*Hollywood Corral*, p. 230.)

Johnny's next film, **Gunning for Justice** (Monogram, 1948), had him and his pals, Hatton and Terhune, discover a map showing the location of gold, hijacked during the Civil War. The plot revolves around their efforts to retrieve it.

Hidden Danger (Monogram, 1948) was the last picture Raymond Hatton made with Johnny Mack Brown. Their long association in the Monogram series had run its course and Hatton departed to end his film career doing character roles, mainly in television series and non-western features.

This film was standard fare as a ranch yarn about an extortion racket operated by a

Edmund Cobb watches as Johnny Mack Brown disarms a player in this scene from **Montana Desperado** (Monogram, 1951). (Courtesy of Jerry Ohlinger's Movie Material Store.)

cattleman's protective association. Its head, Myron Healey, is forcing ranchers to sell their cattle to the association for less than market value. Then he resells the cattle for a handsome profit. Johnny comes on the scene to put a stop to the fraud.

Law of the West (Monogram, 1949) had Johnny play a federal marshal on vacation where he finds ranchers losing their spreads to a bogus real estate agent who has forged phony flaws into their deeds. Johnny becomes the bodyguard to the crooked agent to uncover the real leader behind the plot.

Trail's End (Monogram, 1949) brought Johnny Mack in to aid a young woman in saving her ranch from chislers who have discovered gold on the property. He helps the lady rancher and then rides on to further adventures as she weds her young swain in the picture. If it sounds familiar by now, it is.

In 1949 Johnny had begun to explore the idea of returning to character roles in larger budget films. Monogram had started releasing some medium budget Westerns under the Allied Artists name. With his extensive acting experience in such films, Johnny was a natural for such parts.

Stampede (Allied Artists, 1949) was just the sort of film for Johnny to begin his character roles. It starred Rod Cameron and Gale Storm. Johnny played the sheriff who tries to maintain peace between cattlemen and settlers anxious for free government land upon which the ranchers had been grazing their cattle. Shady land dealers egg the nesters on until a range war breaks out. As a third lead, Johnny turned in a good performance as a character actor.

Meanwhile, his "B" western film series continued. In **West of Eldorado** (Monogram, 1949) Johnny Mack was on the trail of stolen bank loot, taken in a Kansas City robbery. He befriends a youth who was in on the bank job, captures the robbers and reforms the lad in the process. As

Jimmy Ellison and Brown get the drop on a band of desperados in **Whistling Hills** (Monogram, 1951). The gang is led by a masked bandit who uses a mysterious whistle to summon his evil followers. (Courtesy of Bobby Copeland.)

usual now, Alibi (Max Terhune) was along for the ride.

Range Justice (Monogram, 1949) was a repeat of the oft told story of good guy Brown saving heroine, Sarah Padden's ranch from heavy, Fred Kohler, Jr. and his gang. Tristram Coffin was also featured as a villain.

Western Renegades (Monogram, 1949) had Johnny as a U.S. Marshal who aids a brother and sister. They arrive in town just as their father has been murdered and a con-woman passes herself off as their long-missing mother. Following this film, Max Terhune also departed to continue his career playing character roles in other projects.

West of Wyoming (Monogram, 1950) was the familiar story of the homesteaders versus the cattlemen again. Johnny Mack played the government agent who protects the settlers from an unscrupulous cattleman trying to run them off their land.

Over the Border (Monogram, 1950) was a silver smuggling tale in which Johnny has to uncover the secret boss behind the scheme. Myron Healey played a "mean" villain in this one.

Six Gun Mesa (Monogram, 1950) had a lawman aid the foreman of a cattle herd when the ramrod is blamed for the murder of his wranglers.

Law of the Panhandle (Monogram, 1950) made Johnny a U.S. Marshal again to help sheriff Riley Hill break up an outlaw gang terrorizing ranchers. This film has a rather tricky scene when villain Myron Healey plugs Johnny with six shots from his pistol. Suddenly, there is our hero again, blocking Healey's flight, having escaped death by previously loading the outlaw chief's gun with blanks. They were looking for almost anything different in the series.

Outlaw Gold (Monogram, 1950) had Myron Healey, a gunman recently released from prison, out to get revenge upon Johnny Mack for sending him up. Brown, a. U.S. Marshal, and his new sidekick, Milburn Morante as Sandy Parker, are at the

Brown, Jimmy Ellison and Marshall Reed in a scene from **Whistling Hills** (Monogram, 1951). It was late in Brown's career and Ellison was called on to add some action to the series. (Courtesy of Bobby Copeland.)

time on the trail of hijackers of Mexican government gold. Johnny uncovers Marshall Reed, a newspaperman, as the leader of the hijackers as Healey lies in ambush for the lawman.

Another featured role in a medium budget western came for Johnny in 1950 at Allied Artists. **Short Grass** was another Rod Cameron picture in which Johnny again played a lawman in a town at the center of a range war. He aids rancher Cameron in stopping a crooked land grab. Once again, he was billed after the stars.

But in 1951 it was back to the by now very familiar "B" series. **Colorado Ambush** (Monogram), the initial oater of the year, was distinctive only in that Myron Healey, the stock villain in the series, was also the screen writer of the film. A five way gun battle among Johnny Mack, the local sheriff, the kid, the blonde and the outlaw at the climax of the picture was about the only new thing in the film.

Man from Sonora (Monogram, 1951) had Johnny as a marshal who helps the local sheriff find out who is behind the theft of a bullion

shipment and the killing of an undercover lawman.

Blazing Bullets (Monogram, 1951) was the story of a kidnapping and stolen gold bullion. Johnny played the marshal who aids the daughter of the kidnapped victim in getting both her father and the gold back.

Montana Desperado (Monogram, 1951) told the tale of a mysterious masked rider who is involved in the deaths of four tenants of a ranch. Two more die before Johnny can unravel the mystery and bring the killer to justice. Veteran western actor Edmund Cobb had a fine character role in the film.

Oklahoma Justice (Monogram, 1951) brought lawman Johnny a new sidekick, James "Shamrock" Ellison, as a stagecoach driver. Ellison had previously been a sidekick to "Hopalong Cassidy" in the early films of that series and more recently co-starred with another "Hoppy" sidekick, Russell Hayden, in a short lived western series for Lippert Films in 1950.

In this film Johnny once again infiltrates the

Johnny Mack Brown is ready for action in this scene from **Man From the Black Hills** (Monogram, 1952). (Courtesy of Jerry Ohlinger's Movie Material Store.)

gang and rounds them up with Ellison's assistance.

Whistling Hills (Monogram, 1951) had Brown, the roving cowboy, help local sheriff Ellison track down masked stagecoach robbers, led by a legendary whistling hills mystery man. Noel Neill, the Lois Lane of the *Superman* television series, played the heroine.

Texas Lawmen (Monogram, 1951) was another story by actor Myron Healey who did not appear in this one. The yarn revolved around a manhunt for three desperados, two of whom are father and son. Another son is the local sheriff, torn between family loyalty and duty. Johnny played the federal marshal who helps sheriff Ellison bring the outlaws in.

Texas City (Monogram, 1952) had Ellison, playing a dishonorably discharged cavalry officer out to vindicate himself, assist U.S. Marshal Brown hunt down the gang that has been hijacking the army gold bullion.

Man from the Black Hills (Monogram, 1952) added another "Hoppy" sidekick to the cast along with Ellison. Rand Brooks, the last of the "Lucky Jenkins" characters played a villain who passes himself off as Ellison in order to secure an inheritance of a gold mine. Johnny comes to town with Ellison to help him claim his rightful inheritance. The film is loaded with character actors as villains, including Stanford Jolley, Robert Bray, Denver Pyle, and Stanley Price.

Dead Man's Trail (Monogram, 1952) was the story of an outlaw's brother who aids a sheriff in tracking down the gang that killed his brother.

Johnny Mack Brown's last "B" Western was **Canyon Ambush** (Monogram, 1952). Ellison did not appear in the film. But it was full of Johnny Mack's old associates from the studio: Dennis Moore, Denver Pyle, Pierce Lyden, Marshall Reed and Stanley Price. After this film, Johnny hung up his sixgun as a "B" western hero. Although, he did reappear in a cameo role in 1953 in a "B" western spoof, **The Marshal's Daughter** (United Artists), starring Hoot Gibson and Laurie Anders. Other cameos in the picture were Preston Foster, Jimmy Wakely and Tex Ritter as narrator.

7 • Ragtime Cowboy Fuzzy

During the "B" western sound film era there were two comic sidekicks nicknamed "Fuzzy." Al St. John was a bewhiskered little slapstick comedian that some might call the "clown prince" of the western sidekicks. The other comic of the same moniker was Fuzzy Knight who was devoid of a hairy face. Instead, he derived his nickname from his voice which had a distinctive, fuzzy quality.

Fuzzy Knight's film personna is best described as follows. Down the dusty western street runs a short, stubby man who trips on his spurs and takes a pratfall. He struggles to his feet and runs to the rugged hero, Johnny Mack Brown, to warn him of the peril of being shot down from ambush. But he stutters so much that he can't get the words out.

In another situation Fuzzy would sit down at a piano and belt out a humorous song with that unique flannel quality to his voice. He might even roll his eyes while singing for comic effect. This was Fuzzy Knight.

John Forrest Knight was born in Fairmont, West Virginia on May 9, 1901. He entered show business at the tender age of 15 when he appeared in a traveling minstrel show as an end man. He also played the calliope for the troupe.

Studying law at West Virginia University, Knight was a great favorite among his classmates as a singer and piano player with the local college dance band. He invented the "vo-do-de-o" style of swing singing which became widely popular with college groups. Upon graduation from the university with his degree, rather than enter his intended profession, he was urged by his classmates to pursue a musical career. Following several tryouts, he was offered a chance to appear on the stage.

As a beginning professional, Knight was an immediate hit with his comedy song and piano act in vaudeville. He soon graduated into nightclubs where he was equally well received. Following this early success, he was offered a chance to do his act in Earl White's *Vanities* on Broadway in 1927. Knight then followed this hit performance with a role in the 1928 musical comedy, *Here's How*, and Ned Wayburn's *Gambols* in 1929. Next, he toured on the Keith Vaudeville Circuit.

During the years 1928 to 1931 Knight also signed for a series of Paramount musical shorts, entering motion pictures in this manner. In the depression years the motion picture industry had become a haven for nightclub and Broadway entertainers who were hard-pressed for live work.

In 1932 he began a film career of supporting roles that would span several decades and many western film stars in both "A" and "B" films. During his career Fuzzy would have co-starring and featured roles with Gary Cooper, John Wayne, Randolph Scott, Buster Crabbe, Richard Dix, Tex Ritter, Kirby Grant, Bob Baker, Johnny Mack Brown, Rod Cameron, James Ellison and Russell Hayden, Whip Wilson and Bill Elliott among others. His film credits read like a WHO'S WHO of western films. Also, Knight would frequently appear in non-western films and play dramatic roles.

His first films were **Hell's Highway** (RKO, 1932) and **Her Bodyguard** (Paramount, 1933) both starring Richard Dix. Then he was featured as "Ragtime Kelly" in the Mae West film, **She Done Him Wrong** (Paramount, 1933) along with Cary Grant. Fuzzy's first western films were **Under the Tonto Rim** (Paramount, 1933) starring Stuart Erwin, **To the Last Man** (Paramount, 1933) and **Sunset Pass** (Paramount, 1933), the latter two starring Randolph Scott.

Knight continued his roles in the Zane Grey western series at Paramount from 1934 to 1936 in support of several western stars. He played "Bunco McGee" in **The Last Round-Up** and "Cracker" in **Home on the Range** with Scott in 1934. Then he was loaned out to M-G-M to appear in the Civil War drama, **Operator 13** with Gary Cooper. He made several non-western films in 1934, most notably **Moulin Rouge** (United Artists/20th Century) with Franchot Tone.

Fuzzy Knight points something out to Johnny Mack in this scene from **Wild West Days** (1937, Universal -serial). (WOY Collection.)

Throughout 1935 and 1936 he continued to make westerns at Paramount, **Wanderer of the Wasteland** and **Arizona Mahoney**, both starring Buster Crabbe.

However, in 1935 he also began to serve as a comic sidekick to "B" western stars, beginning with Kermit Maynard in **Trails of the Wild** (Ambassador). Then he supported Tex Ritter in his initial "B" western, **Song of the Gringo** (Grand National, 1936). He played the ranch hand who aids Tex in running down a crooked ranch foreman and his gang.

The year 1936 also provided Knight with roles in two large budget films. He played "Tater" in the classic mountain story, **The Trail of the Lonesome Pine** (Paramount), starring Fred MacMurray and Henry Fonda. Fuzzy sang the two popular songs from the film, "Melody in the Sky" and "Twilight on the Trail." He later said that this was his favorite role of all his films. That same year he was selected to play a small part in the

Cecil B. DeMille epic western, **The Plainsman** (Paramount) with Gary Cooper and Jean Arthur. In the film he played "Dave," a townsman who tries to avoid paying Calamity Jane for his drink in her saloon. He also had a small part in the John Wayne non-western film, **The Sea Spoilers** (Universal). All in all it was a big year for Fuzzy.

Meanwhile he continued his non-western roles in several "hill-billy" features released in 1937, **Mountain Justice**, **County Fair**, and **Mountain Music**, the latter with Bob Burns, Martha Raye, George Hayes and Rufe Davis. In 1937 he also began a western series at Universal Studios where he was destined to become the "house" comedian for many years. He became the regular sidekick to Bob Baker, beginning with **Courage of the West** (Universal). Baker was an early singing cowboy who was only mildly successful in "B" westerns.

Indeed, reviewers of this initial series were not kind to Fuzzy either. One reviewer, upon seeing a double feature with both films containing Fuzzy,

54

Johnny Mack, Stanley Andrews and Fuzzy Knight in a scene from **Son of Roaring Dan** (Universal, 1939). (Courtesy of Jerry Ohlinger's Movie Material Store.)

said "Two helpings of Mr. Knight's singing at one sitting are enough in themselves to abolish the digestive possibilities of an already indigestible bill of fare." (Bosley Crowther, December 27, 1937, *The New York Times Film Reviews*, New York: Arno Press, 1970, p. 1456.)

In 1938, while continuing his "B" western film roles, Knight was loaned to support Gary Cooper and Merle Oberon in the modern western comedy, **The Cowboy and the Lady** (United Artists). His role was that of "Buzz," a rodeo sidekick of Cooper's. He got to play the piano and lead the singing in one scene. That same year he played the sidekick to Jack Randall in a Monogram "B" western film, **Where the West Begins**.

However, it was his support of Johnny Mack Brown in the 1939 western serial at Universal that started his continuing role as a regular sidekick. In **The Oregon Trail** Fuzzy played "Deadwood," a typical Fuzzy characterization. He would remain with Johnny Mack Brown until the star left

Universal and then continue in the Universal "B" western series with other stars until the studio discontinued their "B" Westerns.

That same year Brown and Fuzzy continued their series of "B" western features, starting with **Desperate Trails** (Universal). Brown and Baker would share the action at first, but gradually Baker would fade away, leaving Johnny Mack and Fuzzy as a duo team for several years until they were joined by Tex Ritter in the final years of the series. It was during this series that Knight would put the final touches upon his "Fuzzy" characterization for which most western film fans remember him. Although his "Fuzzy" was not a very complex fellow, Knight would manage to add shadings to the film characters he played. Many times he would be a typical sidekick, but other times he would play a comical character in the film, already established when Brown would appear.

In the first film of the series Fuzzy received an

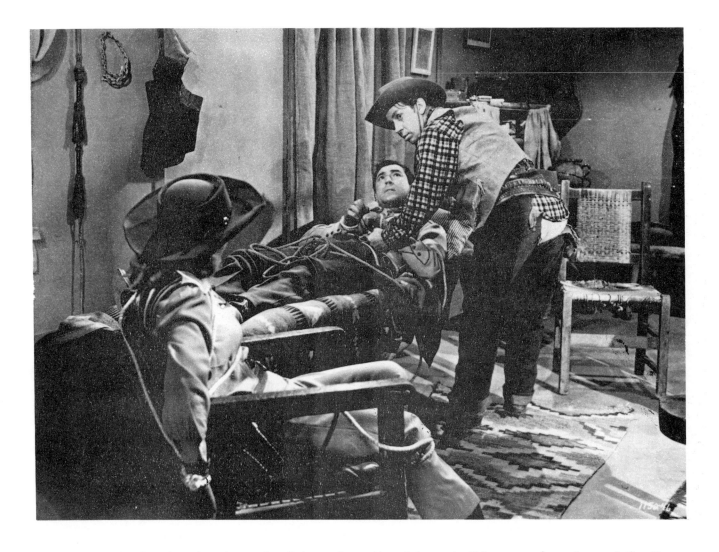

Fuzzy Knight is showing the signs of a fight as he unties Johnny in this scene from **Law of the Range** (Universal, 1941). (Courtesy of Jerry Ohlinger's Movie Material Store.)

accolade from The Hollywood Reporter reviewer: "Fuzzy Knight is an ideal western type and although he accounts for many of the laughs in this release, one of the best comedy scenes is one in which break-away wagons, buggies, carts, etc. figure when a vigilante party is broken up. (August 12, 1939).

In his non-typical characters Fuzzy was equally adept. He played the title role in **Ragtime Cowboy Joe** (Universal, 1940), that of an inept ranch foreman who "oversees" Brown as he aids Fuzzy's boss, the heroine, to save her ranch. Fuzzy is the personification of the title song of the film, which he sings wildly. In **Riders of Pasco Basin** (Universal, 1940) Fuzzy played a hair tonic drummer who helps both Brown and Baker clean up a town beset by local badmen. In **The Lone Star Trail** (Universal, 1943) he was the local barber and partner to Johnny Mack in a ranch. His comedy included a bath house which kept dropping pails of water at inappropriate times. He even

dumped water upon co-star Tex Ritter in this one.

Knight was featured in another epic western in 1937 at Paramount, **Wells Fargo**, starring Joel McCrea and Bob Burns. He also appeared in several bigger pictures in 1940, notably **My Little Chickadee** (Universal) with Mae West and W.C. Fields in which he was "Cousin Zeb" to the sexy Miss West. He also supported Tyrone Power in two films that year, as a cellmate in **Johnny Apollo** (20th Century-Fox) and a western character, "Pete" in the epic western, **Brigham Young** (20th Century-Fox).

Fuzzy began 1941 with a mystery film, **Horror Island** (Universal), playing a non-western sidekick role as "Stuff" with Dick Foran. He also supported George Montgomery in a modern western, **The Cowboy and the Blonde** (20th Century-Fox) that year. In addition, he appeared with Harry Carey and John Wayne in the mountain story of revenge, **The Shepherd of the Hills** (Paramount). Finally, he had a comic role in

Fuzzy Knight, Nell O'Day and Johnny Mack made an impressive series of films for Universal in 1941 and 1942. (Courtesy of Bobby Copeland.)

the Universal all star western, **Badlands of Dakota** with Richard Dix, Robert Stack, Broderick Crawford, Hugh Herbert and Andy Devine. He played "Hurricane Harry" in this one.

In 1942 Tex Ritter joined Brown and Fuzzy in their Universal "B" series, starting with **Deep in the Heart of Texas** (Universal). This was to be the last Universal series for Brown. Some of the films such as the initial entry were among the best, but some were panned by reviewers. Even Fuzzy came in for his share of criticism. About **Raiders of San Joaquin** (Universal, 1943) The Hollywood Reporter reviewer said: "In this case the stuttering, bungling Knight isn't half as funny as he usually is..." (May 25, 1943). The closing of the series seemed to have had its effect upon the usually effective Fuzzy.

Meanwhile, Fuzzy continued his role of "house" comic in the Universal comic western, **Butch Minds the Baby** (1943) with Broderick Crawford and Dick Foran. Then he was loaned to

Warner Brothers for a supporting role in **Juke Girl** (1943) with Ronald Reagan and Ann Sheridan. Back at Universal he supported Dick Foran and Joan Davis in the comedy film, **He's My Guy** (Universal, 1943) and made his first war film with Randolph Scott, **Corvette K-225** (Universal, 1943). He also was loaned to M-G-M for a role in **Apache Trail** with Gilbert Roland.

Knight returned to the serial format in 1944, supporting Milburn Stone in **The Great Alaskan Mystery** (Universal). While continuing his "B" western sidekick roles at Universal, he began to make more non-western films in 1944, several of them musicals, **Hi Good Lookin'!**, **Take It Big**, and **The Singing Sheriff** with Bob Crosby, Bing's band leader brother.

His "B" western star was now Rod Cameron who had been moved up to star status following Rex Ritter's departure to PRC for another series. This Universal series lasted only a short time as Cameron was soon elevated to "A" film status in

Fuzzy Knight pulls Nell O'Day off a player in this scene from **Rawhide Rangers** (Universal, 1941). (Courtesy of Jerry Ohlinger's Movie Material Store.)

such pictures as **Frontier Gal** (1945). Fuzzy, of course, had a comic role in that one as the resident "house" comic. He also teamed up again with Andy Devine for comedy in **Frisco Sal** (Universal, 1945).

Kirby Grant was brought in to replace Cameron in the Universal "B" western series, but this series lasted only one year, the films containing many, many outakes from previous Universal "B" westerns.

In 1947 Knight had a small role in the classic Universal comedy, **The Egg and I** (Universal), starring Fred MacMurray and Claudette Colbert and which introduced the "Ma and Pa Kettle" characters to movie fans.

With competition from television giving the film industry problems, Fuzzy's output of films was curtailed considerably in 1948 and 1949. His only film in 1948 was **The Adventures of Gallant Bess** (M-G-M). In 1949 he began working for a small studio, Lippert, where he

made several western films, **Rimfire** and **Apache Chief**, neither very well received at the time.

In 1950 he began a new "B" western series with co-stars James Ellison, Russell Hayden and Raymond Hatton, all veterans of "B" western series. Ellison and Hayden were former sidekicks of William Boyd in the long running "Hopalong Cassidy" series, while Hatton had been a sidekick to many, many "B" western stars as well as a star in his own right in a silent comedy series with Wallace Beery. However, the Lippert films were poorly made and, despite the talent of the foursome, were not well received by the public. After six films, the series discontinued.

Then Knight signed to support Monogram's "B" western star, Whip Wilson, when the previous sidekick, Andy Clyde, dropped out of the series. This was to be his final "B" series, although he had supported Rex Allen in the Republic western, **Hills of Oklahoma** in 1950.

In 1951 Knight appeared in several non-series

Fuzzy Knight gets the best of the villain Harry Woods in this scene from **Deep in the Heart of Texas** (Universal, 1942). (Courtesy of Jerry Ohlinger's Movie Material Store.)

roles, including **Honeychile** (Republic) with Judy Canova, the western spoof, **Skipalong Rosenbloom** (United Artists) and the western farce, **Gold Raiders** (United Artists), with George O'Brien and the Three Stooges.

By 1952 the Whip Wilson series had ended, so Fuzzy continued his non-western featured roles in **Oklahoma Annie** (Republic) with Judy Canova and **Feudin' Fools** (Monogram) with the Bowery Boys. That same year he began to support Bill Elliott in his larger budget westerns, including **Kansas Territory** (Allied Artists) and **Fargo** (Allied Artists). In 1953 he continued with Elliott in **Topeka** (Allied Artists) and also the following year in **Vigilante Terror** (Allied Artists).

After 1954 Knight began to appear in films only occasionally. He was in **The Naked Hills** (Allied Artists) in 1956, **The Notorious Mr. Monks** (Republic) in 1958 and **Three Thousand Hills** (20th Century-Fox) in 1959.

His last three films were A.C. Lyles westerns which brought many of his former co-stars back together again. Such former stars as Rod Cameron, Richard Arlen, Buster Crabbe, Johnny Mack Brown, Bob Steele and Broncho Billy Anderson were featured in the films, **The Bounty Killer** (Paramount, 1965), **WACO** (Paramount, 1966) and **Hostile Guns** (Paramount, 1967).

It seems fitting that "Fuzzy" Knight ended his film career of 35 years with these "last hurrah" Westerns in the 1960's. The films were like alumni gatherings of the oldtimers of the "B" western films.

"Fuzzy" Knight was once voted the "King of the Cowboy Comedians." Many western film buffs might protest that he couldn't touch "Gabby," "Fuzzy" St. John or "Smiley," but others might ask where could you find such an awkward, foolish or stuttering, singing sidekick for the western film hero? Those stars who were fortunate to ride with "Fuzzy" Knight lived in constant danger from their pal. You could never

Johnny Mack, Jennifer Holt and Tex Ritter seem amused at Fuzzy Knight in this scene from **Little Joe, the Wrangler** (Universal, 1942). (Courtesy of Jerry Ohlinger's Movie Material Store.)

tell what trouble Fuzzy would get mixed up with next.

Fuzzy died in 1976. He had had a western film career of many years, bringing pleasure to several generations of youngsters and adults alike.

Filmography

1. **Hell's Highway** (1932, RKO)
2. **Her Bodyguard** (1932, Paramount)
3. **She Done Him Wrong** (1933, Paramount)
4. **Speed Demon** (1933, Columbia)
5. **Sunset Pass** (1933, Paramount)
6. **Under the Tonto Rim** (1933, Paramount)
7. **This Day and Age** (1933, Paramount)
8. **To the Last Man** (1933, Paramount)
9. **Moulin Rouge** (1933, United Artists/20th Century)
10. **The Last Round-Up** (1934, Paramount)
11. **I Hate Women** (1934, Ken Goldsmith)
12. **Operator 13** (1934, M-G-M)
13. **Night Alarm** (1934, Majestic)
14. **Music in the Air** (1934, Fox)
15. **Behold My Wife** (1935, Paramount)
16. **Home on the Range** (1935, Paramount)
17. **George White's Scandals** (1935, RKO)
18. **The Murder Man** (1935, Monogram)
19. **Mary Burns, Detective** (1935, Paramount)
20. **Wanderer of the Wasteland** (1935, Paramount)
21. **Danger Ahead** (1935, Victory)
22. **The Old Homestead** (1935, Liberty)
23. **Hot Off the Press** (1935, Victory)
24. **Trails of the Wild** (1935, Ambassador)
25. **The Trail of the Lonesome Pine** (1936, Paramount)
26. **And Sudden Death** (1936, Paramount)
27. **The Plainsman** (1936, Paramount)
28. **Song of the Gringo** (1936, Grand National)
29. **The Sea Spoilers** (1936, Universal)
30. **Song of the Trail** (1936, Ambassador)
31. **Rio Grande Romance** (1936, Victory)

Jimmy Wakely, Jennifer Holt, Tex Ritter, Fuzzy Knight and Johnny Bond look on as Johnny Mack and Budd Buster listen in this scene from **The Old Chisholm Trail** (Universal, 1942). (WOY Collection.)

32. **Wildcat Trooper** (1936, Ambassador)
33. **Kelly of the Secret Service** (1936, Victory)
34. **Put on the Spot** (1936, Victory)
35. **With Love and Kisses** (1936, Ambassador)
36. **Arizona Mahoney** (1936, Paramount)
37. **The Gold Racket** (1937, Grand National)
38. **Mountain Justice** (1937, Warner Brothers)
39. **County Fair** (1937, Republic)
40. **Mountain Music** (1937, Paramount)
41. **Courage of the West** (1937, Universal)
42. **Wells Fargo** (1937, Paramount)
43. **Singing Outlaw** (1938, Universal)
44. **Quick Money** (1938, RKO)
45. **Spawn of the North** (1938, Paramount)
46. **Where the West Begins** (1938, Monogram)
47. **The Cowboy and the Lady** (1938, United Artists)
48. **Silks and Saddles** (1938, Treo)
49. **Flying Fists** (1938, Treo)
50. **Border Wolves** (1938, Universal)
51. **The Last Stand** (1938, Universal)

52. **The Oregon Trail** (1939, Universal) Serial
53. **Desperate Trails** (1939, Universal)
54. **Oklahoma Frontier** (1939, Universal)
55. **Union Pacific** (1939, Paramount)
56. **Chip of the Flying U** (1940, Universal)
57. **My Little Chickadee** (1940, Universal)
58. **Johnny Apollo** (1940, 20th Century-Fox)
59. **West of Carson City** (1940, Universal)
60. **Riders of Pasco Basin** (1940, Universal)
61. **Badman of Red Butte** (1940, Universal)
62. **Son of Roaring Dan** (1940, Universal)
63. **Brigham Young** (1940, 20th Century-Fox)
64. **Law and Order** (1940, Universal)
65. **Ragtime Cowboy Joe** (1940, Universal)
66. **Pony Post** (1940, Universal)
67. **Boss of Bullion City** (1941, Universal)
68. **Horror Island** (1941, Universal)
69. **The Cowboy and the Blonde** (1941, 20th Century-Fox)
70. **The Shepherd of the Hills** (1941, Paramount)
71. **Law of the Range** (1941, Universal)

Fuzzy Knight and Johnny protect Jennifer Holt in this scene from **Tenting Tonight on the Old Campground** (Universal, 1943). (Courtesy of Jerry Ohlinger's Movie Material Store.)

72. **New York Town** (1941, Paramount)
73. **Badlands of Dakota** (1941, Universal)
74. **The Masked Rider** (1941, Universal)
75. **Rawhide Rangers** (1941, Universal)
76. **The Man from Montana** (1941, Universal)
77. **Bury Me Not on the Lone Prairie** (1941, Universal)
78. **Arizona Cyclone** (1942, Universal)
79. **Butch Minds the Baby** (1942, Universal)
80. **Juke Girl** (1942, Warner Brothers)
81. **Fighting Bill Fargo** (1942, Universal)
82. **Apache Trail** (1942, M-G-M)
83. **Stagecoach Buckaroo** (1942, Universal)
84. **The Silver Bullet** (1942, Universal)
85. **Boss of Hangtown Mesa** (1942, Universal)
86. **Deep in the Heart of Texas** (1942, Universal)
87. **Little Joe, the Wrangler** (1942, Universal)
88. **The Old Chisholm Trail** (1942, Universal)
89. **He's My Guy** (1943, Universal)
90. **Tenting Tonight on the Old Campground** (1943, Universal)

91. **Cheyenne Roundup** (1943, Universal)
92. **The Lone Star Trail** (1943, Universal)
93. **Corvette K-225** (1943, Universal)
94. **Slick Chick** (1943)
95. **Raiders of San Joaquin** (1943, Universal)
96. **Frontier Law** (1943, Universal)
97. **Hi Good Lookin'!** (1944, Universal)
98. **The Great Alaskan Mystery** (1944, Universal) Serial
99. **Arizona Trail** (1944, Universal)
100. **The Cowboy and the Senorita** (1944, Republic)
101. **Allergic to Love** (1944, Universal)
102. **Take It Big** (1944, Paramount)
103. **The Singing Sheriff** (1944, Universal)
104. **Oklahoma Raiders** (1944, Universal)
105. **The Marshal of Gunsmoke** (1944, Universal)
106. **Boss of Boomtown** (1944, Universal)
107. **Trail to Gunsight** (1944, Universal)
108. **Trigger Trail** (1944, Universal)

Fuzzy Knight points something out to the judge in this scene from **Tenting Tonight on the Old Campground** (Universal, 1943). (Courtesy of Jerry Ohlinger's Movie Material Store.)

109. **Riders of the Santa Fe** (1944, Universal)
110. **The Old Texas Trail** (1944, Universal)
111. **Frisco Sal** (1945, Universal)
112. **Frontier Gal** (1945, Universal)
113. **The Senorita From the West** (1945, Universal)
114. **Song of the Sarong** (1945, Universal)
115. **Swing Out Sister** (1945, Universal)
116. **Beyond the Pecos** (1945, Universal)
117. **Renegades of the Rio Grande** (1945, Universal)
118. **Code of the Lawless** (1945, Universal)
119. **Badman of the Border** (1946, Universal)
120. **Girl on the Spot** (1946, Universal)
121. **Gunman's Code** (1946, Universal)
122. **Guntown** (1946, Universal)
123. **The Lawless Breed** (1946, Universal)
124. **Her Amorous Night** (1946, Universal)
125. **Trail to Vengeance** (1946, Universal)
126. **The Egg and I** (1947, Universal)
127. **Rustler's Roundup** (1947, Universal)

128. **Adventures of Gallant Bess** (1948, M-G-M)
129. **Down to the Sea in Ships** (1949, 20th Century-Fox)
130. **Apache Chief** (1949, Lippert)
131. **Feudin' Rhythm** (1949, Columbia)
132. **Rimfire** (1949, Lippert)
133. **Hostile Country** (1950, Lippert)
134. **Hills of Oklahoma** (1950, Republic)
135. **West of the Brazos** (1950, Lippert)
136. **Marshal of Heldorado** (1950, Lippert)
137. **Colorado Ranger** (1950, Lippert)
138. **Crooked River** (1950, Lippert)
139. **Fast on the Draw** (1950, Lippert)
140. **Wanted: Dead or Alive** (1951, Monogram)
141. **Canyon Raiders** (1951, Monogram)
142. **Nevada Badman** (1951, Monogram)
143. **Gold Raiders** (1951, United Artists)
144. **Stagecoach Driver** (1951, Monogram)
145. **Honeychile** (1951, Republic)
146. **Skipalong Rosenbloom** (1951, United Artists)

Johnny Mack Brown and Fuzzy Knight are playing with White Flash (Tex Ritter's horse) in this publicity still for **The Lone Star Trail** (Universal, 1943). (Courtesy of Jerry Ohlinger's Movie Material Store.)

147. **Rodeo** (1951, Monogram)
148. **Lawless Cowboy** (1951, Monogram)
149. **Stage From Blue River** (1951, Monogram)
150. **Oklahoma Annie** (1952, Republic)
151. **Kansas Territory** (1952, Allied Artists)
152. **Fargo** (1952, Allied Artists)
153. **The Gunman** (1952, Allied Artists)
154. **Night Raiders** (1952, Allied Artists)
155. **Feudin' Fools** (1952, Monogram)
156. **Topeka** (1953, Allied Artists)
157. **Vigilante Terror** (1954, Allied Artists)
158. **The Naked Hills** (1956, Allied Artists)
159. **The Notorious Mr. Monks** (1958, Republic)
160. **Three Thousand Hills** (1959, 20th Century-Fox)
161. **The Bounty Killer** (1965, Paramount)
162. **Waco** (1966, Paramount)
163. **Hostile Guns** (1967, Paramount)

8 • Tex Rides with Johnny Mack

In 1942 Universal contracted with Tex Ritter to co-star with Johnny Mack Brown in a series of "B" Westerns. Republic had the successful "mesquiteer" series and Monogram had the popular "Rough Riders" series with Buck Jones and Tim McCoy. Columbia had just completed a duo series with both Bill Elliott and Tex Ritter. However, the series ended as Elliott moved over to Republic for a new series there.

Tex Ritter had begun his western film career in 1936 in **Song of the Gringo** (Grand National) as a singing cowboy in competition with Gene Autry. Although never as successful in western films as Autry, Ritter had nevertheless carved out an appropriate niche for himself among the cowboy warblers. In 1938 he had moved on to Monogram for another series of musical western films which lasted until 1941. Then he had joined Elliott at Columbia. Now he was ready to step up to Universal.

Tex was born Woodward Maurice Nederland Ritter in Murval, Texas on January 12, 1907. He graduated from Beaumont High School and went to the University of Texas to study law. (Corneau, Ernest N., *The Hall of Fame of Western Stars.* Quincy, Massachusetts: The Christopher Publishing House, 1969, p. 166.)

At the University of Texas Tex encountered J. Frank Dobie, the renowned western folklorist who had a strong effect upon Tex Ritter's love of folk music. Previously, Tex had worked on his family farm as a youngster with a black farm hand who had taught him many old folk songs. (Parrish, James Robert. *Great Western Stars* New York: Ace Books, 1976, p. 180.)

During the depression Tex had to drop out of college to work in a steel mill. Soon he began to sing folk ballads over the radio in Houston. A musical road tour led Tex to Chicago where he entered Northwestern University to resume his study of law. But hard times forced him to return to his musical career. He next went to New York where he secured a small role and understudied Franchot Tone in *Green Grow the Lilacs*. It was in this show that he was nicknamed "Tex" by the cast and stagehands. Short runs in two more plays, *The Round-Up* and *Mother Lode*, followed. (*Ibid.*)

Then back to radio went Tex. He sang songs and told tales on **Lone Star Rangers** and served as announcer for a New York City barn dance program over WHN. He also did dramatic roles in audio-plays, including **Gang Busters, ENO Crime Clues** and **Death Valley Days**. He was then featured as Texas Mason in the popular children's show on CBS, **Bobby Benson's B-Bar-B Riders**. This led to another series where he used the same character, **Song of the B-Bar-B**. Then he created and starred in **Cowboy Tom's Roundup**, a very popular children's radio show in the East for three years. About this same time Rex began his recording career on various labels. (*Ibid.*, pp. 181-2.)

At a New Jersey dude ranch appearance Tex met Edward Finney, a movie producer, who signed him for a series of "B" Westerns for Grand National. The old-time outlaw, Al Jennings, who played the judge in the initial film, taught Tex how to draw and fire his sixguns. (*Ibid.*)

By 1937 Tex had made the Top Ten Western Star list and remained on the list through 1941, regaining his position in 1944 and 1945. It is notable that it was during his years at Columbia and Universal when he was at the highest point in his film career that he dropped off the list. Perhaps, this was due to the fact that he sang much less in both of the duo series or that he had to co-star with the better known Elliott and Brown.

His films with Johnny Mack Brown began with **Deep In the Heart of Texas** (Universal, 1942), the story of Brown returning to Texas after the Civil War only to find his father embroiled in a rebellion against the state government. Tex plays the governor's agent sent to break up the rebellion. In the end he and Brown team up to destroy the rebellion and nab its leaders. In this series Tex was to sing only one song per film, often with the

Tex Ritter is being held at bay by Johnny Mack Brown in this scene from **Little Joe, the Wrangler** (1942, Universal). (WOY Collection.)

Jimmy Wakely Trio in support. In this film Tex sings "The Cowboy's Lament". A rousing musical finale of the title song, somewhat like the Roy Rogers films had, concludes the film.

Next was **Little Joe, The Wrangler** (Universal, 1942) a title taken from an old cowboy ballad. Tex plays a discredited sheriff who has been unable to halt a series of outlaw raids. When Johnny Mack is framed for a murder during an ore shipment robbery, Tex refuses to believe that Brown is guilty. He and Johnny Mack team up to uncover the real outlaws. Tex sings the title song.

The Old Chisholm Trail (Universal, 1943) was the third picture of the series. Tex plays a gunman who in the end comes to the aid of cattleman Johnny Mack as he attempts to get his thirsty cattle to water. A villainous female has blocked the waterholes along the famed trail from Texas. In this film Tex sings "The Rovin' Gambler".

Cheyenne Roundup (Universal, 1943) was the next film for the duo. Tex plays a tough sheriff who mortally wounds an outlaw (Johnny Mack in

a duo role) just as the good Johnny Mack brother appears. Johnny Mack masquerades as the bad twin to help sheriff Ritter bring the outlaw gang in control of the town to justice. The film was a remake of Brown's earlier **Badman of Red Butte** (Universal, 1940). Tex sings "Rose of the Hills" as he romances Jennifer Holt.

Raiders of San Joaquin (Universal, 1943) followed as the next duo oater. Tex plays a rancher whose father is murdered because he opposes the railroad coming through the ranch country. Tex seeks revenge on the railroad as he fights a gang of land grabbers seeking right-of-way for the railroad line. Johnny Mack is the undercover railroad agent who aids railroad agents. Tex sings "A Carefree Cowboy".

The final film of the series was **The Lone Star Trail** (Universal, 1943), a remake of the famous "Destry Rides Again" story by Max Brand, which Universal had twice filmed before, once a "B" with Tom Mix and once an "A" with James Stewart. It was a dandy. Tex plays a government

Johnny Mack, Tex Ritter and Fuzzy Knight fight off the bad guys in this action scene from **Tenting Tonight on the Old Campground** (1943, Universal). (Courtesy of Jerry Ohlinger's Movie Material Store.)

agent on the trail of recently paroled Johnny Mack as he returns to his hometown after two years in the pen for a framed up robbery charge. Tex helps Johnny Mack prove his innocence and bring the real culprits to justice. Tex sings "Adios Vaquero" in this one.

In summary, the Johnny Mack Brown-Tex Ritter series was an excellent one. The stories, the production values and the acting were first rate. Each film had Johnny Mack and Tex square off with each other in a rip-roaring fist fight. Tex could hold his own with Johnny Mack, having spent years fighting with Charles King in his Grand National and Monogram days, as well as mixing it up also with Bill Elliott in the Columbia series. It is a shame that Universal let Johnny Mack get away from them, for the series could likely have run on for several years for both stars. But Brown went to Monogram for his "Nevada" series. Tex Ritter made a few more Universals originally planned for Brown and Ritter together. Then Tex moved to PRC for the "Texas Rangers"

series, which was to be his last.

In 1938 Tex had married actress Dorothy Fay. The marriage produced two sons, Thomas and Jonathan. The latter had gone on to become a famous television and film star in his own right.

Following the end of his western film career in 1945, Tex spent his time on personal appearances and recordings. In 1945 three of his records were the three top tunes listed in Billboard's top ten jukebox tunes. His most popular songs were "Jealous Heart", "Green Grow the Lilacs", "Boll Weevil" and "Rye Whiskey". (Parrish, p. 184.)

Tex next toured throughout the United States with western comic, Max "Alibi" Terhune. In 1949 he formed his Western Festival and Circus, later called Western Revue. In 1950 he returned to films for a guest role in **Holiday Rhythm** (Lippert). He also toured Europe. (*Ibid.*)

In 1952 Tex was selected to sing the theme song for the classic western film, **High Noon** (United Artists, 1952), which won the Academy Award for best song. He performed it for the

The Jimmy Wakely Trio, Fuzzy Knight, Jennifer Holt watch as Johnny Mack and Tex Ritter finish with the villains (Robert Mitchum on the floor in the foreground) in this scene from **Lone Star Trail** (1943, Universal). (WOY Collection.)

awards ceremony in 1953. His recording of the song was his most successful. (*Ibid.*)

During the 1950's he appeared on NBC's *Town Hall Party*, narrated **The Cowboy** in 1954, played a gunfighter in **Apache Ambush** (Columbia, 1955), and sang title themes for films such as **Trooper Hook** (MGM, 1957). (*Ibid.*, pp. 184-85.)

At the same time Tex became a regular performer on the *Grand Ole Opry* radio broadcast in Nashville. He also appeared on Red Foley's *Ozark Jubilee* radio program. In 1958 Tex appeared in the television series *Zane Grey Theatre* and guest-starred in the ABC series, *The Rebel* (*Ibid.*)

Following this, he co-hosted a television series, *Four Star Jubilee* and, in 1959, began a four year starring role in *Tex Ritter's Ranch Party*, a syndicated country music show (*Ibid.*)

In 1966 Tex narrated *What's the Country Coming To?* and starred as the preacher in *Girl from Tobacco Road*. He played himself in *What Am I Bid?* in 1967 in which he sang a nostalgic

ballad, "I Never Got to Kiss the Girl", a lament that he never kissed any of his leading ladies in his Westerns. (*Ibid.*)

He moved to Nashville and served as the Chairman of the National Committee for the Recording Arts and president of the Country Music Association. He was elected to both the Cowboy Hall of Fame and the Country and Western Hall of Fame. (*Ibid.*)

In 1970 Tex sought the Republican nomination for the Senate from Tennessee, but was defeated. (*Ibid.*)

His final film appearance was in **The Nashville Story** (1972). On January 2, 1974 Tex Ritter died of a heart attack while visiting a friend in the Nashville jail. His last record, "The Americans," became a best seller after his death. Tex was sometimes called "America's Most Beloved Cowboy". His zest for life and fun-loving attitude was evident in everything he did. That was why, perhaps, that it was impossible not to like Tex Ritter.

68

9 • Don't Call Me "Oldtimer"!

No one who saw any of the Monogram Johnny Mack Brown film series of the 1940s can have missed a scene repeated over and over. "Nevada" (Brown) would make a comment to "Sandy Hopkins" (Raymond Hatton) in which he smilingly referred to Sandy as "oldtimer." Immediately Sandy would bristle and fire back, "Don't call me Oldtimer!" I still look forward to these little interchanges in the same way that I listen for "Gabby" Hayes to say "You're Dern Tootin'!"

The "oldtimer" nickname was especially appropriate for Raymond Hatton as his film career spanned over 50 years. He was in films from 1911 until 1967, although his first feature film listed was **Oliver Twist** in 1916.

Raymond Hatton was born on July 7, 1892 in Red Oak, Iowa, the son of a prominent physician. He was raised in Des Moines where he attended grammar school. At the age of twelve he made his debut on the vaudeville stage and toured the Midwest as an actor in a stock company. Finding himself stranded in New York, he tried for a job in motion pictures and landed a job at Kalem Studios. From there he went to the Biograph Company where he made many silent films.

In 1914 he joined Mack Sennett in his "slapstick" comedy one-reelers and soon was regarded as one of the screen's best character actors. He played villains opposite famous silent stars, became expert in the use of make-up and costume which helped create many unusual characters, and worked for many different studios. Among his roles was that of the "artful dodger" in the 1916 version of **Oliver Twist**.

He signed with Paramount in 1918 and moved to the West Coast where he appeared in many features for C.B. DeMille who is credited with "discovering" him. In 1919 he appeared in his first film with Wallace Beery, **The Love Burglar**. DeMille cast him in **Male and Female** in the same year in which he played the Honorable Ernest Wooley. His acting was called excellent in the film review of the 1920 Will Rogers film, **Jes'**

Call Me Jim. He played a serious role somewhat different for him.

DeMille cast Hatton again in his 1921 film, **The Affairs of Anatole** and he was cited once more for his acting in the review of **Doubling for Romeo**. During this period he played a variety of character roles including a caricature of an orchestra leader, Bunt's own "Weelum," a cockney and a butler. In 1923 he was cast in Lon Chaney's classic **The Hunchback of Notre Dame**.

Following a number of films in 1924 he appeared with Warner Baxter in **A Son of His Father**. Hatton was cast in the role of an invalid who looked seedy but regained his health and captured the villain after a fall into the river. He poked his finger into the villain's back, making him think he had a gun.

Raymond Hatton became a star in 1926 when he co-starred with Wallace Beery in a knockabout comedy at Paramount entitled **Behind the Front**. Hatton played Shorty McGee, a pickpocket, who lifts his buddy's watch just before being recruited for the Army. A classic comedy scene occurs in the Army prison where Hatton and Beery try to open a can of biscuits unsuccessfully without even making a dent in it. Other comedy films in the series followed. **We're in the Navy Now** (1926) contained a hilarious scene with a Navy hammock. **Fireman, Save My Child** (1927), had Hatton as Sam, an imaginative crook. In **We're in the Air Now** (1927) Beery and Hatton were shot down behind the lines in Germany. A very funny scene involving milking a cow from both ends occurs. **Partners in Crime** (1928) had Hatton playing a dual role. In one role he is a cocksure, eager reporter, Scoop McGee, an energetic scamp. The other role has Hatton playing the dreaded "Knife" Regan, a mean gangster with a tattoo mark on his hand who sends chills up the spines of his victims before knifing them.

The last film of this series, **The Big Killing** (1928) has Beery and Hatton playing road show

Johnny and Raymond Hatton thwart a scheme to beat a rancher out of his land for it's silver ore in **Flashing Guns** (Monogram, 1947). (Courtesy of Bobby Copeland.)

barkers who become involved in a mountain feud. The success of the series relied upon the contrast in size and style between the huge bumbling Beery and the agile, wise-cracking Hatton.

In 1926 Hatton had appeared in his first western feature with Jack Holt in the Zane Grey story, **Born to the West.** He played Jim Fallon, a man who has learned all about women and decides to snub all of them until he looks into the eyes of one of the dancing girls in the Paradise Saloon and changes his mind. It was an early taste of western sidekick roles to come.

William Wyler cast Hatton in one of the leads in his classic western, **Hell's Heroes** (1929) with Charles Bickford and Fred Kohler, Sr.

Three desert rats try to save a baby from the desert and atone for their crimes of robbery and murder. A famous story, it was filmed several times, the most famous of which is John Ford's **Three Godfathers** with John Wayne.

During the 1930s Hatton alternated mainly between westerns and gangster roles with a variety of other character roles between them. He appeared as a sidekick with Joel McCrea in the western **The Silver Horde** in 1930. He was Shorty in the C. B. DeMille film, **The Squaw Man** with Warner Baxter in 1931. The classic western, **Law and Order** (1932) provided Hatton with a role as Deadwood. It starred Walter Huston and Harry Carey. Following this he was in **The Vanishing Frontier** (1932) with Johnny Mack Brown, a star with whom he was later to have a long association in "B" westerns. Also he made **Cornered** with Tim McCoy and **Hidden Gold** with Tom Mix in 1933.

In his non-westerns during this period he appeared with many famous stars including George Bancroft, Loretta Young, Charles Bickford, Jack Oakie and Clark Gable. In the Gable film, **Polly of the Circus,** he played Downey, the bleary sexton who interrupted the church service because he disliked Polly.

Johnny, Kathy Frye and Raymond Hatton are paying close attention to what is being said in this scene from **Crossed Trails** (Monogram, 1948). (Courtesy of Jerry Ohlinger's Movie Material Store.)

In 1933 he continued his western roles with Randolph Scott (**The Thundering Herd**) and Tom Mix (**Terror Trail**). He also continued his gangster roles as a gunman in **State Trooper** and a bodyguard in **Penthouse**. An unusual role found him as the Mouse in **Alice in Wonderland** along with such stars as W. C. Fields and Gary Cooper.

During 1934 he made a western film with Randolph Scott, **Wagon Wheels**, but most of his output was in non-westerns notably **Lady Killer** with James Cagney, **Lazy River** with Robert Young, **The Defense Rests** with Jack Holt and **Straight is the Way** with Franchot Tone.

The year 1935 found Hatton back into westerns in a big way. He made the serial, **Rustlers of Red Dog** with Johnny Mack Brown and began a Zane Grey western series at Paramount with Buster Crabbe that continued until 1936 including **Wanderer of the Wasteland, Nevada, Desert Gold** and **Arizona Raiders**. He also completed a second western serial, **The Vigilantes Are Coming** with Robert Livingston, his first work at Republic Studios.

In non-westerns during 1935 Hatton appeared with Robert Taylor (**Times Square Lady**), James Cagney (**G-Men**), and Will Rogers (**Steamboat Round the Bend** – a John Ford film). Among his non-westerns in 1936 was **Laughing Irish Eyes**.

Hatton strayed from westerns in 1936 with only **Roaring Timber** with Jack Holt as his output. He made a number of non-western films that year most notably **Marked Women** with Bette Davis and Humphrey Bogart in which he played the shyster lawyer.

The year 1938 marked an increase in western films for Hatton with **The Texans** starring Randolph Scott, **Bad Men of Brimstone** with Wallace Beery and **Come On Rangers**, beginning a series of Roy Rogers "B" westerns for Republic. In 1939 he replaced Max Terhune in the Three Mesquiteer series as Rusty Joslin, the comic side-kick, in **Wyoming Outlaw** with John Wayne. The

71

Raymond Hatton and Kathy Frye listen to instructions from Johnny in this scene from **Crossed Trails** (Monogram, 1948). (Courtesy of Jerry Ohlinger's Movie Material Store.)

film also was notable to western film buffs in that Don "Red" Barry had a supporting role. Hatton was less rustic a clown than his predecessor adding more ginger and bite to the role. He was as apt as not to kick the villain in the seat of the pants when he "had the drop on him!"

It was during this series that Hatton honed his grizzly, prairie, oldtimer role to a fine edge. He called upon his long experience with costume and make-up to build the character he wanted in the Mesquiteer series. For example, he used leather cuffs on his sleeves as the real cowboys had and they were heavily scarred with rope burns, adding realism to his dress.

Hatton's role in the Mesquiteer series continued throughout 1940 with Robert Livingston starring. His non-western roles included parts in **Over the Wall** with Dick Foran and **Love Finds Andy Hardy** with Mickey Rooney and Judy Garland. In 1939 he appeared with Bing Crosby, Lloyd Nolan and Walter Pidgeon in a variety of character roles.

A big western became Hatton's major film of 1940, **Kit Carson**, starring Jon Hall and Dana Andrews. He played Jim Bridger, the famous frontier scout.

White Eagle, a third western serial with Buck Jones, was his initial effort in 1941. Following this, he teamed with Buck Jones and Tim McCoy in the Monogram Rough Rider western series which lasted until 1942. Hatton was selected as a veteran character actor who was handy to have around and not just for comedy relief. He played "Sandy Hopkins," a folksy character to compliment Jones and McCoy who were in their older period. Actually Hatton was the youngest of the three, although playing the "oldtimer" of the bunch. Eight Rough Rider features were made with **Arizona Bound** giving Hatton his best comic bit—while being served tea by a lady, he is asked if he prefers one lump or two. "Six," he replies, with a twinkle in his eye. Judging from the look on the lady's face, it could easily have

Kathy Frye holds back Steve Clark, and, perhaps Douglas Evans as Raymond Hatton throttles another man in this scene from **Crossed Trails** (Monogram, 1948). (Courtesy of Jerry Ohlinger's Movie Material Store.)

been an ad lib.

The series continued until 1942 when Tim McCoy was recalled into the Army as a reservist in World War II. Jones and Hatton continued their roles following McCoy's departure until Jones was killed in the disastrous Copacabana fire.

In 1943 the Rough Riders series was left with Hatton only. A new star was brought to Monogram to star with Hatton — his old partner — Johnny Mack Brown. Brown played "Nevada" Jack MacKenzie and Hatton continued playing "Sandy Hopkins" a retired federal lawman. Beginning with **The Ghost Rider**, Brown and Hatton would make 45 Monogram Westerns until 1949 and **The Law of the West**.

It was during these years that Hatton modified his role as the grizzled oldtimer in a variety of undercover roles. Calling upon his rich experience as a character actor he helped Nevada capture the villains. Most western fans today remember Hatton best for these roles in which he portrayed a preacher, a tinker, a bar fly or swamper and a wide assortment of others as an undercover detective helping Brown.

In 1944 he was cast as a grizzled old coot named Zeke in John Wayne's **Tall in the Saddle** and Buckly in **Black Gold**.

Following the Brown Monogram western series, he made several non-westerns including **Operation Haylift** and **County Fair** in 1950. Then Hatton signed on with Lippert for a western series starring James Ellison and Russell Hayden beginning with **Hostile Country**. In the interim he had appeared with Lash LaRue in **The Dalton's Women**. This was to be his last western film.

After 1950 Hatton made fewer films with westerns and non-westerns interspersed. His most notable film during this period of semi-retirement was his last film, **In Cold Blood** in 1967, a classic study of murder done in semi-documentary style.

Raymond Hatton died on October 21, 1971 in

Two villains accost Raymond Hatton in this scene from **Crossed Trails** (Monogram, 1948). (Courtesy of Jerry Ohlinger's Movie Material Store.)

Palmdale, California of a heart attack. His wife the former screen actress, Francis Hatton had died one week before. His career was one of the longest in films and corresponded with the rise of the film industry itself. He rose from bit parts to starring roles in silent films, played western sidekicks for many years and ended his career as a character actor in a wide variety of films. Few film stars deserved the title "oldtimer" more than he.

Partial Filmography: Raymond Hatton

Note: we will probably never be able to complete this filmography because of the scarcity of information on the years from 1911 to 1916.

Silent Films

1. **Oliver Twist** (1916).
2. **Woman God Forgot** (1917).
3. **Joan the Woman** (1917).
4. **The Little American** (1917).
5. **The Whispering Chorus** (1918).
6. **We Can't Have Everything** (1918).
7. **The Source** (1918).
8. **You're Fired** (1919).
9. **The Love Burglar** (1919).
10. **Male and Female** (1919).
11. **Every Woman** (1919).
12. **The Dancing Fool** (1920).
13. **Jes' Call Me Jim** (1920).
14. **The Ace of Hearts** (1921).
15. **The Affairs of Anatol** (1921).
16. **Bunty Pulls the Strings** (1921).
17. **The Concert** (1921).
18. **Peck's Bad Boy** (1921).
19. **Salvage** (1921).
20. **All's Fair in Love** (1921).
21. **Pilgrim's of the Night** (1921).
22. **Doubling for Romeo** (1922).
23. **Ebb Tide** (1922).

What is Johnny Mack Brown saying as he holds a deed while Kathy Frye, Steve Clark, and perhaps, Douglas Evans, and Raymond Hatton listen in this scene from **Crossed Trails** (Monogram, 1948). Courtesy of Jerry Ohlinger's Movie Material Store.)

24. Head Over Heels (1922).
25. Pink Gods (1922).
26. To Have and to Hold (1922).
27. Manslaughter (1922).
28. The Hottentot (1922).
29. His Back Against the Wall (1922).
30. At Bay (1922).
31. The Barefoot Boy (1923).
32. Java Head (1923).
33. The Virginian (1923).
34. Trimmed in Scarlet (1923).
35. The Tie That Binds (1923).
36. Three Wise Fools (1923).
37. A Man of Action (1923).
38. Big Brother (1923).
39. Enemies of Children (1923).
40. The Hunchback of Notre Dome (1923).
41. True As Steel (1924).
42. Triumph (1924).
43. The Mine with the Iron Door (1924).
44. Cornered (1924).

45. The Fighting American (1924).
46. Half A Dollar Bill (1924).
47. Adventure (1925).
48. Contraband (1925).
49. In the Name of Love (1925).
50. Devil's Cargo (1925).
51. A Son of his Father (1925).
52. The Thundering Herd (1925).
53. The Top of the World (1925).
54. Tomorrow's Love (1925).
55. Lord Jim (1925).
56. Behind the Front (1926).
57. Born to the West (1926).
58. Silence (1926).
59. Forlorn River (1926).
60. We're in the Navy Now (1926).
61. Fashions for Women (1927).
62. Fireman, Save My Child (1927).
63. Now We're in the Air (1927).
64. The Big Killing (1928).
65. Wife Savers (1928).

Raymond Hatton, Lynne Carver, Kathy Frye and Johnny Mack in a publicity still for **Crossed Trails** (Monogram, 1948). (Courtesy of Jerry Ohlinger's Movie Material Store.)

66. **Partners in Crime** (1928).
67. **The Office Scandal** (1929).
68. **Trent's Last Case** (1929).
69. **When Caesar Ran a Newspaper** (1929).
70. **Dear Vivian** (1929).

Sound Films

71. **Christie Talking Plays** (1929).
72. **Hell's Heroes** (1929).
73. **Christie Shorts** (1929).
74. **The Silver Horde** (1930).
75. **Rogue of the Rio Grande** (1930).
76. **Murder on the Roof** (1930).
77. **Her Unborn Child** (1930).
78. **Midnight Mystery** (1930).
79. **The Road to Paradise** (1930).
80. **Pineapples** (1930).
81. **The Mighty** (1930).
82. **The Squaw Man** (1931).
83. **Honeymoon Lane** (1931).

84. **The Lion and the Lamb** (1931).
85. **Arrowsmith** (1931).
86. **The Challenge** (1931).
87. **Woman Hungry** (1931).
88. **Law and Order** (1932).
89. **Polly of the Circus** (1932).
90. **Made on Broadway** (1932).
91. **The Fourth Horseman** (1932).
92. **Uptown New York** (1932).
93. **Exposed** (1932).
94. **The Crooked Circle** (1932).
95. **Vanity Street** (1932).
96. **Malay Nights** (1932).
97. **Stranger in Town** (1932).
98. **Drifting South** (1932).
99. **Vanishing Frontier** (1932).
100. **Alias Mary Smith** (1932).
101. **Long Loop Laramie** (1932).
102. **Divorce a la Mode** (1932).
103. **State Trooper** (1933).
104. **Under the Tonto Rim** (1933).

Raymond Hatton has stopped the villain, Steve Clark, from escaping in this scene from **Crossed Trails** (Monogram, 1948). (Courtesy of Jerry Ohlinger's Movie Material Store.)

105. **Alice in Wonderland** (1933).
106. **Lady Killer** (1933).
107. **Penthouse** (1933).
108. **Day of Reckoning** (1933).
109. **Tom's in Town** (1933).
110. **Terror Trail** (1933).
111. **Cornered** (1933).
112. **Hidden Gold** (1933).
113. **The Big Cage** (1933).
114. **The Defense Rests** (1934).
115. **Women in His Life** (1934).
116. **Lazy River** (1934).
117. **Once to Every Bachelor** (1934).
118. **Fifteen Wives** (1934).
119. **The Thundering Herd** (1934).
120. **Straight is the Way** (1934).
121. **Wagon Wheels** (1934).
122. **Times Square Lady** (1935).
123. **Murder in the Fleet** (1935).
124. **Calm Yourself** (1935).
125. **Rustlers of Red Dog** (serial) (1935).

126. **Nevada** (1935).
127. **Wanderer of the Wasteland** (1935).
128. **Red Morning** (1935).
129. **G-Men** (1935).
130. **The Daring Young Men** (1935).
131. **Steamboat 'Round the Bend** (1935).
132. **Stormy** (1935).
133. **Exclusive Story** (1936).
134. **Women Are Trouble** (1936).
135. **Mad Holiday** (1936).
136. **Laughing Irish Eyes** (1936).
137. **Desert Gold** (1936).
138. **Timothy's Quest** (1936).
139. **The Vigilantes Are Coming** (serial) (1936).
140. **The Arizona Raiders** (1936).
141. **Yellowstone** (1936).
142. **Jungle Jim** (serial) (1936).
143. **Marked Women** (1937).
144. **Fly Away Baby** (1937).
145. **Badman of Brimstone** (1937).
146. **Torchy Blane: the Adventurous Blonde** (1937).

Raymond Hatton and Brown ponder a way to break up a gang operating a cattleman's protective racket in **Hidden Danger** (Monogram, 1948). Marshall Reed (standing on the right) looks on. (Courtesy of Bobby Copeland.)

147. **Love Is on the Air** (1937).
148. **The Missing Witness** (1937).
149. **Roaring Timber** (1937).
150. **Public Wedding** (1937).
151. **Over the Goal** (1937).
152. **He Couldn't Say No** (1938).
153. **Come On Rangers** (1938).
154. **Love Finds Andy Hardy** (1938).
155. **The Texans** (1938).
156. **Touchdown Army** (1938).
157. **Tom Sawyer, Detective** (1938).
158. **Over the Wall** (1938).
159. **I'm From Missouri** (1939).
160. **Ambush** (1939).
161. **Undercover Doctor** (1939).
162. **Rough Rider's Round-Up** (1939).
163. **Frontier** (1939).
164. **Paris Honeymoon** (1939).
165. **New Frontier** (1939).
166. **Wyoming Outlaw** (1939).
167. **Wall Street Cowboy** (1939).

168. **Kansas Terrors** (1939).
169. **The Cowboys From Texas** (1939).
170. **Six Thousand Enemies** (1939).
171. **Career** (1939).
172. **Heroes of the Saddle** (1940).
173. **Pioneers of the West** (1940).
174. **Covered Wagon Days** (1940).
175. **Rocky Mountain Rangers** (1940).
176. **Oklahoma Renegades** (1940).
177. **Queen of the Mob** (1940).
178. **Kit Carson** (1940).
179. **Arizona Bound** (1941).
180. **Gunman From Bodie** (1941).
181. **Forbidden Trails** (1941).
182. **Ghost Town Law** (1942).
183. **Cadets on Parade** (1942).
184. **Girl From Alaska** (1942).
185. **Down Texas Way** (1942).
186. **Raiders of the West** (1942).
187. **Dawn on the Great Divide** (1942).
188. **Below the Border** (1942).

Johnny Mack and Raymond Hatton made a good action team in this scene from **Frontier Feud** (Monogram, 1948). (Courtesy of Jerry Ohlinger's Movie Material Store.)

189. **West of the Law** (1942).
190. **The Ghost Rider** (1943).
191. **The Texas Kid** (1943).
192. **Outlaws of Stampede Pass** (1943).
193. **Six Gun Gospel** (1943).
194. **Stranger From Pecos** (1943).
195. **Raiders of the Border** (1944).
196. **Rough Riders** (1944).
197. **Partners of the Trail** (1944).
198. **West of the Rio Grande** (1944).
199. **Land of the Outlaws** (1944).
200. **Tall in the Saddle** (1944).
201. **Range Law** (1944).
202. **Ghost Guns** (1944).
203. **The Law Men** (1944).
204. **Law of the Valley** (1945).
205. **The Navajo Trail** (1945).
206. **Flame of the West** (1945).
207. **Sunbonnet Sue** (1945).
208. **Frontier Feud** (1945).
209. **Gunsmoke** (1945).

210. **The Last Trail** (1945).
211. **Northwest Trail** (1945).
212. **Rhythm Round-Up** (1945).
213. **Stranger From Santa Fe** (1945).
214. **Drifting Along** (1946).
215. **Under Arizona Skies** (1946).
216. **The Haunted Mine** (1946).
217. **Border Bandits** (1946).
218. **Shadows of the Range** (1946).
219. **Raiders of the South** (1946).
220. **The Gentleman From Texas** (1946).
221. **Silver Range** (1946).
222. **Trigger Fingers** (1946).
223. **Trailing Danger** (1947).
224. **Land of the Lawless** (1947).
225. **Rolling Home** (1947).
226. **Valley of Fear** (1947).
227. **Black Gold** (1947).
228. **The Law Comes to Gunsight** (1947).
229. **Code of the Saddle** (1947).
230. **Prairie Express** (1947).

Johnny disarms Dennis Moore as Raymond Hatton looks on in this scene from **Frontier Feud** (Monogram, 1948). (Courtesy of Jerry Ohlinger's Movie Material Store.)

231. **Gun Talk** (1947).
232. **Unconquered** (1947).
233. **Crossed Trails** (1948).
234. **Triggerman** (1948).
235. **Overland Trails** (1948).
236. **Frontier Agent** (1948).
237. **Back Trail** (1948).
238. **Range Justice** (1948).
239. **Sheriff of Medicine Bow** (1949).
240. **Trail's End** (1949).
241. **Gunning for Trouble** (1949).
242. **Western Renegades** (1949).
243. **Hidden Danger** (1949).
244. **West of El Dorado** (1949).
245. **The Fighting Ranger** (1949).
246. **Law of the West** (1949).
247. **Operation Haylift** (1950).
248. **County Fair** (1950).
249. **West of the Brazos** (1950).
250. **Marshal of Heldorado** (1950).
251. **Crooked River** (1950).

252. **Colorado Ranger** (1950).
253. **Fast on the Draw** (1950).
254. **Hostile Country** (1950).
255. **Skipalong Rosenbloom** (1951).
256. **Kentucky Jubilee** (1951).
257. **The Golden Hawk** (1952).
258. **Cow Country** (1953).
259. **Thunder Pass** (1954).
260. **The Twinkle in God's Eye** (1955).
261. **Treasure of the Ruby Hills** (1955).
262. **Dig That Uranium** (1956).
263. **Shake, Rattle and Rock** (1956).
264. **Flesh and the Spur** (1956).
265. **Girls in Prison** (1956).
266. **Pawnee** (1957).
267. **Invasion of the Saucer Men** (1957).
268. **Motorcycle Gang** (1957).
269. **Alaska Passage** (1959).
270. **The Quick Gun** (1964).
271. **Requiem For a Gunfighter** (1965).
272. **In Cold Blood** (1967).

10 • The Rest of the Posse

In addition to Fuzzy Knight and Raymond Hatton as regular sidekicks in the Universal and Monogram series, Johnny Mack had numerous other sidekicks throughout his long film career in "B" Westerns. Syd Saylor provided some laughs in several of Brown's early oaters, including **Branded a Coward** (Superior, 1935), **Rogue of the Range** (Superior, 1935) and **Guns in the Dark** (Republic, 1937). Horace Murphy played both comedy and serious roles in several early films also: **Everyman's Law** (Superior, 1936) and **Lawless Land** (Superior, 1936). Even Al St. John, in his pre-"Fuzzy" days, played a Jewish storekeeper in **A Lawman is Born** (Republic, 1937).

Syd Saylor had played "Lullaby Joslin" in the initial Three Mesquiteers series film, but had been replaced by Max Terhune in the continuing role. However, Saylor had been in films for some time when he supported Johnny Mack in his pictures. He had made his feature film debut in 1926 in **Red Hot Leather** and had previously made a comedy short series for two years before that. Then in 1928 he had appeared in the western serial, **The Mystery Rider**.

His film credits in the early years of sound films included **Border Legion** (Paramount, 1930), with Richard Arlen, **The Light of the Western Skies** (Paramount, 1930), **Fighting Caravans** (Paramount, 1931) with Gary Cooper, all Zane Grey stories, and **Men Without Law** (Columbia, 1930) with Buck Jones.

In 1934 Saylor had supported George O'Brien in **The Dude Ranger** (Fox), playing "Nebraski Kemp", who says sagely when a rattlesnake pops up in the dude's bed his first night in the bunkhouse, "Rattlers don't climb in windows!" That same year he also made **When A Man Sees Red** (Universal) with Buck Jones and **Mystery Mountain** (Mascot), a serial with Ken Maynard.

In 1935 Syd appeared in support of Kermit Maynard in several of his Ambassador films, **Code of the Mounted** and **Wilderness Mail**.

Then in 1936 he returned to the Zane Grey series for **Nevada** (Paramount) with Buster Crabbe and also made **Headin' for the Rio Grande** (Grand National) with Tex Ritter.

Although his western film credentials appeared sound for a comic sidekick, Saylor was really more of a character actor than a comic. His stuttering gimmick wore thin after a while and he was then mostly a wise-cracking pal rather than a true comic.

Following roles with various other western film stars, he concluded his sidekick support with Bob Steele in his final series for PRC in 1946. But he continued to play character roles in many films and television programs until December 21, 1962, when he died of a heart attack in Hollywood, California.

Horace Murphy, who just barely played the sidekick to Johnny Mack, also supported a number of other western stars, most notably Tex Ritter. In that series he played "Ananias," the portly pompous windbag, who began every tall tale by expounding, "Back in '66..."

Horace was born in Findley, Tennessee on June 3, 1880. He entered show business as a child on the Mississippi riverboats, playing in the orchestra. He rose in the business until he was half-owner in the showboat, Cottonblossom Floating Palace. Then he opened a string of tent shows from New Orleans to Los Angeles, each with an orchestra and a baseball team. Next, he entered the theater business in Los Angeles and Burbank. Amidst all this financial dealing, he found time to enter motion pictures as a character actor in 1935.

Other western stars Murphy supported included Bob Steele in **Last of the Warrens** (Supreme, 1936), Kermit Maynard in **Song of the Trail** (Ambassador, 1936), Richard Arlen in **The Mine with The Iron Door** (Paramount, 1936), The Three Mesquiteers in **Ghost Town Gold** (Republic, 1936), Ken Maynard in **The Fugitive Sheriff** (Columbia, 1936), Rex Bell in **Too Much Beef** (Columbia, 1936) and Jack Perrin in **Gun**

Max Terhune and his dummy, Elmer Sneezewood, joined Brown for a few films after Raymond Hatton left the Brown series, here in a scene from **Trail's End** (Monogram, 1949). (Courtesy of Bobby Copeland.)

Grit (Atlantic, 1936).

In 1937 he continued his character roles with such stars as Bob Allen in **The Gun Ranger** (Columbia), Smith Ballew in **Western Gold** (20th Century-Fox), Jack Randall in **Stars Over Arizona** (Monogram), and Tom Kenne in **Romance of the Rockies** (Monogram).

Then he returned to play a sheriff in the Universal Johnny Mack Brown serial, **Flaming Frontiers** in 1938. Other stars he supported that year were Buck Jones and Roy Rogers. In 1939 Horace again supported Johnny Mack Brown as a sidekick named Nebraska in the Universal Western, **Desperate Trails**; a telegraph operator in the Roy Rogers film, **Saga of Death Valley** (Republic); and a peddler in the George O'Brien oater, **Legion of the Lawless** (RKO).

By 1940 Horace Murphy began making fewer western films, mainly **Ghost Town Raiders** (Republic) with Don "Red" Barry, **The Range Buster** (Monogram) and **Melody Ranch** (Republic) with Gene Autry. In 1941 he made a Rough Riders film, **Arizona Bound** (Monogram) and **Badman of Deadwood** (Republic) with Roy Rogers.

After 1941 Murphy left films for several years. During that time he portrayed "Buckskin", Red Ryder's sidekick on the west coast Blue Network radio production. He also performed on Gene Autry's *Melody Ranch* program and *The Roy Rogers* (radio) show.

But in 1945 he returned to western films, supporting Jimmy Wakely in **Springtime in Texas**, **Raiders of the Dawn** and **Lonesome Trail**, all Monogram oaters. That year he also played in the premiere Eddie Dean color film, **Song of Old Wyoming** (PRC).

After 1945 there is little evidence of additional film roles, although Horace Murphy lived to the ripe old age of 94. He died on January 20, 1975. Murphy had not been a major western sidekick, but he had added luster to many a western film.

Johnny's new comic sidekick was now Max Terhune, here in a close up shot. (Courtesy of WOY Collection.)

Frank Yaconelli made one western serial as a sidekick to Johnny Mack, **Wild West Days** (Universal, 1937), in which he played Mike, the musical sidekick. He was born in Italy on October 2, 1898 and began his film career during the silent era. Throughout the early sound era he was used in films mainly for his dialectic comedy. He appeared with Ken Maynard in several of his Westerns, notably **The Strawberry Roan** (Universal, 1933). He also became the sidekick to Jack Randall and Tom Keene in several of their Monogram pictures.

In 1946 when Martin Garralaga bowed out of the Pancho role in the Monogram Cisco Kid series, Yaconelli was given the sidekick role of "Baby" for the next three films in the series, after which he was relegated back to character roles.

He went on to do character bits in such films as **Wild Horse Mesa** (RKO, 1947) with Tim Holt and **Abbott and Costello Meet Captain Kidd** (Universal, 1953) with the comedy duo and Charles Laughton. On November 19, 1965 Frank Yaconelli died of lung cancer in Los Angeles. His contribution as a comic sidekick had been meager, one of filling in where dialectic comedy was useful.

Following his Universal days in which Fuzzy Knight had been his primary sidekick, Johnny Mack was supported mainly by Raymond Hatton at Monogram until 1948 when Hatton left the series. Previously, in **Sheriff of Medicine Bow** (Monogram), Max Terhune had been introduced as an additional humorous character in the Brown series. Then Hatton bowed out and Terhune took over the comic sidekick duties to Johnny Mack.

Max Terhune had become a western sidekick star in the second Three Mesquiteers film, **Ghost Town Gold** (Republic, 1936), in which he was shown winning Elmer, his dummy in a three-card monte card game. Terhune was a relative newcomer to films when he joined the Mesquiteers.

Jimmy Ellison was brought into the Brown series toward the end. Here Johnny keeps Jimmy from fighting with Rand Brooks in **Man From the Black Hills** (Monogram, 1952). (Courtesy of Jerry Ohlinger's Movie Material Store.)

Max Terhune was born on February 12, 1891 in Franklin, Indiana with many talents for show business. He was a juggler, magician, whistler, card manipulator, pitchman, impressionist and ventriloquist as well as an actor. He had toured the Orpheum Circuit with his dummy, Skully Null, who later became Elmer Squeezewood in his films. Max began his entertainment career when he won a whistling contest in Shelbyville, Indiana. Soon his barnyard imitations and other talents brought him to the attention of the *National Barn Dance* radio show in 1932. By 1936 Gene Autry took notice of him and brought him to Hollywood where he made his film debut in Autry's film, **Ride, Ranger, Ride** (Republic, 1936). Following this, he went on to replace Saylor in the Mesquiteer series in which he made 21 films, concluding with **Three Texas Steers** (Republic, 1939).

Terhune was under an annual contract at Republic for seven years, but in 1939, after he had appeared in the "A" western epic, **Man of Conquest** with Richard Dix, the studio did not renew his contract. Then he signed, along with fellow Mesquiteer "Crash" Corrigan, with Monogram for another trio western series, The Range Busters. The first film had the same title. In this series he was given the name, "Alibi," since Republic retained the "Lullaby" character for the Mesquiteer series. After 18 Range Buster films through 1943, Max then supported Charles Starrett and Tex Ritter in the wartime western musical film, **Cowboy Canteen** (Columbia, 1944). He also appeared with Allan "Rocky" Lane in **Sheriff of Sundown** (Republic) that year.

Terhune was away from films then until 1947, when he came back to Republic to back up Monte Hale in **Along the Oregon Trail** (Republic). Then he supported Eddie Dean and Ken Maynard in **White Stallion** (Astor, 1947).

The next year he joined Johnny Mack for eight films. He retained the "Alibi" character and Elmer

Johnny can't seem to keep Jimmy Ellison out of fights in **Man From the Black Hills** (Monogram, 1952). (Courtesy of Jerry Ohlinger's Movie Material Store.)

for the series. In **Law of the West** (Monogram, 1948) he plays a storekeeper who uses his ventriloquism to trick the outlaws into surrendering. In **West of Eldorado** (Monogram, 1948) Terhune uses Elmer and his ventriloquism to break down the isolation of an orphaned youngster aided by Johnny Mack and himself. The last film of his series had Terhune play a slow-moving sheriff who aids Johnny Mack in rounding up the outlaws. This was to be his last "B" Western also.

From 1951 to 1957 Terhune appeared in several "A" film productions: **Rawhide** (20th Century-Fox 1951) with Tyrone Power, **Jim Thorpe-All American** (Warner Brothers, 1951) with Burt Lancaster, **Giant** (Warner Brothers, 1956) with Rock Hudson, Elizabeth Taylor and James Dean and **King and Four Queens** (United Artists, 1956) with Clark Gable. In addition, he had appeared in various television programs such as *I Love Lucy* and *Ramar of the Jungle*.

On June 5, 1973 Max Terhune died of a heart attack and stroke in Cottonwood, Arizona. In all he made 70 films and is best remembered as "Lullaby" in the Mesquiteer films. His portrayal was bucolic, easy-going and added just the right touch to the relationship already established between Livingston and Corrigan in the series. His amusing comedy with Elmer was a novelty to Westerns and brought him special fame at the same time that "Charlie McCarthy" was so popular on the radio.

Before his death he had said of his film career: "I loved every minute of it and have many wonderful memories. I have had the opportunity of working with some of the most talented people on earth." (McClure, Arthur and Jones, Ken D. *Heroes, Heavies and Sagebrush*, New York: A.S. Barnes and Company, 1972, p. 126.)

Johnny Mack Brown continued his western series at Monogram without a sidekick until Milburn Morante developed from a character into a sidekick, briefly. In **West of Wyoming**

What has landed Jimmy and Johnny in jail in this scene from **Man From the Black Hills**,(Monogram, 1952)? (Courtesy of Jerry Ohlinger's Movie Material Store.)

(Monogram, 1950) Morante plays Panhandle, an old codger who helps Johnny thwart a crooked cattleman's attempt to frighten homesteaders off their land. **Law of the Panhandle** (Monogram, 1950) had Morante as Ezra Miller, another old codger, while Riley Hill and Johnny Mack team up to round up a band of outlaws. In **Outlaw Gold** (Monogram, 1950) Morante plays a sidekick named Sandy Parker in the tradition of Raymond Hatton who helps Johnny nab a gang of hijackers. The last film Morante did with Johnny Mack was **Blazing Bullets** (Monogram, 1951). After that Johnny went without a comical sidekick in his films.

The last sidekick for Johnny Mack Brown was James Ellison who joined him in 1951 in **Outlaw Justice** (Monogram). He was more of a co-star than a sidekick and played featured roles in the films.

Ellison was born James Smith in Guthrie Center, Iowa in 1910. He was raised on a ranch in Valier, Montana where he became an accomplished rider as a child. Later his family moved to Los Angeles. When grown, he joined a stock company and traveled east where he was selected to perform with the Moscow Art Theater Group. Then he returned to California and joined the Beverly Hills Little Theater Company. There he was spotted by a talent scout for films. He was signed by Warner Brothers and cast in the juvenile lead in **Playgirl** (1932).

After several years of playing romantic leads, Ellison was selected by Harry Sherman for the role of Johnny Nelson in the Hopalong Cassidy series beginning at Paramount in 1935. He was featured in the first eight "Hoppies" as a co-star with William Boyd in the starring role. In 1936 Cecil B. DeMille cast him as Buffalo Bill in the epic Western, **The Plainsman** (Paramount), in support of Gary Cooper and Jean Arthur.

Following this, he played in comedies and dramas as a romantic lead until the late 1940's

Jimmy Ellison and Johnny Mack Brown in a publicity still for **Man From the Black Hills**, (Monogram, 1952). (Courtesy of Jerry Ohlinger's Movie Material Store.)

when he returned to Westerns. In 1948 he had the lead in Lippert's **Last of the Wild Horses**.

Then in 1950 Ellison teamed with another Hopalong Cassidy sidekick, Russell Hayden and two former Johnny Mack Brown sidekicks, Fuzzy Knight and Raymond Hatton, for a series of "quickie" Westerns at Lippert. Shot in one month, all six films featured the same casts in different stories. According to Don Miller in *Hollywood Corral*: "Being charitable about it, the score came up three up and three down... When the series was over, Ellison and Hayden had shown they had deserved better treatment." (New York: Popular Library, 1976, pp. 236-237.)

In 1951 James Ellison then joined Johnny Mack in a series of six features through 1952. It was to be the last series for both Ellison and Brown, although Ellison looked much younger than Brown who had put on considerable weight and was showing his age noticeably.

In **Whistling Hills** (Monogram, 1951) Ellison plays the local sheriff who is aided by cowboy Brown in tracking down a band of stagecoach robbers. The outlaws are led by a masked rider who used a weird whistle to signal his men. **Texas Lawmen** (Monogram, 1952) also had Ellison as a local sheriff, assisted by federal marshal Brown, as he is torn between loyalty to his outlaw family members and his sworn duty.

Texas City (Monogram, 1952) had Ellison as a discredited army officer out to prove that he was not dishonorable, aided by Brown, again a federal marshal, in recovering a stolen army gold shipment.

Man From Black Hills (Monogram, 1952) had Ellison playing the son of a dead gold miner who comes home only to find a crook posing as himself to steal the mine. Interestingly enough, the imposter is played by another former Hopalong Cassidy sidekick, Rand Brooks. Brown is the cowboy who helps Ellison regain his inheritance.

Dead Man's Trail (Monogram, 1952) was the

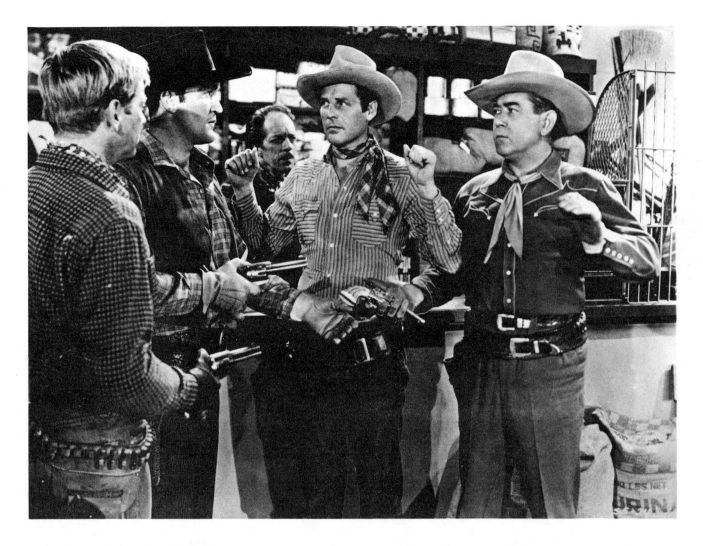

Rand Brooks, Lane Bradford, I. Stanford Jolly, Jimmy and Johnny in a scene from **Man From the Black Hills** (Monogram, 1952). (Courtesy of Jerry Ohlinger's Movie Material Store.)

last Brown film with Ellison as the co-star. It tells the story of an outlaw's brother who aids a sheriff in tracking down his brother's killer.

Ellison did not appear in Johnny Mack's last "B" Western. He retired from the screen after this series.

Johnny Mack Brown had many sidekicks in his more than 17 years as a "B" western film hero. Some were of the highest niche such as Hatton and Knight. Others were lower on the pecking order such as Saylor and Morante. But all added to the Brown films in their own way. Westerns would not have been nearly as much fun without the sidekicks.

11 • Sunset on the Range

Throughout his career as a western film star, Johnny Mack Brown had remained physically active in his daily life. Despite his increasing weight problem as he grew older, Johnny continued to play tennis and golf, swim and ride horses. His love of horses had manifested itself in polo as a young man at the Riviera Country Club in Hollywood. There he was always a tough contender in the matches.

Johnny Mack Brown was a devoted family man and spent much time with his four children as they grew up in Beverly Hills. The family lived in a spacious Tudor home overlooking the Beverly Hills. Johnny and his wife, Connie, were justly proud of their beautiful home, filled as it was with priceless antiques, a noted china collection and a circular library, complete with many first editions and fine bindings. Johnny was also proud of his collection of hand made stagecoaches on display in his home. Framed on the wall was a receipt signed by Paul Revere for making a teapot for a Brown family member in 1792.

During his later years in films, Johnny had made a series of personal appearances around the country. In 1950 he performed along with the Tennessee Ramblers at the Alabama State Fair in Birmingham. There he told western tales about his trick horse, Rebel, and demonstrated his fancy gun handling. His wife and oldest daughter often traveled with him.

After his film career in "B" Westerns was over, Johnny went to work in television like many of his peers. He appeared in a variety of series shows including *Tales of Wells Fargo* with Dale Robertson and *Perry Mason* with Raymond Burr. He had had a brief radio show of his own in 1939 on CBS entitled *Under Western Skies*. It lasted only one year, but the experience with the show made broadcasting a familiar medium for him.

After his children had grown up and moved on with their own lives and with a smaller income since he was no longer a film star, Johnny sold his Beverly Hills mansion. He and his wife moved to a modest LaBrea apartment. Then in 1961 Johnny accepted a position as the maitre d' for a Los Angeles restaurant.

In 1965 he was cast in two "A" western features as a character actor. In the Dan Duryea film, **The Bounty Killer** (Embassy) Johnny played his familiar sheriff character. The film also featured a whole host of former "B" western actors, including several from his old Universal days, Fuzzy Knight and Rod Cameron. Also the picture included Buster Crabbe and Richard Arlen from his old Paramount days. Bob Steele was in the film from his old Supreme days. Finally, Edmund Cobb and I. Stanford Jolley also were featured in the film. They were from his old Monogram days. It must have been like a school reunion for them all.

The second film, **Requiem for a Gunfighter** (Embassy) had Johnny play a character named Enkoff rather than a lawman. Again, along with him in the film were oldtime cowboy stars Tim McCoy, Lane Chandler and Bob Steele and his longest running sidekick, Raymond Hatton.

These two roles led Johnny Mack to the most infamous role he ever played in a motion picture, as well as his last. In **Apache Uprising** (Paramount, 1966), an A.C. Lyles production, Johnny was cast as the lecherous sheriff who attacks heroine Corinne Calvet only to be soundly thrashed by hero Rory Calhoun. It is well that most of his former fans could only recognize him in the film by his distinctive voice so serious had his weight problem become. It is rather sad to realize that this scene has become his film finale after such a fine western film career, especially when you stop to remember all the film heroines he had rescued in many, many films. The producer and director of the film might have given Johnny a more sympathetic character role before he hung up his spurs for good. Johnny is reputed to have been unhappy that he allowed himself to be cast in the role.

Like the earlier two films he appeared in, **Apache Uprising** sported many of the old timer

Johnny Mack Brown, 70, football and film star

WOODLAND HILLS, Calif. (UPI) — Johnny Mack Brown, who went from All-America college football player and Rose Bowl hero to star of hundreds of Saturday-matinee Western movies in the 1930s and 1940s, died Thursday at age 70.

Brown died of kidney failure, said a spokesman for the motion picture country home and hospital, where he had been under treatment for a month.

JOHNNY MACK BROWN

Mr. Brown, a native of Dothan, Ala., first won fame as a halfback on the University of Alabama team that beat the University of Washington 20-19 in a come-from-behind thriller in the 1926 Rose Bowl in which Mr. Brown caught two touchdown passes. Mr. Brown was named to the College Football Hall of Fame in 1957.

Mr. Brown went on to become an actor and once estimated he had appeared in more than 300 pictures, mostly B-grade Westerns with his horse "Reno."

His first Western was "Billy the Kid" with Wallace Beery in 1930. From 1942 to 1950 he was consistently named to the Motion Picture Herald's list of the 10 top money-making Western stars. Almost all of his pictures were aimed at the Saturday afternoon children's market.

He retired in the 1950s and was host and manager of a restaurant in the San Fernando Valley.

The 1926 Rose Bowl game was the highlight of his football career, Mr. Brown said in later years, because "we were the first Southern team ever invited to participate. We were supposed to be kind of lazy down South — full of hookworms and all. Nevertheless, we came out here and beat one of the finest teams in the country, making it a kind of historic event for Southern football. We didn't play just for Alabama, but for the whole South."

The Crimson Tide went into the game the underdog and Washington was leading 12-0 at the half before Alabama began to roll, with Brown catching the two touchdown passes, carrying one for 59 yards.

A Los Angeles sports writer called Brown's play "a thrilling feat that positively numbed" spectators and sparked "a do-or-die onslaught" that carried the game for the Alabamans.

Mr. Brown is survived by his wife, Cornelia, his college sweetheart whom he married shortly after graduation, and four children.

The obituary for Johnny Mack Brown as it appeared in newspapers on November 16, 1974.

"B" stars in character roles: Richard Arlen, Arthur Hunnicutt, Don "Red" Barry and former heroine, Jean Parker.

In 1957 Johnny Mack Brown had been elected to the Football Hall of Fame for his outstanding play at the University of Alabama and in the Rose Bowl Game. He was greatly appreciative of this honor. But in poor health and badly overweight, his final years were not easy. On November 14, 1974 he died of a kidney ailment, complicated by his cardiac condition, in Woodland Hills, California. He was 70 years of age.

Johnny Mack Brown was second only to Charles Starrett in the number of "B" western film starring roles. According to Richard B. Smith, III, he made 111 "B" Westerns, five western serials and appeared in numerous "A" western and non-western features between 1927 and 1966. He had worked in western pictures at M-G-M, Paramount, Mascot, Supreme, Republic, Universal, Monogram, Allied Artists, United Artists and Embassy. (Unpublished "Filmography of Johnny Mack Brown.") According to Don Miller, he made 16 "B" Westerns for Supreme "...half of which were distributed by Republic. For Universal, four serials and six co-starred with Bob Baker, 15 solo, 7 co-starred with Tex Ritter — total 28. For Monogram 66 features as a star, two supporting roles in Monogram-Allied Artists big scale Westerns." (*Hollywood Corral*, p. 230.)

When it comes down to it, Johnny Mack Brown began making sound western films earlier than most of the cowboy stars, lasted longer and ended his career rather quietly with style, when the time came.

Johnny Mack Brown will be remembered as the football hero with the soft southern drawl who became a cowboy movie star, could fight like the blazes, handle his sixgun with the best, ride like thunder and either get the girl or not. At the end of the picture he often mounted Rebel and rode off down the trail, that is, if he didn't get the girl. He was truly the hero, on the football field or on the silver screen. We'll be seeing you, Partner!

MGM was giving John Mack Brown the star build up when this publicity photo was taken with Gwen Lee in 1928. (WOY Collection.)

490-200

John Mack Brown and Kay Johnson in a scene from the all-talking picture **Billy the Kid**. Dated December 7, 1930. (WOY Collection.)

Although his Southern ancestors raised blooded horses, screen actor John Mack Brown, specialized in pedigreed dogs. He is shown here with "Baron Von Munchausen 2nd," his champion Schnauzer who won first place for his breed at the Los Angeles Kennel Club's show at the Ambassador Hotel in December 1934. In addition to many cups and ribbons, "The Baron" won seven first places against the country's finest dogs, and was California's first champion Schnauzer. Actor Brown was elected president of a club made up of fanciers of this breed. He is pictured with "The Baron" at home. (WOY Collection.)

John Wayne and Johnny Mack Brown in a publicity photo for **Born to the West** (1937, Paramount). This is the only film in which the two ex-football stars appeared together. (WOY Collection.)

Johnny Mack Brown on his summer replacement radio show, "Under Western Skies" on CBS on Friday nights at 8 to 8:30 p.m. His co-star was Isleta Gayle. (WOY Collection.)

A Universal Publicity Photo captioned: John Mack Brown, Universal western star, displays a spectacular bit of horsemanship during first day's shooting on his new Universal film **Desperate Trails** (1939). The horse is "Wheezer," his favorite mount. (WOY Collection.)

A Publicity Photo captioned: Cowboy Johnny Mack Brown tries to answer the questions that only a three-year old could ask. His daughter Sally listens intently as daddy reads answers to her questions from the encyclopedia. Dated July 10, 1950. (WOY Collection.)

A Publicity Photo captioned: Like Father, Like Daughter — Johnny Mack Brown, a former All-American football star from Alabama, helps his ten-year-old daughter Cynthia onto his horse, Rebel. Dated February 21, 1950. (WOY Collection.)

With appreciation
and very best
wishes – always –
Johny Mack Brown

A Publicity Photo Johnny used to send to fans who wrote. (Courtesy of Merrill McCord.)

Johnny Mack taking it easy at home in a Publicity Photo distributed to fan magazines around 1950. (Courtesy of Merrill McCord.)

12 • Filmography

1. SLIDE, KELLY, SLIDE

Copyrighted . . . . .April 1, 1927
Distributor . . . . Metro-Goldwyn-Mayer
Length . . . . .82 Minutes
Director . . . . Edward Sedgewick
Original Screenplay . . . . , A. P. Younger
Photography . . . . .Henry Sharp
Film Editor . . . . Frank Sullivan

Cast

William Haines . . . . .Jim Kelly
Sally O'Neil . . . . Mary Munson
Harry Carey . . . . Tom Munson
Junior Coghlan . . . . .Mickey Martin
Warner Richmond . . . . .Cliff Macklin
Paul Kelly . . . . Fresbie
Carl Dane . . . . Swede Hansen
Guinn Williams . . . . .McLean
Bob Meusel .himself
Tony Lazzeri . . . . .himself
Johnny Mack Brown . . . . .uncredited

2. THE BUGLE CALL

Copyrighted . . . . .August 1, 1927
Distributor . . . . , . . . Metro-Goldwyn-Mayer
Length . . . . .61 Minutes
Director . . . . Edward Sedgewick
Screenplay . . . . .Josephine Lovett
Story . . . . .C. Gardiner Sullivan
Photography . . . . André Barlatier
Film Editor . . . . Sam S. Zimbalist

Cast

Jackie Coogan . . . . Billy Randolph
Clair Windsor . . . . .Alice Tremayne
Herbert Rawlinson . . . . Captain Randolph
Tom O'Brien . . . . Sergeant Doolan
Harry Todd . . . . .Corporal Jansen
Nelson McDowell . . . . .Luke
Sarah Padden . . . . Luke's Wife
Johnny Mack Brown . . . . .uncredited

3. AFTER MIDNIGHT

Copyrighted . . . . .August 17, 1927
Distributor . . . . Metro-Goldwyn-Mayer
Length . . . . .66 Minutes
Director . . . . .Monta Bell
Screenplay . . . . Joe Farnham
Photography . . . . .Percy Hilburn
Film Editor . . . . Blanche Sewell

Cast

Norma Shearer . . . . Mary
Lawrence Gray . . . . Joe Miller
Gwen Lae .Maizie
Eddie Sturgis . . . . .Red Smith
Philip Sleeman . . . . Gus Van Gundy
Johnny Mack Brown . . . . .uncredited

4. MOCKERY

Copyrighted . . . . October 12, 1927
Distributor . . . . Metro-Goldwyn-Mayer
Length . . . . .62 Minutes
Director . . . . Benjamin Christensen
Screenplay . . . . .Bradley King
Photography . . . . Merritt B. Gerstad
Film Editor . . . . .John W. English

Cast

Lon Chaney (Sr.) . . . . Sergei
Ricardo Cortez . . . . .Dimitri
Barbara Bradford . . . . Tatiana
Mack Swain . . . . Mr. Gaidaroff
Emily Fitzroy . . . . Mrs. Gaidaroff
Charles Puffy . . . . .Ivan
Kai Schmidt . . . . Butler
Johnny Mack Brown . . . . .uncredited

5. THE FAIR CO-ED

Copyrighted . . . . October 20, 1927
Distributor . . . . Metro-Goldwyn-Mayer
Length . . . . .67 Minutes
Director . . . . .Sam Wood
Screenplay . . . . Byron Morgan, Joe Farnham

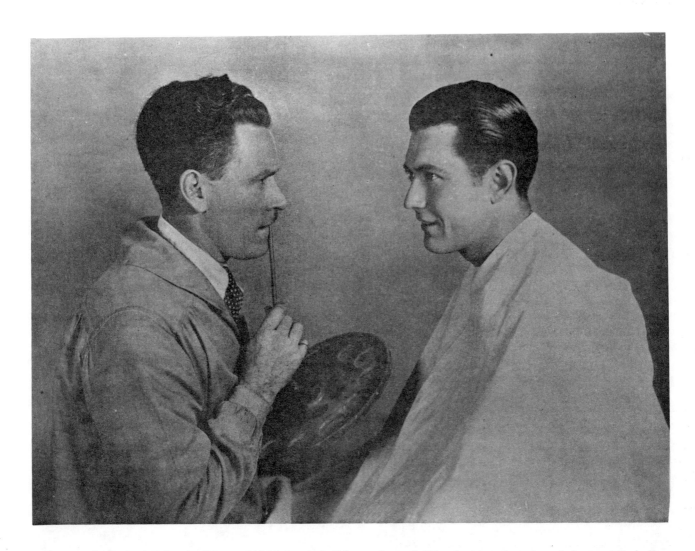

As part of his publicity build up MGM issued this series of (3) photos showing Johnny Mack Brown being made up by Cecil Holland. (WOY Collection.)

Photography	John Seitz
Film Editor	Conrad A. Nervig

Cast

Marion Davies	Marion
John Mack Brown	Bob Dixon
Jane Winston	Betty
Thelma Hill	Rose
Lillian Leighton	Housekeeper
Gene Stone	Herbert

6. THE DIVINE WOMAN

Copyrighted	January 14, 1928
Distributor	Metro-Goldwyn-Mayer
Length	76 Minutes
Director	Victor Seastrom
Screenplay	Gladys Unger, John Colton
Photography	Oliver Marsh
Film Editor	Conrad A. Nervig

Cast

Greta Garbo	Marianne
Lars Hansen	Lucien
Lowell Sherman	Monsieur Le Grande
Polly Moran	Madame Pigonier
Dorothy Cumming	Madame Zizi Rouck
John Mack Brown	Jean Lery
Cesare Gravina	Gigi
Paulette Duval	Paulette
Jean De Briac	Stage Director

7. SOFT LIVING

Copyrighted	February 3, 1928
Distributor	Fox
Length	59 Minutes
Director	James Tinling
Presenter	William Fox
Producer	James Tinling
Screenplay	Grace Mack, Malcolm S. Baylau
Photography	Joseph August
Film Editor	J. Edwin Robbins
Assistant Director	Leslie Selander

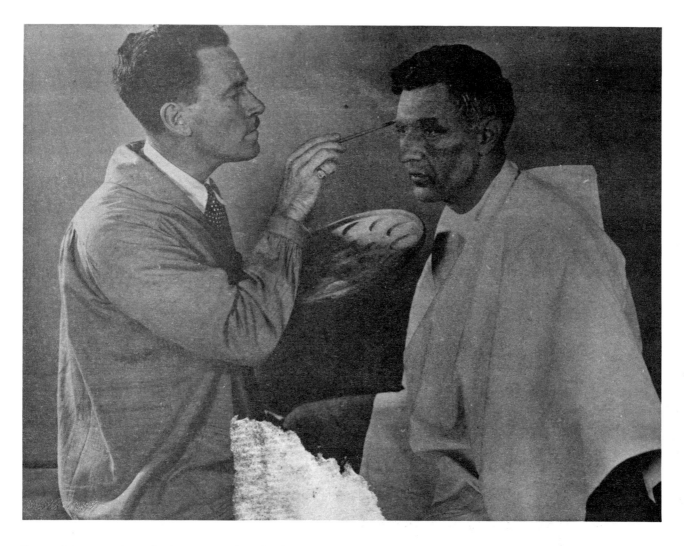

Second in a series of photos used to build up Johnny Mack Brown with Cecil Holland doing the make-up. (WOY Collection.)

Cast

Madge Bellamy . . . . Nancy Woods
John Mack Brown . . . . Stockney Webb
Mary Duncan . . . . .Lorna Estabrook
Henry Kohler . . . . .Rodney S. Bowen
Joyce Compton . . . . Billie Wilson
Thomas Jefferson . . . . Philip Estabrook
Olive Tell . . . . .Mrs. Rodney S. Bowen
Maine Geary . . . . .Office Boy
Tom Dugan . . . . Hired Man
David Wengren . . . . .Hired Man

8. SQUARE CROOKS

Copyrighted . . . . .February 22, 1928
Distributor . . . . Fox
Length . . . . .56 Minutes
Director . . . . .Lewis Seiler
Producer . . . . Philip Klein
Presenter .William Fox
Screenplay . .Becky Gardner, Malcolm S. Boylan

Photography . . . . .Rudolph Bergquist
Film Editor . . . . Jack Dennis

Cast

Robert Armstrong . . . . Eddie Ellison
John Mack Brown . . . . Larry Scott
Dorothy Dwan . . . . .Jane Brown
Dorothy Appleby . . . . .Kay Ellison
Eddie Sturgis . . . . .Mike Ross
Clarance Burton . . . . Harry Welsh
Jackie Coombs . . . . Philip Carson
Lydia Dickson . . . . Slavey

9. THE PLAY GIRL

Copyrighted . . . . .March 29, 1928
Distributor . . . . Fox
Length . . . . .54 Minutes
Director . . . . .Arthur Rosen
Presenter .William Fox
Screenplay . . . . .John Stone, Norman Z. McLeod
Photography . . . . .Rudolph Bergquist

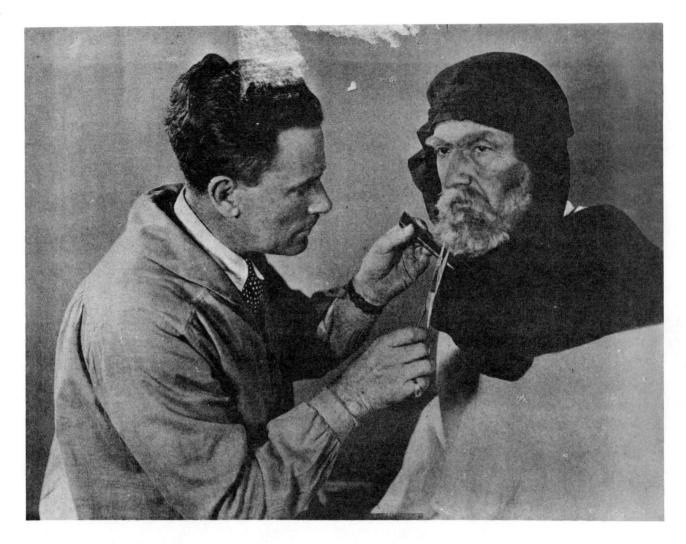

Third of a series of photos of Johnny Mack Brown being made up as an old man by Cecil Holland used by MGM to build up his star power. (WOY Collection.)

Film Editor . . . , ... Ralph Dietrich
Cast
Madge Bellamy . . . . . . Madge Norton (Logan?)
John Mack Brown . . . . Bradley Lane
Walter McGrail . . . . David Courtney
Lionel Belmore . . . . .The Greek Florist
Anna Garvin . . . . .Millie
Thelma Hill . . . . The Salesgirl
Harry Tenbrook . . . . The Chauffeur

10. OUR DANCING DAUGHTERS

Copyrighted . . . . September 28, 1928
Distributor . . . . Metro-Goldwyn-Mayer
Length . . . . .80 Minutes
Director . . . . Harry Beaumont
Screenplay . . . Josephine Lovett, Marian Ainslee, Ruth Cummings
Photography . . . . .George Barnes
Film Editor . . . . William Hamilton
Song: "I Loved You Then as I Love You Now"

by Ballad MacDonald, William Axt and David Mendoza
Cast
Joan Crawford . . . . .Diana Medford
John Mack Brown . . . . Ben Blaine
Nils Asther . . . . .Norman
Dorothy Sebastian . . . . .Beatrice
Anita Page . . . . Ann
Kathryn Williams . . . . .Ann's Mother
Edward Nugent . . . . .Freddie
Dorothy Cummings . . . . .Diana's Mother
Sam DeGrasse . . . . .Freddie's Father

11. ANNAPOLIS

Copyrighted . . . . October 16, 1928
Distributor . . . . .Pathé
Length . . . . .82 Minutes
Director . . . . Christy Cabanne
Producer/Screenplay/Sound Effects/Music . . .
. . . F. McGraw Willis

MGM publicity photo captioned: Ladies are supposed to carry a lot of unnecessary junk in their purses, but it's nothing compared to what men carry in their pockets. Johnny Mack Brown, handsome young MGM player who used to be a football star at the University of Alabama found a discrepancy of two pounds in his weight one day and discovered the fact that it was the junk he carried in his pockets — and Johnny is no different than other men. Imagine It! Most men carry over two pounds of extras with them all the time. (Some editor has added crop marks sometime in the past.) (WOY Collection.)

Original Story . . . . . . Roger S. Pease, John Kraft
Photography . . . . Arthur Miller
Film Editor . . . . .Claude Berkeley
Song: "My Annapolis and You" by Charles and Irving Bibo

Cast

John Mack Brown . . . . Bill
Hugh Allen . . . . Herbert
Jeanette Loft . . . . .Betty
Maurice Ryan . . . . Fat
William Bakewell . . . . Skippy
Byron Munson . . . . First Classman
Charlotte Walker . . . . .Aunt
Herbert Bosworth . . . . Father

12. A LADY OF CHANCE

Copyrighted . . . . .January 28, 1929
Distributor . . . . Metro-Goldwyn-Mayer
Length . . . . . 74 Minutes with Talking Sequences
Director . . . . .Robert Z. Leonard

Screenplay . . . . . . .A.P. Younger, Ralph Spence,
Edmund Scott
Photography . .Peverell Marley, William Daniels
Film Editor . . . . Margaret Booth

Cast

Norma Shearer . . . . Dolly
Lowell Sherman . . . . .Bradley
Gwen Lee . . . . .Gwen
John Mack Brown . . . . Steve Crandall
Eugenie Besserer . . . . Mrs. Crandall
Buddy Messinger . . . . .Hank

13. A WOMAN OF AFFAIRS

Copyrighted . . . . .December 10, 1928
Distributor . . . . Metro-Goldwyn-Mayer
Length . . . . . . 87 Minutes - Sound Effects/Music
Director .Clarence Brown
Screenplay . . . . Bess Meredyth, Marian Ainslee,
Ruth Cummings
Photography . . . . .William Daniels

Johnny has a villain by the throat as Slim Whitaker is about to pistol whip him in the serial **Fighting with Kit Carson** (1933, Mascot).(Courtesy of Jim Stringham.)

Film Editor . . . . Hugh Wynn
Song: "Love's First Kiss" by William Axt and David Mendoza

Cast

Greta Garbo . . . . Diana
John Gilbert . . . . Neville
Lewis Stone . . . . Hugh
John Mack Brown . . . . David
Douglas Fairbanks, Jr. . . . . .Jeffrey
Hobart Bosworth . . . . Sir Morton
Dorothy Sebastian . . . . .Constance

14. COQUETTE

Copyrighted . . . . .March 30, 1929
Distributor . . . . United Artists
Length . . . . 73 Minutes - Sound
Director/Dialogue . . . . Sam Taylor
Screenplay . . . . John Grey, Allen McNeil
Photography . . . . Karl Strauss
Song: "Coquette" by Irving Berlin

Cast

Mary Pickford . . . . .Norma Besant
John Mack Brown . . . . .Michael Jeffrey
Matt Moore . . . . Stanley Wentworth
John Sainpolis . . . . .Dr. John Besant
William Janney . . . . Janney Besant
Harry Kolker . . . . .Jasper Carter
George Irving . . . . Robert Wentworth
Louise Beavers . . . . Julia

15. THE VALIANT

Copyrighted . . . . May 14, 1929
Distributor . . . . Fox
Length . . . . 58 Minutes - Talking sequences
Director . . . . .William K. Howard
Presenter .William Fox
Screenplay . . . . . John Hunter Booth and Tom Barry
Photography . . . . . . Lucien Andriot and Glen MacWilliams

Johnny Mack talks with Betsy King Ross while leading a group of men in this scene from **Fighting with Kit Carson** (1933, Mascot) (Courtesy of Jim Stringham.)

Film Editor . . . . Jack Dennis
Cast
Paul Muni . . . . James Dyke
John Mack Brown . . . . .Robert Word
Edith Yorke . . . . .Mrs. Douglas
Richard Carlyle . . . . .Chaplin
Marguerite Churchill . . . . Mary Douglas
DeWitt Jennings . . . . Warden
Clifford Dempsey . . . . .Police Lieutenant

16. THE SINGLE STANDARD

Copyrighted . . . . .August 12, 1929
Distributor . . . . Metro-Goldwyn-Mayer
Length . . . . .68 Minutes - Music/Sound
Director . . . . John S. Robertson
Screenplay . . . .Josephine Lovett, Marian Ainslee
From the novel . . . . Adele Rogers St. John
Photography . . . . Oliver Marsh
Film Editor . . . . Blanche Sewell
Music . . . . .William Axt

Cast
Greta Garbo . . . . .Arden Stuart
Nils Asther . . . . .Packy Cannon
John Mack Brown . . . . .Tommy Hewlett
Dorothy Sebastian . . . . Mercedes
Lane Chandler . . . . Ding Stewart
Robert Castle . . . . Anthony Kendall
Mahlon Hamilton . . . . .Mr. Glendening
Kathryn Williams . . . . .Mrs. Glendening
Zeffie Tilbury . . . . .Mrs. Handley

17. HURRICANE

Copyrighted . . . . October 14, 1929
Distributor . . . . Columbia
Length . . . . 60 Minutes - Sound
Director . . . . Ralph Ince
Producer . . . . .Harry Cohn
Screenplay . . . . Enid Hibbard, Norman Houston,
Weldon Melick, Evelyn Campbell,
Norman Springer

Johnny Mack talks with a player in this scene from **Fighting with Kit Carson** (1933, Mascot.) (Courtesy of Jim Stringham.)

Photography . . . . .Teddy Tetzlaff	**Photography** . . . . .Jack MacKenzie
Film Editor .David Berg	**Film Editor** . . . . . Ann McKnight, George Marsh

Song: "Someone" by Oscar Levant, Sidney Clare

Cast (left)

Hobart Bosworth . . . . Hurricane Martin	
John Mack Brown .Dan	
Lelia Hyams . . . . Mary Stevens	
Allan Roscoe . . . . Captain Black	
Tom O'Brien . . . . Dugan	
Lelia McIntyre . . . . .Mrs. Stevens	
Joe Bordeau . . . . .Pete	
Eddie Chandler . . . . .Bull	

Cast (right)

John Mack Brown . . . . .Barry Holmes	
Sally O'Neil . . . . Ruth Morgan	
Clyde Cook . . . . Max Langley	
Blanche Frederici . . . . .Mrs. Langley	
Joseph Cawthorn . . . . .Herman Kemple	
Albert Conti . . . . Walter Klucke	
J. Barry Sherry . . . . John Parker	
Adele Watson . . . . Miss Dunn	
Ole M. Ness . . . . Professor Rowland	
Henry Armetta . . . . .Tony	

18. JAZZ HEAVEN

Copyrighted . . . . October 20, 1929
Distributor . . . . .RKO
Length . . . . 66 Minutes - Sound
Director . . . . Melville Brown
Supervisor . . . . .Myles Connolly
Screenplay . . . . . Cyrus Wood, J. Walter Reuben,
Pauline Forney, Dudley Murphy

19. UNDERTOW

Copyrighted . . . . .February 10, 1930
Distributor . . . . .Universal
Length . . . . 53 Minutes - Sound
Director . . . . .Harry Pollard

Johnny Mack talks with Lafe McKee while heroine Joyce Compton watches in this scene from **The Rustlers of Red Dog** (1935, Universal). (Courtesy of Jim Stringham.)

Presenter . . . . Carl Laemmle
Screenplay Winifred Reeve, Edward T. Lowe, Jr.
Photography . . . . Jerome Ash
Film Editor . . . . Daniel Mandell

Cast

Mary Nolan . . . . Sally Blake
Robert Ellis . . . . Jim Paine
John Mack Brown . . . . .Paul Whalen
Churchill Ross . . . . Lindy
Audrey Ferris . . . . .Kitty

20. GREAT DAY

Note: Made by MGM in 1930 but never released.

21. MONTANA MOON

Copyrighted . . . . .March 30, 1930
Distributor . . . . Metro-Goldwyn-Mayer
Length . . . . 82 Minutes - Sound
Director . . . . Malcolm St. Clair

Screenplay . . . . Sylvia Thalberg, Frank Butler,
Joe Farnham
Photography . . . . .William Daniels
Film Editor . . . .Carl L. Pierson, Leslie F. Wilder
Songs: "The Moon is Low," "Happy Cowboy" by
Nacio Herb Brown; "Montana Call," "Let Me
Give You Love," "Trailin' in Old Montana" by
Herbert Stout Last, Clifford Gray

Cast

Joan Crawford . . . . Joan
John Mack Brown . . . . .Larry
Dorothy Sebastian . . . . .Elizabeth
Ricardo Cortez . . . . .Jeff
Benny Rubin . . . ."The Doctor"
Cliff Edwards . . . . Froggy
Karl Dane . . . . .Hank
Lloyd Ingraham . . . . Mr. Prescott

22. BILLY THE KID

Copyrighted . . . . October 23, 1930

Johnny Mack shoots it out with renegade Indians as they attack the wagon train in this scene from **The Rustlers of Red Dog** (1935, Universal serial). (Courtesy of Jim Stringham.)

Distributor . . . . Metro-Goldwyn-Mayer
Length . . . . 92 Minutes - Sound
Director . . . . .King Vidor
Screenplay . . . . .Wanda Tuchock, Lawrence
Stallings, Charles MacArthur
Photography .Gordon Avil
Film Editor . . . . Hugh Wynn

Cast

John Mack Brown . . . . .Billy the Kid
Wallace Beery . . . . .Garrett
Kay Johnson . . . . .Claire
Wyndham Standing . . . . Tunston
Karl Dane . . . . .Swenson
Russell Simpson . . . . McSween
Blanche Frederici . . . . .Mrs. McSween
Roscoe Ates . . . . Old Stuff
Warner P. Richmond . . . . Ballinger
James Marcus . . . . Donovan
Nelson McDowell . . . . .Hatfield
Jack Carlyle . . . . Brewer
John Beck . . . . Butterworth

Christopher Martin . . . . .Santiago
Marguerite Padula . . . . Nicky Whoozie
Aggie Herring . . . . .Mrs. Hatfield

23. THE GREAT MEADOW

Copyrighted . . . . .February 2, 1931
Distributor . . . . Metro-Goldwyn-Mayer
Length . . . . .81 Minutes
Director . . . . .Charles Brabin
Screenplay . . . . . .Charles Brabin, Elizabeth Ellis
From a Novel . . . . . . .Elizabeth Maddox Roberts

Cast

John Mack Brown . . . . Berk Jarvis
Eleanor Boardman . . . . .Diony Hall
Lucille Laverne . . . . Elvira Jarvis
Anita Louise .Betty Hall
Gavin Gordon . . . . Evan Muir
Guinn Williams . . . . Reuben Hall
Russell Simpson . . . . .Thomas Hall
Sarah Padden . . . . Mistress Hall

Johnny Mack and Walter Miller hold up Raymond Hatton in this scene from **The Rustlers of Red Dog** (1935, Universal serial). (Courtesy of Jim Stringham.)

Helen Jerome Eddy . . . . Sally Tolliver

24. THE SECRET SIX

Copyrighted . . . . .April 22, 1931
Distributor . . . . Metro-Goldwyn-Mayer
Length . . . . .83 Minutes
Director . . . . George Hill
Screenplay . . . . .Frances Marion
Cast
Wallace Beery . . . . Scorpio
Lewis Stone . . . . Newton
John Mack Brown . . . . .Hank
Jean Harlow . . . . .Anne
Marjorie Rambeau . . . . Peaches
Paul Hurst . . . . Mizoski
Clark Gable . . . . .Cari
Ralph Bellamy . . . . .Johnny Franks
John Miljan . . . . Colimo
DeWitt Jennings . . . . Donlin
Murray Kinnell . . . . Metz

Fletcher Norton .Delano
Louis Northeaux .Eddie
Frank McGlynn . . . . Judge
Theodore Von Eltz . . . . District Attorney

25. THE LAST FLIGHT

Copyrighted . . . . .August 14, 1931
Distributor . . . . First National
Length . . . . .80 Minutes
Director . . . . William Dieterle
Screenplay .John Monk Saunders, Byron Morgan
From the Novel . . . . . . "Single Lady" by John
Monk Saunders
Cast
Richard Barthelmess . . . . Cary Lockwood
John Mack Brown . . . . Bill Talbot
Helen Chandler .Nikki
Walter Bryon . . . . The Outside, Frink
Elliott Nugent . . . . Francis
David Manners . . . . Shep Lambert

111

Johnny Mack protects heroine Joyce Compton in this scene from **The Rustlers of Red Dog** (1935, Universal serial). (Courtesy of Jim Stringham.)

26. LASCA OF THE RIO GRANDE

Copyrighted . . . . October 8, 1931
Distributor . . . . .Universal
Length . . . . .60 Minutes
Director . . . . .Edward Laemmle
Screenplay .Randall Faye
Based on a Poem . . . . . "Lasca" by Frank Duprey
and a Story . . . . .Tom Reed

Cast

Leo Carillo . . . . .Jose Santa Cruz
Dorothy Burgess . . . . .Lasca
Johnny Mack Brown . . . . .Miles Kincaid
Slim Summerville . . . . .Crabapple
Frank Campeau . . . . .Jehosaphat

27. THE VANISHING FRONTIER

Copyrighted . . . . July 28, 1932
Distributor . . . . .Paramount
Length . . . . .65 Minutes
Director . . . . .Phil Rosen
Producer . . . . Sam Jaffe
Screenplay . . . . Stuart Anthony
Photography . . . . .James S. Brown

Cast

Johnny Mack Brown . . . . .Kirby Tornell
Evelyn Knapp . . . . .Carol Winfield
Zasu Pitts .Aunt Sylvia
Raymond Hatton . . . . .Waco
Ben Alexander . . . . Lucien Winfield
J. Farrell MacDonald . . . . .Hornet
George Irving . . . . General Winfield
Joyselle . . . . Delores

28. FLAMES

Released 1932
Distributor . . . . Monogram
Length . . . . .64 Minutes
Director . . . . Karl Brown
Producer . . . . .Trem Carr

Johnny Mack, Walter Miller and Raymond Hatton have their weapons ready to repel renegades in this scene from **The Rustlers of Red Dog** (1935, Universal serial). (Courtesy of Jim Stringham.)

Screenplay . . . . Karl Brown, J.E. Chadwick
Cast
Johnny Mack Brown . . . . Charlie
Noel Francis . . . . .Pat
George Cooper . . . . .Fishy
Marjorie Beebe .Gertie
Richard Tucker .Garson
Russell Simpson . . . . .Jake
Kit Guard . . . . .Pete

29. 70,000 WITNESSES

Copyrighted . . . . September 1, 1932
Distributor . . . . .Paramount
Length . . . . .71 Minutes
Director . . . . Ralph Murphy
Producer . . . . Charles R. Rogers
Screenplay . . . . .Garrett Fort, Robert N. Lee
Dialogue . . . . .P.J. Wolfson, Allen Rivkin
From the Novel . . . . .Cortland Fitzsimmons
Cast
Phillips Holmes . . . . .Buck Buchanan

Dorothy Jordan . . . . .Dorothy Clark
Charles Ruggles . . . . Johnny Moran
Johnny Mack Brown . . . . Wally Clark
J. Farrell MacDonald . . . . .State Coach
Lew Cody .Slip Buchanan
David Landau . . . . Dan McKenna
Kenneth Thompson . . . . Dr. Collins
Guinn "Big Boy" Williams . . . . Conners
George Rosener . . . . .Ortello
Walter Hiers . . . . Old Guard
Paul Page . . . . Greenwood

30. MALAY NIGHTS

Copyrighted . . . . November 14, 1932
Distributor . . . . .Weeks/Mayfair
Length . . . . .63 Minutes
Director . . . . .E. Mason Hopper
Presenter . . . . George W. Weeks
Screenplay . . . . John Thomas Neville
Based upon a Story . . . . Glenn Ellis
Photography . . . . Jules Cronjager

Johnny Mack and heroine Joyce Compton see a threat coming at them in this scene from **The Rustlers of Red Dog** (1935, Universal serial). (Courtesy of Jim Stringham.)

Film Editor . . . . .Byron Robinson
Assistant Director . . . . William Nolte
Supervisor . . . . .Cliff Broughton
Cast
Johnny Mack Brown . . . . .Jim Wilson
Dorothy Burgess . . . . Eve Blake
Ralph Ince . . . . Jack Sheldon
Raymond Hatton . . . . Rance Danvers
Carmelita Geraghty . . . . Daisy
George Smith . . . . Sonny
Lionel Belmore . . . . .Bartender
Mary Jane . . . . Salvation Lass

31. FIGHTING WITH KIT CARSON

Copyrighted . . . . July 6, 1933
Distributor . . . . Mascot
Length . . . . .12 Chapters - Serial
Directors . . . . . . Armand Schaefer, Colbert Clark
Screenplay . . . . Jack Natteford, Barney Sarecky,
Colbert Clark and Wyndham Gittens

Film Editor .Earl Turner
Cast
Johnny Mack Brown . . . . Kit Carson
Betsy King Ross . . . . Joan Fargo
Noah Beery, Sr. . . . . Kraft
Noah Beery, Jr. . . . . Nakomas
Iron Eyes Cody

32. SATURDAY'S MILLIONS

Copyrighted . . . . October 4, 1933
Distributor . . . . .Universal
Length . . . . .76 Minutes
Director . . . . Edward Sedgewick
Screenplay . . . . .Dale Van Every
Based upon a Story . . . . Lucian Cary
Cast
Robert Young . . . . .Jim Fowler
Leila Hyams . . . . .Joan Chandler
Johnny Mack Brown . . . . Alan
Andy Devine . . . . .Andy Jones

This Lobby card shows Johnny Mack getting the drop on two villains in this 1936 Supreme film. (WOY Collection.)

Grant Mitchell . . . . Ezra Fowler
Mary Carlisle .Thelma
Joe Sauers . . . . .Coach
Mary Doran . . . . .Marie
Paul Porcasi . . . . Felix
Lucille Lund . . . . Myra Blane
Richard Tucker . . . . .Mr. Chandler
Paul Hurst . . . . .Trainer
Herbert Cortbell . . . . .Baldy
William Kent . . . . .Sam

33. FEMALE

Copyrighted . . . . November 22, 1933
Distributor . . . . First National
Length . . . . .65 Minutes
Director . . . . .Michael Curtiz
Screenplay . . . . Gene Markey and Kathryn Scola
Suggested by a Story . . Donald Henderson Clark
Film Editor . . . . Jack Killifer

Cast

Ruth Chatterton . . . . Allison Drake
George Brent . . . . Jim Thorne
Johnny Mack Brown . . . . Cooper
Ruth Donnelly . . . . .Miss Frothingham
Lois Wilson . . . . Harriet Brown
Ferdinand Gottschalk . . . . .Pettigrew
Phillip Reed . . . . Claybourne
Rafaelo Otteans .Delia
Gavin Gordon . . . . Briggs
Kenneth Thompson . . . . .Red
Huey White . . . . .Puggy
Douglas Dumbrille . . . . Mumford
Walter Walker . . . . Jarrett
Fabhee . . . . Charles Wilson
Edward Cooper . . . . Butler
Spencer Charters . . . . Tom

34. SON OF A SAILOR

Copyrighted . . . . .December 16, 1933

Johnny Mack has the drop on villain Jack Ingram in this Universal film, while Jennifer Holt looks on. (WOY Collection.)

Distributor . . . . First National
Length . . . . .70 Minutes
Director . . . . Lloyd Bacon
Producer . . . . James Seymour
Screenplay . . . . Al Cohn, Paul Gerard Smith,
Ernest Pagano, H.M. Walker
Photography . . . . .Ira Morgan
Film Editor . . . . .James Gibbon
Cast
Joe E. Brown . . . . Handsome Callahan
Jean Muir . . . . .Helen Farnsworth
Thelma Todd . . . . Allison Lloyd (The Baroness)
Johnny Mack Brown . . . . .Duke
Frank McHugh . . . . Gaga
Gary Owen . . . . Sailor Johnson
Sheila Terry . . . . .Genieve
George Blackwood . . . . . .Armstrong Farnsworth
Samuel H. Hinds . . . . .Admiral
Arthur Vinton . . . . Vincent
George Irving . . . . .Rear Admiral Lee
Walter Miller . . . . Kramer

Kenneth Thompson . . . . .Williams
John Marston . . . . Lt. Read
Joe Sauers (Sawyer) . . . . Slug
Clay Clement . . . . .Blanding
Purcell Pratt . . . . .Captain Briggs
Merna Kennedy

35. CROSS STREETS

Copyrighted . . . . .January 17, 1934
Distributor . . . . Invincible
Length . . . . .65 Minutes
Director . . . . .Frank R. Strayer
Screenplay . . . . .Anthony Coldeway
Based upon a Story . . . . Gordon Morris
Cast
Claire Windsor . . . . Anne Clement
Johnny Mack Brown . . . . Adam Blythe
Anita Louise . . . . Clara Grattan
Kenneth Thompson . . . . Mort Talbot
Matty Kemp . . . . Ken Barclay

Johnny Mack holds Iris Meredith closely in this Republic feature, **The Gambling Terror** (1936). (Photo courtesy of Merrill McCord.)

Joseph Swickard . . . . .Dean Todd
Niles Welch . . . . .Jerry Clement

36. THREE ON A HONEYMOON

Copyrighted . . . . .March 15, 1934
Distributor . . . . Fox
Length . . . . .65 Minutes
Director .James Tinling
Producer . . . . John Stone
Screenplay . . . . T. Lowe, Jr., Douglas Doty, George Wright, Raymond Van Sickle
Based upon the Novel . . . "Promenade Deck" by Ishbel Ross
Photography . . . Joseph Valentine, Arthur Arling
Film Editor . . . . Alex Troffey
Music Director . . . . Samuel Kaylin
Cast
Sally Eilers . . . . Joan Foster
Zasu Pitts .Alice Mudge
Henrietta Crossman . . . ."Ma" Gillespie

Charles Starrett . . . . Dick Chatterton
Irene Harvey . . . . Millicent Wells
John Mack Brown . . . . .Chuck Wells
Russell Simpson . . . . .Ezra MacDuff
Cornelius Keefe . . . . Phil Lang
Howard Lally
Wini Shaw

37. ST. LOUIS WOMAN

Copyrighted . . . . .April 26, 1934
Distributor . . . . Showmen's Pictures
Length . . . . .68 Minutes
Director . . . . Albert Ray
Supervisor . . . . .Al Alt
Screenplay . . . . .Jack Natteford
Story . . . . .Elwood Ullman
Music . . . . Betty Laidlaw, Bob Lively
Cast
John Mack Brown . . . . Jim Warren
Jeanette Loft . . . . .St. Louis Lou

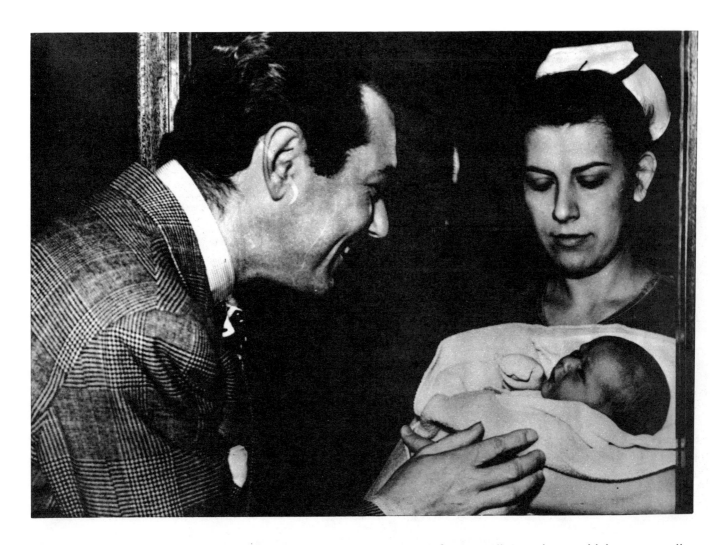

Publicity Photo captioned: John Mack Brown, screen star and former All-American grid hero, proudly peers through a glass pane at the latest star of his household — his baby daughter, age 4 days. The infant is just plain "Miss Brown," not yet having received a name. Dated April 7, 1939. (WOY Collection.)

Earle Foxe . . . . .Harry Crandall
Roberta Gale . . . . .Eleanor Farnham

38. MARRYING WIDOWS

Released 1934
Distributor . . . . Tower
Length . . . . .65 Minutes
Director . . . . Sam Newfield
Screenplay . . . . .Adele Buffington
Photography . . . . Harry Forbes
Assistant Director . . . . .Leslie Simmonds
Cast
Judith Allen . . . . .Widow
Minna Gombell . . . . .Press Agent
Lucien Littlefield . . . . Brother-in-law
John Mack Brown . . . . Husband
Bert Roach . . . . His Partner
Sarah Padden
Virginia Sales

Nat Carr
Arthur Hoyt
Otto Hoffman
Syd Saylor
Gladys Blake
George Grandee

39. BELLE OF THE NINETIES

Copyrighted . . . . September 21, 1934
Distributor . . . . .Paramount
Length . . . . .73 Minutes
Director . . . . .Leo McCarey
Presenter . . . . Adolph Zukor
Producer . . . . .William LeBaron
Screenplay . . . . Mae West
From a Story . . . . Mae West
Music/Lyrics . . . . . Arthur Johnson, Sam Coslow
Cast
Mae West .Ruby Carter
Roger Pryor . . . . Tiger Kid

Johnny Mack holds sidekick Bob Kortman by the neck on the swinging bridge in this scene from **Wild West Days** (1937, Universal-serial). (Courtesy of Jim Stringham.)

John Mack Brown	. . . .	.Brooks Claybourne
Katherine DeMille	. . . .	Molly Brant
John Miljan	. . . .	.Ace Lamont
James Donlan	. . . .	. Kirby
Tom Herbert	. . . .	.Gilbert
Stuart Holmes	. . . .	.Dirk
Harry Woods	. . . .	.Slade
Edward Gargan	. . . .	.Stogie
Libby Taylor	. . . .	Jasmine
Frederick Burton	. . . .	Colonel Claybourne
Augusta Anderson	. . . .	.Mrs. Claybourne
Benny Baker	. . . .	.Blackie
Morris Cohan	. . . .	. Butch
Warren Hymer	. . . .	St. Louis Fighter
Wade Boteler	. . . .	Editor
George Walsh	. . . .	Leading Man

40. AGAINST THE LAW

Copyrighted	. . . .	October 15, 1934
Distributor	. . . .	Columbia
Length	. . . .	.61 Minutes

Director	. . . .	.Lambert Hillyer
Supervisor	. . . .	Irving Briskin
Assistant Director	. . . .	Wilbur McGaugh
Screenplay	. . . .	.Harold Shumate
Photography	. . . .	.Al Seigler
Film Editor	. . . .	.Otto Meyer

Cast

Johnny Mack Brown	. . . .	Steve Wayne
Sally Blane	. . . .	Martha Gray
Arthur Hohl	. . . .	.Kelly
George Meeker	. . . .	.Bert Andrews
James Bush	. . . .	Bill Barrie
Bradley Page	. . . .	.Mike Eagan
Ward Bond	. . . .	.Tony Rizzo
Hooper Atchley	. . . .	O'Brien
Al Hill	. . . .	Reardon
Joseph Crehan	. . . .	Captain Elliot
Walter Walker	. . . .	Chief Surgeon
Joseph Sauers	. . . .	.McManus
Pat O'Malley	. . . .	.Fireman
Eddie O'Hearn	. . . .	Fireman

Johnny Mack, Lafe McKee, Frank Yaconelli and Bud Osborne appear happy at what they are seeing in this scene from **Wild West Days** (1937, Universal-serial). (Courtesy of Jim Stringham.)

Charles E. Brinley . . . . .Janitor
Howard Mitchell . . . . .Cameraman
Eddie Foster . . . . .Cameraman
Lee Shumway .Policeman
Frank O'Connor . . . . Policeman
Dick Rush . . . . .Policeman
Kernan Cripps . . . . .Policeman
Billy West . . . . Crook
Edwin J. Brady . . . . .Crook
Harry Bowen . . . . .Window Washer
Frances Morris . . . . .Nurse
Dick Allen . . . . .Lieutenant Gage
Hal Price . . . . Bartender
Irene Coleman . . . . Check room girl
Jerry Storm . . . . Waiter
Stanley Mack . . . . Driver
Cliff Lyons . . . . . . .double for John Mack Brown
Bert Young . . . . .double for Al Hill
Ray Ellis
Dick Stewart
Steve Clark

Harry Tenbrook

41. THE RUSTLERS OF RED DOG

Copyrighted . . . . . . January 7 to March 28, 1935
Distributor . . . . .Universal
Length . . . . .12 Chapters - Serial
Director . . . . .Louis Friedlander
Screenplay . . . . George Plympton, Basil Dickey,
        Ella O'Neill, Nate Gatzert, Vin Moore
Story . . . . .Nathaniel Eddy
Cast
Johnny Mack Brown . . . . Jack Woods
Joyce Compton . . . . .Mary Lee
Walter Miller . . . . Deacon
Raymond Hatton . . . . .Laramie
H. L. Woods . . . . .Rocky
Frederic McKaye . . . . Snakey
Charles K. French . . . . .Tom Lee
Lafe McKee . . . . .Bob Lee
William Desmond . . . . Ira Dale

Johnny Mack and sidekick Bob Kortman have the drop on a gang of villains in **Wild West Days** (1937, Universal-serial). (Courtesy of Jim Stringham.)

J. P. McGowan . . . . Captain Trent
Edmund Cobb . . . . Buck
Bud Osborne . . . . Jake
Monte Montague . . . . .Kruger

42. BRANDED A COWARD

Released . . . . .July 1935
Distributor . . . . Supreme Pictures
Length . . . . .57 Minutes
Director . . . . Sam Newfield
Producer . . . . A. W. Hackel
Screenplay . . . . .Earle Snell
Story . . . . Richard Martinson
Photography . . . . William Nobles
Film Editor .Earl Turner
Cast

Johnny Mack Brown . . . . .Johnny Hume
Billie Seward . . . . Ethel Carson
Lloyd Ingraham . . . . . . Mr. Carson (her father)
Syd Saylor . . . . Oscar

Mickey Rentschler . . . . Young Johnny
Lee Shumway
Yakima Canutt
Frank McCarroll
Roger Williams
Rex Downing
Edward Piel, Sr.

43. BETWEEN MEN

Released . . . . .November 29, 1935
Distributor . . . . Supreme Pictures
Length . . . . .59 Minutes
Director . . . . .Robert N. Bradbury
Producer . . . . A. W. Hackel
Screenplay . . . . .Charles Francis Royal
Story . . . . Robert N. Bradbury
Photography . . . . Bert Longnecker
Film Editor . . . . .S. Roy Luby
Assistant Director . . . . .Harry S. Knight

Johnny Mack in a classic close up stance in the serial **Wild West Days** (1937, Universal). (Courtesy of Jim Stringham.)

Cast

Johnny Mack Brown	John Wellington, Jr.
Beth Marion	Gale Winters
William Farnum	John Wellington/Rand
Earl Dwire	Trent
Lloyd Ingraham	Sir George Thorn
Frank Ball	Gentry/Winters
Barry Downing	Young Johnny
Horace B. Carpenter	Doctor Strong
Forrest Taylor	Lawyer Wyndham
Wally Wales	Blacksmith Luke
Jim Corey	Brawler
Milburn Morante	Prospector Pete
Sherry Tansey	Henchman Tampas
Silver Tip Baker	Johnson
Budd Buster	Virginia Townsman & New Mexico Brawler
Clyde McClary	Brawler
Horace Murphy	Burton
Tex Phelps	Henchman
Francis Walker	Henchman
Jack Kirk	Henchman
Artie Ortego	Henchman
Archie Ricks	Henchman
George Morrell	Townsman

44. THE COURAGEOUS AVENGER

Released	December 13, 1935
Distributor	Supreme Pictures
Length	58 Minutes
Director	Robert N. Bradbury
Producer	A. W. Hackel
Screenplay/Story	Charles Francis Royal
Photography	Bert Longnecker
Film Editor	S. Roy Luby
Assistant Director	Glen Cook

Cast

Johnny Mack Brown	Kirk Baxter
Helen Erickson	Betty Stonewell
Warner Richmond	Gorman
Edward Cassidy	Sheriff

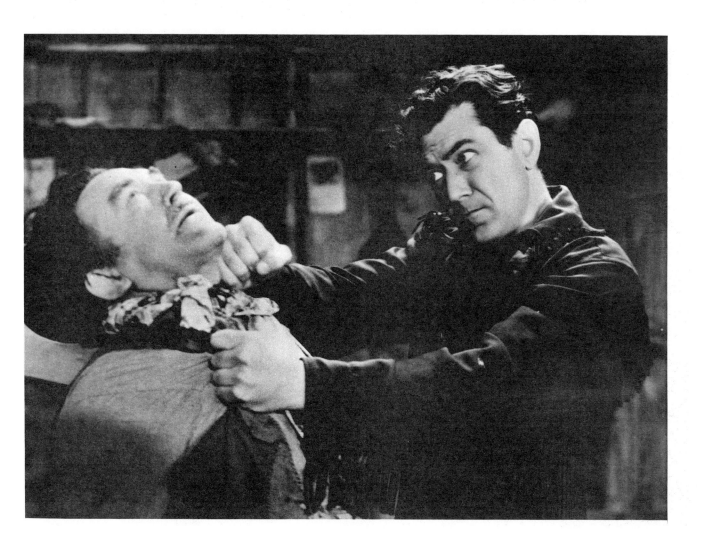

Johnny Mack lays a hard right to the jaw of villain Bud Osborne in the Universal serial **Wild West Days** (1937). (Courtesy of Jim Stringham.)

Eddie Parker . . . . Wellford
Frank Ball . . . . Davis
Earl Dwire . . . . .Prisoner
Forrest Taylor . . . . Marshal Taggert
Bob Burns . . . . Posse Rider
Herman Hack . . . . Henchman

45. VALLEY OF THE LAWLESS

Released . . . . .January 25, 1936
Distributor . . . . Supreme Pictures
Length . . . . .56 Minutes
Director . . . . .Robert N. Bradbury
Producer . . . . A. W. Hackel
Screenplay . . . . .Charles Francis Royal
Story . . . . Robert N. Bradbury
Photography . . . . Bert Longnecker
Film Editor . . . . .S. Roy Luby
Assistant Director . . . . .Glen Cook
Cast
Johnny Mack Brown . . . . Bruce Reynolds

Joyce Compton . . . . .Joan Jenkins
George Hayes . . . . Old Man Jenkins
Dennis Meadows (Dennis Moore) . .Cliff Graves
Bobby Nelson . . . . .Billy Jenkins
Frank Hagney . . . . .Tiger Carlow
Charles King . . . . .Regan
Jack Rockwell . . . . .Sheriff Graves
Frank Ball . . . . Amos Jenkins
Robert McKenzie . . . . .Croupier
Forrest Taylor . . . . Gambler
George Morrell . . . . .Gambler
Jack Evans .Spectator
Milburn Morante . . . . .Ed Reynolds
Tex Phelps .Henchman
Rube Dalroy . . . . Townsman
Anita Carmargo . . . . Dancer

46. DESERT PHANTOM

Released .March 10, 1936

Johnny Mack as sheriff with a group of townsmen, including Jonathan Hale, in his supporting role with Rod Cameron in this scene from **Short Grass** (1950, Allied Artists.) (Courtesy of Bobby Copeland.)

Distributor	Supreme Pictures
Length	59 Minutes
Director	S. Roy Luby
Producer	A. W. Hackel
Screenplay	Earle Snell
Story	E. B. Mann
Photography	Bert Longnecker
Film Editor	Roy Claire (S. Roy Luby)
Production Manager	Jerome S. Bresler
Assistant Director	Harry S. Knight

Cast

Johnny Mack Brown	Billy Donovan
Sheila Manors	Jean Haloran
Ted Adams	Salizar
Karl Hackett	Tom Jackson
Hal Price	Jim Day
Nelson McDowell	Doc Simpson
Charles King	Dan
Fred Parker	Man at Bar
Forrest Taylor	Townsman
Frank Ball	Townsman
George Morrell	Townsman
Art Dillard	Henchman
Roger Williams	Henchman

47. ROGUE OF THE RANGE

Released	April 25, 1936
Distributor	Supreme Pictures
Length	57 Minutes
Director	S. Roy Luby
Producer	A. W. Hackel
Screenplay/Story	Earle Snell
Photography	Jack Greenhaigh
Film Editor	Roy Claire (S. Roy Luby)
Production Manager	Jerome S. Bresler
Assistant Director	Harry S. Knight

Cast

Johnny Mack Brown	Dan Doran
Lois January	Stella Lamb
Alden Chase	Lige Branscomb
Phyllis Hume	Tess

Johnny Mack talks with Buffalo Bill (**John Rutherford**) in the serial, **Flaming Frontiers** (1938). (Courtesy of Jim Stringham.)

George Ball .Jim Mitchell
Jack Rockwell . . . . Sloan
Horace Murphy . . . . Sheriff Tom
Frank Ball . . . . .Express Agent John
Lloyd Ingraham . . . . Doctor
Horace B. Carpenter . . . . .Blacksmith Lem
Forrest Taylor . . . . .Prison Guard Pinky
George Morrell . . . . Stage Driver
Oscar Gahan . . . . .Stage Guard
Blackie Whiteford . . . . Stage Bandit
Tex Palmer . . . . .Stage Bandit
Max Davidson . . . . .Peddler
Art Dillard . . . . Henchman Artie
Slim Whitaker . . . . .Henchman
Herman Hack . . . . Prison Guard
Wally West . . . . Prison Guard

48. EVERYMAN'S LAW

Released . . . . June 10, 1936
Distributor . . . . Supreme Pictures

Length . . . . .62 Minutes
Director . . . . .Albert Ray
Producer . . . . A. W. Hackel
Screenplay/Story . . . . .Earle Snell
Photography . . . . .Jack Greenhaigh
Film Editor .L. R. Brown

Cast

Johnny Mack Brown . . . . . . The Dog Town Kid
Beth Marion . . . . Marian Henley
Frank Campeau . . . . Gibbs
Roger Gray . . . . .The Lobo Kid
Lloyd Ingraham .Morgan
John Beck . . . . .Pike
Horace Murphy . . . . .Sheriff Bradley
Dick Alexander . . . . Barber
Slim Whitaker . . . . .Pete
Edward Cassidy . . . . Homesteader
Jim Corey . . . . Homesteader
Francis Walker . . . . .Henchman
Herman Hack . . . . Henchman
Buck Bucko . . . . .Henchman

Johnny Mack has a friendly conversation with heroine Eleanor Hansen in this scene from **Flaming Frontiers** (1938, Universal serial). (Courtesy of Jim Stringham.)

George Morrell . . . . .Bartender
Art Dillard . . . . .Saloon Bit
Jack Evans . . . . .Saloon Bit
Tex Palmer .Saloon Bit

49. THE CROOKED TRAIL

Released . . . . .July 26, 1936
Distributor . . . . Supreme Pictures
Length . . . . .60 Minutes
Director . . . . .S. Roy Luby
Producer . . . . A. W. Hackel
Screenplay . . . . George Plympton
Photography . . . . .Jack Greenhaigh
Film Editor . . . . Roy Claire (S. Roy Luby)
Assistant Director . . . . Edwin Tyler
Cast
Johnny Mack Brown . . . . .Jim Blake
Lucille Brown . . . . .Helen Carter
John Merton . . . . .Harve Tarleton
Ted Adams . . . . .Esteban Solano

Charles King . . . . .Lanning
John Van Pelt . . . . .Tex
Edward Cassidy . . . . .Grimby
Horace Murphy . . . . Carter
Roger Williams . . . . .Henchman
Dick Curtis . . . . Henchman
Earl Dwire
Artie Ortego
Hal Price
Fred Parker
Tex Palmer

50. UNDERCOVER MAN

Released . . . . September 24, 1936
Distributor . . . . Republic
Length . . . . .56 Minutes
Director . . . . .Albert Ray
Producer . . . . A. W. Hackel
Screenplay . . . . Andrew Bennison
Photography . . . . .Jack Greenhaigh

Johnny Mack mixes it up with two henchmen in the Universal serial, **Flaming Frontiers** (1938). (Courtesy of Jim Stringham.)

Film Editor .S. Roy Luby

Cast
Johnny Mack Brown . . . . .Steve McLain
Suzanne Kaaren . . . . Linda Forbes
Ted Adams .Ace Pringle
Frank Darien . . . . .Dizzy Slocum
Horace Murphy . . . . Sheriff Pegg
Lloyd Ingraham . . . . Judge Forbes
Dick Morehead . . . . .Rusty Wilson
Edward Cassidy . . . . Slim
Tom London
Frank LaRue
Milburn Morante
Margaret Mann
George Morrell
Frank Ball

51. THE GAMBLING TERROR

Released . . . . .February 15, 1937
Distributor . . . . Republic

Length . . . . .53 Minutes
Director . . . . Sam Newfield
Producer . . . . A. W. Hackel
Screenplay/Story . . . . Fred Myton, George
Plympton
Photography . . . . Bert Longnecker
Film Editor .S. Roy Luby

Cast
Johnny Mack Brown . . . . Jeff
Iris Meredith . . . . Betty Garrett
Charles King . . . . .Brett
Horace Murphy . . . . .Missouri Bill
Dick Curtis . . . . Dirk
Budd Buster . . . . .Shorty
Ted Adams . . . . .Sheriff
Earl Dwire . . . . Bradley
Bobby Nelson . . . . Jerry Garrett
Frank Ellis . . . . Blackie
Lloyd Ingraham . . . . .Mr. Nelson
Emma Tansey . . . . .Mrs. Nelson
Frank Ball . . . . Garrett

Johnny Mack stops the stage at gunpoint in the Universal serial **The Oregon Trail** (1939). (Courtesy of Merrill McCord.)

Sherry Tansey	Pete	Warner Richmond	Link Carson
Steve Clark	McClure	Karl Hackett	Mart Pierson
George Morrell		Earle Hodgins	Buck Andrews
Art Dillard		Frank LaRue	Tilden
Tex Palmer		Frank Ellis	Red Cassidy
Jack Montgomery		Lew Mechan	Bill O'Donnell
		Frank Ball	Steve Warner
		Dick Curtis	Cartwright

52. TRAIL OF VENGEANCE

Jim Corey
Horace Murphy
Dick Cramer
Steve Clark
Budd Buster
Jack C. Smith
Jack Kirk
Francis Walker
Tex Palmer

Copyrighted . . . . .March 29, 1937
Distributor . . . . Republic
Length . . . . .54 Minutes
Director . . . . Sam Newfield
Producer . . . . A. W. Hackel
Screenplay . . . . . .George Plympton, Fred Myton
Based upon a Story . . . . E. B. Mann
Photography . . . . Bert Longnecker
Film Editors . . . . S. Roy Luby, Tom Neff
Cast

Johnny Mack Brown . . . . .Dude Ramsey
Iris Meredith . . . . .Jean Warner

53. LAWLESS LAND

Released . . . . .April 6, 1937

Hoping to trap Sam Morgan (James Blaine) on the right, Johnny asks to look at the land grant which Morgan claims he got from the government. Heroine Louise Stanley and Ed LeSaint look on expectantly in this scene from the Universal serial, **The Oregon Trail** (1939). (Courtesy of Jim Stringham.)

Distributor .... Republic			Released .... April 22, 1937	
Length .... 55 Minutes			Distributor .... Republic	
Director .... Albert Ray			Length .... 51 Minutes	
Producer .... A. W. Hackel			Director .... Sam Newfield	
Screenplay/Story .... Andrew Bennison			Producer .... A. W. Hackel	
Photography .... Jack Greenhaigh			Screenplay .... George Plympton	
Film Editor .... S. Roy Luby			Story .... James P. Olsen	

Cast

Film Editor .... S. Roy Luby

Cast

Johnny Mack Brown .... Jeff		Johnny Mack Brown .... Jim Walters	
Louise Stanley .... Letty		Lois January .... Beth Harvey	
Ted Adams .... Clay		Tom London .... Sig Bostell	
Julian Rivero .... Ortego		Frank LaRue .... Hamp Harvey	
Horace Murphy .... Lafe		Ernie Adams .... Pete	
Frank Ball .... Bill		Dick Curtis .... Brent	
Edward Cassidy .... Sheriff		Milburn Morante .... Deputy	
Ana Camargo .... Lolita		Jack Rockwell .... Ed Parks	
Roger Williams		Horace Murphy .... Bit	
Frances Kellogg		Budd Buster .... Bit	
Chiquita Hernandez Orchestra		Frank Ball .... Judge	

54. BAR Z BAD MEN

Tex Palmer

In this scene from **The Oregon Trail** Johnny Mack Brown and Fuzzy Knight have the drop on the villains (including Charles King, Horace Murphy, James Blaine and Charles Stevens). Johnny shoots Murphy through the hand when they try to resist him. (1939, Universal-serial). (Courtesy of Jim Stringham.)

George Morrell
Horace B. Carpenter
Art Dillard
Oscar Graham

55. GUNS IN THE DARK

Released . . . . May 13, 1937
Distributor . . . . Republic
Length . . . . .56 Minutes
Director . . . . Sam Newfield
Producer . . . . A. W. Hackel
Screenplay . . . . .Charles Francis Royal
Based upon a Story . . . . E. B. Mann
Photography . . . . Bert Longnecker
Film Editor . . . . .S. Roy Luby
Assistant Director . . . . Bob Ray
Cast
Johnny Mack Brown . . . . .Johnny Darrel
Claire Rochelle . . . . Joan Williams
Dick Curtis . . . . .Stevens

Julian Madison . . . . .Dick Martin
Ted Adams . . . . Manuel Mendez
Syd Saylor .Oscar Roscoe
Steve Clark . . . . .Pete
Jim Corey . . . . Jim
Roger Williams . . . . .Ranger Adams
Sherry Tansey
Slim Whitaker
Lew Meehan
Tex Palmer
Francis Walker
Frank Ellis
Budd Buster
Oscar Gahan
Merrill McCormick
Dick Cramer
Jack C. Smith
Chick Hannon

Bill Cody, Jr. points out the Indians to scouts John Mack Brown and Fuzzy Knight in this scene from **The Oregon Trail** (1939, Universal-serial). (Courtesy of Jim Stringham.)

56. A LAWMAN IS BORN

Released . . . . June 21, 1937
Distributor . . . . Republic
Length . . . . .61 Minutes
Director . . . . Sam Newfield
Producer . . . . A. W. Hackel
Screenplay . . . . George Plympton
Based upon a Story . . . . Henry F. Olmstead
Photography . . . . Bert Longnecker
Film Editor . . . . Roy Claire (S. Roy Luby)
Cast
Johnny Mack Brown . . . . .Tom Mitchell
Iris Meredith . . . . .Beth Graham
Warner Richmond . . . . Kane Briscoe
Mary MacLaren . . . . .Martha Lance
Dick Curtis . . . . .Lefty Doogan
Earle Hodgins . . . . .Sheriff Lance
Charles King . . . . Bart Moscrip
Frank LaRue . . . . .Graham
Al St. John . . . . .Root

Steve Clark . . . . Sam Brownlee
Jack C. Smith . . . . .Ike Manton
Sherry Tansey
Wally West
Budd Buster
Lew Meehan
Tex Palmer

57. WILD WEST DAYS

Copyrighted . . . . May 20 to September 10, 1937
Distributor . . . . .Universal
Length . . . . 13 Chapters - Serial
Directors . . . . .Ford Beebe and Cliff Smith
Screenplay . . . . . . Wyndham Gittens, Norman S.
Hall, Ray Trampe
Based on the Novel . . . ."Saint Johnson"
by W. R. Burnett
Cast
Johnny Mack Brown . . . . Kentucky
George Shelley . . . . .Dude

The pioneers, including Helen Gibson, Fuzzy Knight and a wagon driver on the right, George Plues, are huddled together watching the Indians as John Mack protects heroine Louise Stanley in **The Oregon Trail** (1939, Universal-serial). (Courtesy of Jim Stringham.)

Robert Kortman	Trigger	Cast	
Frank Yaconelli	Mike	Johnny Mack Brown	Lon Cardigan
Lynn Gilbert	Lucy	Claire Rochelle	Bobbie Reynolds
Frank McGlynn	Larry	Dick Curtis	Bull Berke
Russell Simpson	Keeler	Horace Murphy	Calico Haynes
Francis MacDonald	Purvis	Frank LaRue	Jeff Reynolds
Walter Miller	Doc Hardy	Ed Cassidy	John Porter
Chief Thundercloud	Red Hatchet	Bobbie Nelson	Tug Murdock
Al Bridge	Steve	Frank Ball	Murdock
		Steve Clark	Holbrook
		Frank Ellis	Brown

58. BOOTHILL BRIGADE

Released/Copyrighted . . . . .August 2, 1937
Distributor . . . . Republic
Length . . . . .53 Minutes
Director . . . . Sam Newfield
Producer . . . . A. W. Hackel
Screenplay . . . . George Plympton
Based upon a Story . . . . . . .Harry M. Olmstead
Photography . . . . Bert Longnecker
Film Editor . . . . .S. Roy Luby

59. BORN TO THE WEST (aka HELLTOWN)

Copyrighted . . . . .December 10, 1937
Distributor . . . . .Paramount
Length . . . . .57 Minutes
Director . . . . .Charles Barton
Screenplay . . . . .Stuart Anthony, Robert Yost
Based upon a Novel . . . . .Zane Grey
Photography . . . . .J. D. Jennings

John Mack congratulates Colonel Custer (Roy Barcroft) for his part in helping the government track down the outlaw band. Among the players looking on are Bill Cody, Jr., Ed LeSaint, Louise Stanley. **The Oregon Trail** (1939, Universal-serial). (Courtesy of Jim Stringham.)

Film Editor . . . . .John Link

Cast

John Wayne . . . . .Rudd
Marsha Hunt . . . . .Nellie
Johnny Mack Brown . . . . Fillmore
John Patterson . . . . Hardy
Monte Blue . . . . .Hammond
Syd Saylor . . . . .Hooley
Lucien Littlefield . . . . John, the cattle buyer
Nick Lukats . . . . Fallon
James Craig . . . . Brady
Johnny Boyle . . . . .Sam
Jack Kennedy . . . . Sheriff
Lee Prather . . . . .Stranger
Alan Ladd . . . . Inspector
Jack Daley . . . . .Gambler
Vester Pegg . . . . .Bartender

60. WELLS FARGO

Copyrighted . . . . .December 31, 1937

Distributor . . . . .Paramount
Length . . . . .115 Minutes
Director/Producer . . . . Frank Lloyd
Associate Producer . . . . Howard Estabrook
Screenplay . . . Paul Schoefield, Gerald Geraghty,
Frederick Jackson
Based upon a Story . . . . Stuart Lake
Song . . . . .Ralph Freed, Burton Lane
Photography . . . . Theodore Sparkuhl
Film Editor . . . . .Hugh Bennett

Cast

Joel McCrea . . . . Ramsey MacKay
Bob Burns . . . . .Hank York
Frances Dee . . . . .Justine
Lloyd Nolan .Del Slade
Porter Hall . . . . .James Oliver
Ralph Morgan . . . . .Mr. Pryor
Mary Nash . . . . .Mrs. Pryor
Robert Cummings . . . . Trimball
Henry O'Neill . . . . .Henry Wells
John Mack Brown . . . . Talbot Carter

Discovering the outlaws in the powder wagon, John Mack and his pal, Charlie Murphy (center) fight with Colin Kenny (Slade) and Charles Stevens (Breed). Breed is knocked over the side in this scene from **The Oregon Trail** (1939, Universal-serial). (Courtesy of Jim Stringham.)

Jane Dewey	Lucy Dorsett Trimball
Peggy Stewart	Alice MacKay
Bernard Siegal	Pawnee
Stanley Fields	Abe
Frank McGlynn	Lincoln
Jack Clark	William Fargo
Clarence Kolb	John Butterworth
Granville Bates	Bradford the Banker
Harry Davenport	Ingalls the Banker
Frank Conroy	Ward the Banker
Brandon Tynan	Edwards the Newspaper Publisher
Hal K. Dawson	Correspondent
Lucien Littlefield	San Francisco Postmaster
Jimmy Butler	Nick, Jr.
Willie Fung	Wong
Sheila Dorcey	Lola Montez
Robert Emmett O'Connor	Sea Captain

61. FLAMING FRONTIERS

Copyrighted	May 12 to July 26, 1938
Distributor	Universal
Length	15 Chapters - Serial
Directors	Ray Taylor and Alan James
Screenplay	Wyndham Gittens, George Plympton, Basil Dickey, Paul Perez
Suggested by the Story	"The Tie That Binds" by Peter B. Kyne

Cast

Johnny Mack Brown	Tex Houston
Eleanor Hansen	Mary Grant
Ralph Bowman	Tom Grant
Charles Middleton	Ace Daggett
James Blaine	Bart Eaton
Charles Stevens	Breed
William Royal	Tom Crosby
Horace Murphy	Sheriff
Michael Slade	Postmaster
John Rutherford	Buffalo Bill

Bob Baker, Johnny Mack Brown, and Fuzzy Knight prevented a gang of badmen from grabbing water rights from honest ranchers in **Oklahoma Frontier** (1939, Universal-serial). (This Lobby Card Courtesy of Bobby Copeland.)

Chief Thundercloud . . . . Thundercloud

62. THE OREGON TRAIL

Copyrighted . . . . May 3 to July 6, 1939
Distributor . . . . .Universal
Length . . . . .15 Chapters - Serial
Directors . . . . Ford Beebe and Saul A. Goodkind
Screenplay . . . . George Plympton, Basil Dickey,
Edmund Kelso, W. W. Watson
Dialogue . . . . .Dorothy Cormack
Cast
Johnny Mack Brown . . . . Jeff Scott
Louise Stanley . . . . Margaret Mason
Bill Cody, Jr. . . . . Jimmy Clark
Fuzzy Knight . . . . "Deadwood" Hawkins
Ed LeSaint . . . . .John Mason
James Blaine . . . . Sam Morgan
Jack C. Smith . . . . "Bull" Bragg
Roy Barcroft . . . . .Colonel Custer
Colin Kenny . . . . .Slade

63. DESPERATE TRAILS

Copyrighted . . . . .August 9, 1939
Distributor . . . . .Universal
Length . . . . .60 Minutes
Director/Producer . . . . Albert Ray
Screenplay . . . . Andrew Bennison
Based upon the Story . . . ."Christmas Eve at Pilot
Butte" by Courtney Riley Cooper
Photography . . . . Jerry Ash
Film Editor . . . . Louis Sackin
Cast
Johnny Mack Brown . . . . .Steve Hayden
Bob Baker . . . . Clem Waters
Fuzzy Knight . . . . Cousin Willie
Bill Cody, Jr. . . . . .Little Bill
Frances Robinson . . . . Judith Longton
Russell Simpson . . . . .Big Bill Tanner
Clarence H. Wilson . . . . Major Culp
Charles Stevens . . . . .Ortega
Horace Murphy . . . . .Nebraska

Johnny Mack and Bob Baker look pained as they ride along with a warbling Fuzzy Knight in this scene from **Bad Man From Red Butte** (1940, Universal). (Courtesy of Jerry Ohlinger's Movie Material Store.)

Ralph Dunn . . . . Lon
Fern Emmett . . . . .Mrs. Plunkett
Ed Cassidy .Marshal Cort
Anita Camargo . . . . .Rosita
Jack Shannon . . . . Ab
Wilbur McCauley .Joe
Al Haskell
Frank Ellis
Frank McCarroll
Cliff Lyons
Eddie Parker

64. OKLAHOMA FRONTIER

Copyrighted . . . . September 19, 1939
Distributor . . . . .Universal
Length . . . . .59 Minutes
Director/Screenplay . . . . .Ford Beebe
Associate Producer . . . . .Albert Ray
Photography . . . . Jerome Ash
Film Editor . . . . Louis Sackin

Music Director . . . . Charles Previn

Cast

Johnny Mack Brown . . . . .Jeff McLeod
Bob Baker . . . . .Tom Rankin
Fuzzy Knight . . . . .Windy
Anne Gwynne . . . . Janet Rankin
James Blaine . . . . .George Frazier
Robert Kortman . . . . J. W. Saunders
Charles King . . . . .Soapy
Harry Tenbrook . . . . .Grimes
Horace Murphy . . . . .Mushy
Lloyd Ingraham . . . . Judge
Anthony Warde . . . . .Wayne
Robert Cummings, Sr. . . . . .Rankin
Lane Chandler . . . . Sergeant
Hank Bell . . . . Corporal
Dick Burk . . . . .Settler
Frank Mayo .Marshal
Joe De La Cruz
Al Bridge
Hank Worden

Johnny Mack and Nell O'Day seem to be watching intently in this Universal feature **Pony Post** (1940). (Courtesy of Jerry Ohlinger's Movie Material Store.)

Blackie Whiteford
Roy Harris (Riley Hill)
George Magrill
George Cheesebro
Tom Smith
The Texas Rangers

65. CHIP OF THE FLYING U

Copyrighted . . . . October 5, 1939
Distributor . . . . Universal
Length . . . . .55 Minutes
Director . . . . Ralph Staub
Screenplay . . . . . Larry Rhine, Andrew Bennison
Based upon a Story . . . . B. M. Bower
(pseudonym of Bertha "Muzzy" Sinclair)
Photography . . . . William Sickner
Cast
Johnny Mack Brown . . . . Chip Bennett
Bob Baker . . . . Dusty
Fuzzy Knight . . . . Weary

Doris Weston . . . . Margaret Whitmore
Forrest Taylor . . . . J. G. Whitmore
Anthony Warde .Duncan
Karl Hackett . . . . Hennessey
Henry Hall . . . . .Wilson
Claire Whitney . . . . .Miss Robinson
Ferris Taylor . . . . .Sheriff
Cecil Kellogg . . . . Red
Hank Bell
Harry Tenbrook
Chester Conklin
Vic Potel
Hank Worden
Charles K. French
Frank Ellis
Kermit Maynard

66. WEST OF CARSON CITY

Copyrighted . . . . November 6, 1939
Director . . . . Universal

Johnny Mack pounces upon villains Ray Teal and Jack Rockwell as they hold Nell O'Day in this scene from **Pony Post** (1940, Universal). (Courtesy of Jerry Ohlinger's Movie Material Store.)

Length . . . . .56 Minutes
Director . . . . .Ray Taylor
Screenplay . . . . . Milton Raison, Sherman Lowe,
Jack Bernhard
Based upon the Story . . . . Milton Raison
Photography . . . . .Jerry Ash
Music/Lyrics . . . . . . "On the Trail of Tomorrow"
by Milt Rossen, Everett Carter
Cast
Johnny Mack Brown . . . . .Jim Bannister
Bob Baker . . . . .Nevada
Fuzzy Knight . . . . .Banjo
Peggy Moran . . . . .Millie Harkins
Harry Woods . . . . .Mack Gorman
Robert E. Homans . . . . .Judge Harkins
Al K. Hall .Lem Howard
Roy Barcroft . . . . .Bill Tompkins
Charles King . . . . .Drag
Frank Mitchell . . . . Breed
Edmund Cobb . . . . .Sleepy
Jack Roper . . . . .Larkin

Ted Wells . . . . .Slim
Jack Shannon . . . . .Pete
Vic Potel
Kermit Maynard
Ernie Adams
Donald Kerr
Dick Carter
Al Bridge
The Four Singing Notables

67. RIDERS OF PASCO BASIN

Copyrighted . . . . November 14, 1939
Distributor . . . . .Universal
Length . . . . .56 Minutes
Director . . . . .Ray Taylor
Screenplay . . . . Ford Beebe
Photography . . . . .William Sickner
Film Editor . . . . Louis Sackin
Songs: "Tying Up My Bridle to the Door of Your
Heart" and "Song of the Prairie" by Milton Rosen

Johnny Mack is about to slug the villain Ray Teal as Fuzzy Knight looks on in this scene from **Pony Post** (1940, Universal). (Courtesy of Jerry Ohlinger's Movie Material Store.)

and Everett Carter, sung by Bob Baker, Rudy Scooter and His Californians

Cast

Johnny Mack Brown	Lee Jamison
Bob Baker	Bruce Moore
Fuzzy Knight	Luther
Frances Robinson	Jean Madison
Arthur Loft	Matt Kirby
Frank LaRue	Joel Madison
James Guilfoyle	Evans
Lafe McKee	
Chuck Morrison	
Edward Cassidy	
Robert Winkler	
William Gould	
Ted Adams	
Kermit Maynard	
David Sharpe	
Hank Bell	
Edward Piel	
John Judd	

Gordon Hart
Rudy Scooters and His Californians

68. BAD MAN FROM RED BUTTE

Copyrighted	May 16, 1940
Distributor	Universal
Length	58 Minutes
Director	Ray Taylor
Associate Producer	Joseph G. Sanford
Screenplay	Sam Robins
Photography	William Sickner
Film Editor	Paul Landers
Songs	Everett Carter and Milton Rosen

Cast

Johnny Mack Brown . .	Gil Brady/Buck Halliday
Bob Baker	Gabriel Hornsby
Fuzzy Knight	Spud Jenkins
Anne Gwynne	Tibby Mason
Lloyd Ingraham	Turner
Lafe McKee	Dan Todhunter

Villain Stanley Blystone tells off Johnny Mack and Tom Chatterton as Dorothy Short looks on in this scene from **Pony Post** (1940, Universal). (Courtesy of Jerry Ohlinger's Movie Material Store.)

Bill Cody, Jr. . . . . Skip Todhunter
Roy Barcroft . . . . Hank
Buck Moulton . . . . Jitters
Earl Hodgins . . . . Hiram Cochran
James Morton . . . . Baldy
Mira McKinney . . . . Miss Woods
Eric Alden . . . . Brady
George Billings . . . . Tough Boy

69. SON OF ROARING DAN

Copyrighted . . . . July 30, 1940
Distributor . . . . Universal
Length . . . . 63 Minutes
Director . . . . Ford Beebe
Associate Producer . . . . Joseph G. Sanford
Screenplay . . . . Clarence Upton Young
Photography . . . . William Sickner
Film Editor . . . . Paul Landers
Music Director . . . . Charles Previn
Songs: "Yippee," "I Worry All the Time" and

"Powder River" by Milton Rosen and Everett Carter

Cast

Johnny Mack Brown . . . . Jim Reardon
Fuzzy Knight . . . . Tick Belden
Nell O'Day . . . . Jane Belden
Jeanne Kelly . . . . Eris Brooks
Robert Homans . . . . Dan McPhail
Tom Chatterton . . . . Stuart Manning
John Eldredge . . . . Thorndyke
Ethan Laidlaw . . . . Matt Gregg
Lafe McKee . . . . Brooks
Dick Alexander . . . . Big Taylor
Eddie Polo . . . . Charlie Gregg
Bob Reeves
Chuck Morrison
Frank McCarroll
Lloyd Ingraham
Jack Shannon
Ben Taggert

Johnny Mack talks with sidekick Fuzzy Knight in the Universal feature **Pony Post** (1940). (Courtesy of Jerry Ohlinger's Movie Material Store.)

Ralph Peters
Ralph Dunn
Jack Montgomery
The Texas Rangers (Musicians)

70. RAGTIME COWBOY JOE

Copyrighted . . . . September 12, 1940
Distributor . . . . .Universal
Length . . . . .58 Minutes
Director . . . . .Ray Taylor
Associate Producer . . . . .Joseph G. Sanford
Screenplay . . . . Sherman Lowe
Photography . . . . Jerome Ash
Film Editor . . . . Paul Landers
Music Director . . . . Charles Previn
Songs: "Ooh La La" (sung by Viola Vonn), "Cross-Eyed Kate," "Trail Drivers" by Milton Rosen, Everett Carter and Bob Crawford
Cast
Johnny Mack Brown . . . . .Steve

Fuzzy Knight . . . . .Joe
Nell O'Day . . . . .Helen
Dick Curtis . . . . .Bo
Marilyn (Lynn) Merrick . . . . .Mary
Walter Soderling .Virgil
Roy Barcroft . . . . .Putt
Harry Tenbrook . . . . .Del
Viola Vonn . . . . Cabaret Singer
Jack Clifford
William Gould
Bud Osborne
The Texas Rangers
Bob O'Connor
Eddie Parker
Frank McCarroll
George Plues
Ed Cassidy
Buck Moulton
Harold Goodwin
Wilfred Lucas
Kermit Maynard

In this scene from **Boss of Bullion City** (1941, Universal) Johnny Mack is holding heroine Maria Montez and they both look awfully happy. (Courtesy of Jerry Ohlinger's Movie Material Store.)

71. LAW AND ORDER (aka THE LAW)

Copyrighted	September 18, 1940
Distributor	Universal
Length	57 Minutes
Director	Ray Taylor
Associate Producer	Joseph Sanford
Screenplay	Sherman Lowe, Victor McLeod
Based on the Novel	"Saint Johnson" by W. R. Burnett
Photography	Jerome Ash

Songs: "Those Happy Days" (sung by Fuzzy Knight), "Oklahoma's Oke With Me" (sung by Jimmy Dodd; and Nell O'Day) by Milton Rosen, Everett Carter, Jimmy Dodd

Cast

Johnny Mack Brown	Bill Ralston
Fuzzy Knight	Deadwood
Nell O'Day	Sally Dixon
James Craig	Brant
Harry Cording	Poe Daggett
Earle Hodgins	Eldon
Robert Fiske	Deal
James Dodd	Jimmy
William Worthington	Judge Williams
Ethan Laidlaw	Kurt Daggett
Ted Adams	Walt
Harry Humphrey	Dixon
George Plues	Stage Driver
Kermit Maynard	Henchman
Jack Shannon	Henchman
Scoop Martin	Henchman
Cliff Parkinson	Henchman
Bob Kortman	Henchman
Frank McCarroll	
Frank Ellis	
Jim Corey	
Lew Meehan	
Charles King	
The Notables Quartet	

Johnny Mack and Maria Montez play a love scene in **Boss of Bullion City** (1940, Universal). (Courtesy of Jerry Ohlinger's Movie Material Store.)

72. PONY POST

Copyrighted . . . . October 23, 1940
Distributor . . . . .Universal
Length . . . . .59 Minutes
Director . . . . .Ray Taylor
Screenplay . . . . Sherman Lowe
Photography . . . . .William Sickner
Film Editor . . . . Paul Landes
Songs . . . . . Johnny Bond, Milton Rosen, Everett Carter

Cast

Johnny Mack Brown . . . . .Cal Sheridan
Fuzzy Knight . . . . Shorty
Nell O'Day . . . . .Norma Reeves
Dorothy Short . . . . Alice
Tom Chatterton . . . . .Goodwin
Stanley Blystone . . . . .Atkins
Jack Rockwell . . . . Mack Richards
Ray Teal . . . . Claude Richards
Kermit Maynard . . . . .Whitmore

Lane Chandler . . . . .Fairweather
Eddie Cobb . . . . George Barber
Lloyd Ingraham . . . . Dr. Nesbet
Charles King . . . . Hamilton
Jimmy Wakely and His Rough Riders
Frank McCarroll
Iron Eyes Cody

73. BOSS OF BULLION CITY

Copyrighted . . . . October 13, 1940
Released . . . . .January 10, 1941
Distributor . . . . .Universal
Length . . . . 61 Minutes
Director . . . . .Ray Taylor
Producer . . . . .Harry Sherman
Screenplay . . . .Arthur St. Claire, Victor McLeod
Based upon a Story . . . . Arthur St. Claire

Cast

Johnny Mack Brown . . . . Tom Bryant
Fuzzy Knight . . . . .Burt Penneycracker

A Publicity Photo captioned: Johnny Mack Brown is selected by the sculptor Salamunich to portray the typical "man of the West." Johnny Mack is currently appearing in Universal's **The Masked Rider** (1941). (WOY Collection.)

Nell O'Day . . . . Martha Hadley		**Length** . . . . .61 Minutes	
Maria Montez . . . . .Linda Calhoun		**Director** . . . . .Ray Taylor	
Earle Hodgins . . . . Mike Calhoun		**Screenplay** . . . . . Sherman Lowe, Victor McLeod	
Harry Woods . . . . .Sheriff Salter		**Based upon a Story** . . . . Sherman Lowe	
Melvin Lang . . . . .Fred Wallace, deputy		**Photography** .Jerry Ash	
Dick Alexander . . . . Steve Hogan		**Film Editor** . . . . Charles Maynard	
Karl Hackett . . . . .Tug Crawford, deputy		**Music Director** . . . . Charles Previn	
George Humbert . . . . .Mario Fernandez			Cast
Frank Ellis . . . . .Deputy		**Johnny Mack Brown** . . . . Joe Henderson	
Kermit Maynard . . . . .Cowboy		**Fuzzy Knight** . . . . .Lem Fielding	
Tex Terry . . . . .Cowboy		**Nell O'Day** . . . . Edna Fielding	
Bill Nestell . . . . .Cowboy		**Kathryn Adams** . . . . Dorothy Walker	
Bob Kortman		**Lee Shumway** . . . . Andy Walker	
Michael Vallon		**Frank O'Connor** . . . . Wendel	
The Guadalajara Trio		**Ernie Adams** .Mustang	
		Don House . . . . Bob Henderson	

74. BURY ME NOT ON THE LONE PRAIRIE

Pat O'Brien . . . . Braffet

Bud Osborne .Calvert

Ed Cassidy . . . . .Sheriff Edison

Copyrighted . . . . November 25, 1940   **William Desmond** . . . . .Bartender

Distributor . . . . .Universal   **Jack Rockwell** . . . . Tiger Cain

Johnny Mack is about to be pistol whipped as he fights with villain Charles King in this scene from **Law of the Range** (1941, Universal). (Courtesy of Jerry Ohlinger's Movie Material Store.)

Harry Cording . . . . Red Clinton
Slim Whitaker
Kermit Maynard
Bob Kortman
Jim Corey
Charles King
Ethan Laidlaw
Frank Ellis
Jimmy Wakely's Rough Riders

75. LAW OF THE RANGE

Copyrighted . . . . June 11, 1941
Distributor . . . . .Universal
Length . . . . .59 Minutes
Director . . . . .Ray Taylor
Associate Producer . . . . .Will Cowan
Screenplay . . . . Sherman Lowe
Suggested by a Story . . . . .Charles E. Barnes
Photography . . . . .Charles Van Enger
Music Director . . . . Charles Previn

Songs: Robert Crawford, Gomer Cook, Milton Rosen, Everett Carter

Cast

Johnny Mack Brown . . . . .Steve
Fuzzy Knight .Chaparral
Nell O'Day . . . . Mary
Roy Harris (Riley Hill) . . . . .The Kid
Pat O'Malley . . . . Steve's Father
Elaine Morey . . . . .Virginia
Ethan Laidlaw . . . . .Hobart
Al Bridge . . . . Squint Johnson
Hal Taliaferro
Tim O'Brien
Lucille Walker and the Texas Rangers
Jack Rockwell
Charles King
Terry Frost
Jim Corey
Bud Osborne
Slim Whitaker
Bob Kortman

Nell O'Day has the drop on Riley Hill as Johnny Mack looks on from his tied up position in this scene from **Law of the Range** (1941, Universal). (Courtesy of Jerry Ohlinger's Movie Material Store.)

76. RAWHIDE RANGERS

Copyrighted . . . . June 26, 1941
Distributor . . . . .Universal
Length . . . . .57 Minutes
Director . . . . .Ray Taylor
Associate Producer . . . . .Will Cowan
Original Screenplay . . . . Ed Earl Repp
Photography . . . . .William Sickner
Film Editor . . . . Ed Curtis
Songs: "A Cowboy is Happy" (sung by Nell O'Day); "Huckleberry Pie" (sung by Fuzzy Knight); "It's a Ranger's Life" (sung by The Texas Rangers)

Cast

Johnny Mack Brown . . . . Brand
Fuzzy Knight . . . . .Porky
Kathryn Adams .Joan
Nell O'Day . . . . .Patti
Roy Harris (Riley Hill) . . . . .Steve
Harry Cording .Blackie

Al Bridge . . . . Rawlings
Frank Shannon . . . . Captain
Ed Cassidy . . . . .Martin
Bob Kortman . . . . .Dirk
Chester Gan . . . . .Sing Lo
James Early . . . . .Banker
Jack Rockwell
Frank Ellis
Fred Burns
Tex Palmer
Tex Terry
The Picard Family
The Texas Rangers

77. MAN FROM MONTANA

Copyrighted . . . . .August 4, 1941
Distributor . . . . .Universal
Length . . . . .57 Minutes
Director . . . . .Ray Taylor
Associate Producer . . . . .Will Cowan

Johnny Mack has villain Bud Osborne at gunpoint as sidekick, Fuzzy Knight, looks on in this scene from **Law of the Range** (1941, Universal). (Courtesy of Jerry Ohlinger's Movie Material Store.)

Original Screenplay . . . . .Bennett Cohen
Photography . . . . .Charles Van Enger
Film Editor . . . . Paul Landers
Songs: "Call of the Range," "Western Trail," "Bananas Make Me Tough," "Little Joe"
Cast

Johnny Mack Brown . . . . .Bob Dawson
Fuzzy Knight . . . . Grubby
Billy Lenhart . . . . .Butch
Kenneth Brown . . . . Buddy
Jeanne Kelly (Jean Brooks) . . . . .Linda
Nell O'Day . . . . Sally
William Gould . . . . .Thompson
James Blaine . . . . Durham
Dick Alexander . . . . Kohler
Karl Hackett . . . . Trig
Edmund Cobb . . . . .Dakota
Frank Ellis . . . . .Decker
Kermit Maynard . . . . .Chris
Jack Shannon . . . . .Tex
Murdock MacQuarrie . . . . .Preston

Charles McMurphy . . . . .Dugan
The King's Men

78. THE MASKED RIDER

Copyrighted . . . . .August 6, 1941
Distributor . . . . .Universal
Length . . . . .58 Minutes
Director . . . . .Ford Beebe
Associate Producer . . . . .Will Cowan
Screenplay . . . Sherman Lowe, Victor I. McLeod
Based upon a Story . . . . .Sam Robins
Photography . . . . .Charles Van Enger
Songs: "La Golondrinda," "Carmelita," "Casenoble," "Cancanita," "Chiapanacas" by Milton Rosen, Everett Carter
Cast

Johnny Mack Brown . . . . .Larry
Fuzzy Knight . . . . .Patches
Nell O'Day . . . . .Jean
Grant Withers . . . . .Douglas

Johnny Mack seems to be enjoying Fuzzy's entanglement in the Universal feature, **Law of the Range** (1941). (Courtesy of Jerry Ohlinger's Movie Material Store.)

Virginia Carroll . . . . Margerita
Guy D'Ennery . . . . .Don Sebastian
Carmela Cansino . . . . .Carmencita
Roy Barcroft . . . . .Luke
Dick Botiller . . . . Pedro
Fred Cordova . . . . Pablo
Al Haskell. . . . . Jose
Rico De Montez . . . . Manuel
Bob O'Connor . . . . Guard
The Guadalajara Trio
The Jose Cansino Dancers

79. ARIZONA CYCLONE

Copyrighted . . . . October 27, 1941
Distributor . . . . .Universal
Length . . . . .57 Minutes
Director . . . . .Ray Taylor
Associate Producer . . . . .Will Cowan
Original Screenplay . . . . .Sherman Lowe
Photography . . . . .Charles Van Enger

Film Editor . . . . Paul Landers
Songs: "Let's Go," "On the Trail of Tomorrow"
by Milton Rosen, Everett Carter; "Wooden Leg
Pete" by Austin Grant
Cast
Johnny Mack Brown . . . . Tom
Fuzzy Knight .Muleshoe
Nell O'Day . . . . .Claire
Kathryn Adams . . . . Elsie
Herbert Rawlinson . . . . .Randolph
Dick Curtis . . . . .Quirt
Robert Strange . . . . Draper
Glenn Strange . . . . .Jessup
The Notables

80. STAGECOACH BUCKAROO

Copyrighted . . . . October 29, 1941
Distributor . . . . .Universal
Length . . . . .58 Minutes
Director . . . . .Ray Taylor

Johnny Mack and Fuzzy seem to have villain Riley Hill in custody as Nell O'Day looks on in this scene from **Law of the Range** (1941, Universal). (Courtesy of Jerry Ohlinger's Movie Material Store.)

Associate Producer . . . . .Will Cowan
Screenplay . . . . .Al Martin
Based on a Story . . . . . "Shotgun Messenger" by
Arthur St. Claire
Photography . . . . Jerome Ash
Songs: "Don't Ever be a Cowboy," "Just Too Darn Bashful," "Wyoming Will be a New Home," "Put it There" by Milton Rosen, Everett Carter

Cast

Johnny Mack Brown . . . . .Steve
Fuzzy Knight . . . . Clem
Nell O'Day . . . . .Molly
Anne Nagel . . . . Nina
Herbert Rawlinson . . . . Kincaid
Glenn Strange .Braddock
Ernie Adams . . . . Blinky
Henry Hall . . . . Denton
Lloyd Ingraham . . . . .Simpson
Kermit Maynard
Frank Brownlee
Jack C. Smith

Harry Tenbrook
Frank Ellis
Blackie Whiteford
Hank Bell
Ray Jones
Jim Corey
William Nestell
Carl Sepulveda
The Guardsmen

81. FIGHTING BILL FARGO

Copyrighted . . . . November 3, 1941
Distributor . . . . .Universal
Length . . . . 57-59 Minutes
Director . . . . .Ray Taylor
Associate Producer . . . . .Will Cowan
Screenplay . . . . . .Paul Franklin, Arthur V. Jones,
Dorcas Cochran
Based upon a Story . . . . .Paul Franklin
Photographer . . . . .Charles Van Enger

Johnny Mack struggles with villain, Dick Curtis, in the Universal feature, **Arizona Cyclone** (1941). (WOY Collection.)

Film Editor . . . . Paul Landers
Songs: "Happiness Corral," "Geraldine," "Welcome Home" (Sung by Eddie Dean Trio) by Milton Rosen, Everett Carter

Cast

Johnny Mack Brown . . . . Bill Fargo
Fuzzy Knight . . . . Grubby
Jeanne Kelly (Jean Brooks) . . . . Linda
Kenneth Harlan . . . . Hackett
Nell O'Day . . . . Julie
Ted Adams . . . . Vic Savage
James Blaine . . . . Cash Scanlon
Al Bridge . . . . Houston
Joseph Eggerton . . . . Judge
Bob Kortman
Earle Hodgins
Tex Palmer
Harry Tenbrook
Kermit Maynard
Blackie Whiteford
Merrill McCormack

Bud Osborne
Eddie Dean Trio

82. RIDE 'EM COWBOY

Copyrighted . . . . December 4, 1941
Distributor . . . . Universal
Length . . . . .86 Minutes
Director . . . . Arthur Lubin
Associate Producer . . . . Alex Gottlieb
Screenplay . . . . True Boardman, John Grant, Harold Shumate
Based upon a Story . . . . . . Edmund L. Hartmann
Photography . . . . John Boyle
Film Editor . . . . Phillip Kahn
Songs: "A Tisket, A Tasket" (sung by Ella Fitzgerald); "I'll Remember April," "Beside the Rio Tonto," "Wake Up Jacob" and "Rock 'n' Reelin'" (sung by the Merry Macs); "Give Me My Saddle" (sung by Dick Foran); "Cow Boogie" by Don Raye, Gene De Paul and Patricia Johnson

Here is a cast photo from **Deep in the Heart of Texas** (1942, Universal). From left to right: Eddie Polo, Tex Ritter, William Farnum, Elmer Clifton (director), Johnny Mack Brown, Jennifer Holt, Oliver Drake (associate producer), Pat O'Malley and Kenneth Harlan. (Courtesy of Bobby Copeland.)

Music Director . . . . Charles Previn

Cast

Bud Abbott . . . . .Duke
Lou Costello .Willoughby
Anne Gwynne . . . . .Anne Shaw
Samuel H. Hinds . . . . Sam Shaw
Dick Foran . . . ."Broncho Bob" Mitchell
Richard Lane . . . . .Peter Conway
Judd McMichael . . . . .Tom
Ted McMichael . . . . .Dick
Joe McMichael . . . . Harry
Mary Lou Cook . . . . .Dotty Davis
Johnny Mack Brown . . . . . . .Alabam Brewster
Ella Fitzgerald . . . . .Ruby
Douglas Dumbrille . . . . .Jake Rainwater
Jody Gilbert . . . . Moonbeam
Morris Ankrum . . . . .Ace Henderson
Charles Lane . . . . Martin Manning
Russell Hicks . . . . Rodeo announcer
Tom Hanlon . . . . Announcer
Wade Boteler . . . . Rodeo Manager

James Flavin . . . . Railroad detective
Boyd Davis . . . . .Doctor
Eddie Dunn . . . . 2nd detective
Isabel Randolph . . . . .Lady at rodeo
James Seay . . . . Ranger captain
Harold Daniels . . . . Reporter
Ralph Peters . . . . .1st henchman
Linda Brent . . . . Sunbeam
Lee Sunrise . . . . 2nd Indian girl
Chief Yowlachie . . . . Chief Tomahawk
Harry Monte . . . . .Midget
Sherman Saunders . . . . Square dance caller
Carmen Cansino . . . . 1st Indian girl
Iron Eyes Cody . . . . .Indian
The Hi-Hatters
The Buckaroos Band
The Ranger Chorus of Forty
The Congoroos

Johnny Mack defends his father William Farnum from accusations by Tex Ritter and fellow Texans, including Jennifer Holt in the Universal feature, **Deep in the Heart of Texas** (1942). (Courtesy of Jerry Ohlinger's Movie Material Store.)

83. THE SILVER BULLET

Copyrighted . . . . July 3, 1942
Distributor . . . . .Universal
Length . . . . .60 Minutes
Director .Joseph H. Lewis
Associate Producer . . . . Oliver Drake
Screenplay . . . . .Elizabeth Beecher
Original Story . . . . Oliver Drake
Photography . . . . .Charles Van Enger
Film Editor . . . . Maurice Wright
Songs: "My Gal, She Works in the Laundry" sung by Fuzzy Knight, written by Oliver Drake, Milton Rosen, and Jimmy Wakely; "Sweetheart of the Rio Grande" sung by the Pals of the Golden West, written by Oliver Drake, Milton Rosen and Jimmy Wakely; "Vote for Emily Morgan" sung by the Pals of the Golden West, written by Oliver Drake, Milton Rosen and Jimmy Wakely; "Red River Valley" sung by the Pals of the Golden West (Jimmy Wakely is a member of the Pals)

Cast

Johnny Mack Brown . . . . "Silver Jim" Donovan
Jennifer Holt .Nancy Lee
Fuzzy Knight . . . . .Wild Bill Jones
William Farnum . . . . .Dr. Thad Morgan
Leroy Mason . . . . Walter Kincaid
Rex Lease .Rance Harris
Grace Lenard . . . . .Queenie Canfield
Claire Whitney . . . . Emily Morgan
Charles "Slim" Whitaker . . . . . . .Buck Dawson
Michael Vallon . . . . .Nevada Norton
Merrill McCormick . . . . Pete Sloan
Pals of the Golden West and Nora Lou Martin

84. BOSS OF HANGTOWN MESA

Copyrighted . . . . July 14, 1942
Distributor . . . . .Universal
Length . . . . .59 Minutes
Director . . . . .Joseph H. Lewis
Associate Producer . . . . Oliver Drake

Johnny Mack gets an adoring look from heroine Jennifer Holt in his eastern duds in this scene from **Deep in the Heart of Texas** (1942, Universal). (Courtesy of Jerry Ohlinger's Movie Material Store.)

Screenplay . . . . Oliver Drake
Songs: "Pappa Was a Gun Man" sung by Fuzzy Knight, written by Oliver Drake; "Ain't Got Nothin' and Nothin' Worries Me" sung by Fuzzy Knight and written by Oliver Drake, Jimmy Wakely and Milton Rosen; "Trail Dreamin'" sung by The Pals of the Golden West and written by Oliver Drake, Jimmy Wakely, and Milton Rosen; "Song of the Prairie" sung by the Pals of the Golden West.

Cast

Johnny Mack Brown	Steve Collins
Fuzzy Knight	Dr. I. Wellington Dingle
William Farnum	Judge Ezra Binns
Rex Lease	Bert Lawler
Helen Deverell	Betty Wilkins
Hugh Prosser	The Utah Kid
Robert Barron	Flash Hollister
Michael Vallon	Clint Rayner
Henry Hall	John Wilkins
Fred Kohler, Jr.	Clem

Pals of the Golden West
Nora Lou Martin
Jimmy Wakely

85. DEEP IN THE HEART OF TEXAS

Copyrighted	August 21, 1942
Distributor	Universal
Length	62 Minutes
Director	Elmer Clifton
Associate Producer	Oliver Drake
Original Screenplay	Oliver Drake
Adaptation	Grace Norton
Photography	Harry Newman
Film Editor	Otto Ludwig

Songs: "Deep in the Heart of Texas" (ensemble), "Song of the Sage," "Sweet Genevieve," "Dixie," "Cowboy's Lament," some by Johnny Bond, Don Swander, June Hersey

Cast

Johnny Mack Brown	Jim Mallory

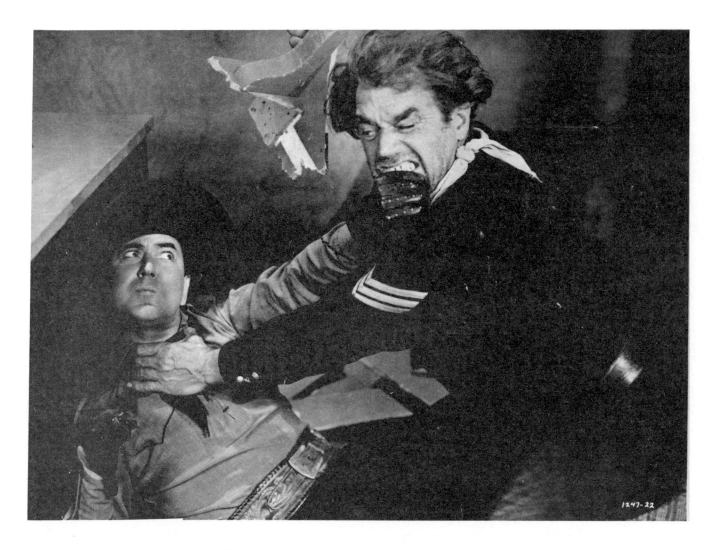

Johnny Mack struggles with villain Harry Woods in this scene from **Deep in the Heart of Texas** (1942, Universal). (Courtesy of Jerry Ohlinger's Movie Material Store.)

Tex Ritter . . . . Brent Gordon	**Length** . . . . 60-64 Minutes
Fuzzy Knight . . . . Happy T. Snodgrass	**Director** . . . . Lewis O. Collins
Jennifer Holt . . . . Nan Taylor	**Associate Producer** . . . . Oliver Drake
William Farnum . . . . Colonel Mallory	**Screenplay** . . .Sherman Lowe, Elizabeth Beecher
Harry Woods . . . . .Idaho	**Based upon a Story** . . . . Sherman Lowe
Kenneth Harlan . . . . Sneed	**Photography** . . . . .William Sickner
Pat O'Malley . . . . .Jonathan Taylor	**Film Editor** . . . . .Russell Schoengarth

Roy Brent . . . . Franklin
Edmund Cobb . . . . Matthews
Jimmy Wakely Trio
Earle Hodgins
Budd Buster
Frank Ellis
Tom Smith
Ray Jones
Eddie Polo

Songs: "I'll Saddle My Pony" by Jimmy Wakely (sung by Wakely Trio); "Git Along Little Doggie" (sung by Wakely Trio); "Little Joe, the Wrangler" (sung by Tex Ritter, later by Fuzzy Knight)

Cast

Johnny Mack Brown . . . . Neal Wallace
Tex Ritter . . . . Bob Brewster
Fuzzy Knight . . . . .Little Joe Smith
Jennifer Holt . . . . .Janet Hammond
Florine McKinney . . . . Mary Brewster
James Craven . . . . .Lloyd Chapin
Hal Taliaferro . . . . .Travis
Glenn Strange . . . . Jeff Corey
Ethan Laidlaw . . . . .Bit

86. LITTLE JOE, THE WRANGLER

Copyrighted . . . . .August 28, 1942
Distributor . . . . .Universal

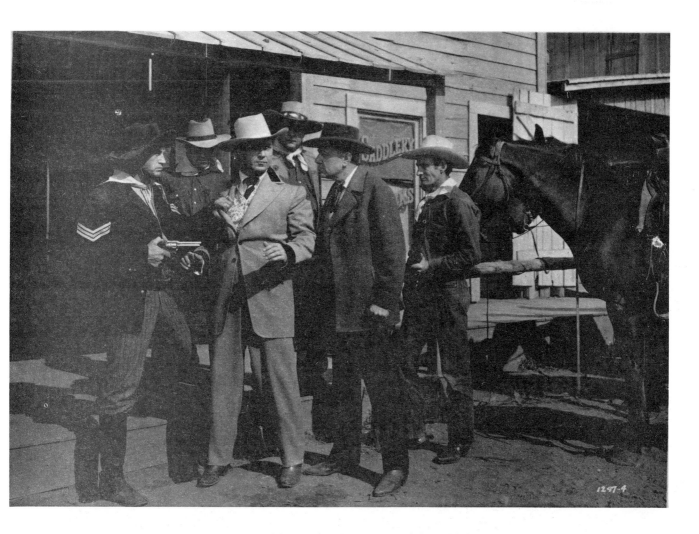

Johnny Mack seems to be in deep trouble as he is menaced by villain Harry Woods and a gang of players in the Universal feature **Deep in the Heart of Texas** (1942). (Courtesy of Jerry Ohlinger's Movie Material Store.)

Evelyn Cooke . . . . Helen
Slim Whitaker . . . . .Charlie
Carl Sepulveda . . . . Norton
Michael Vallon . . . . .Clem
Robert F. Hill .Hammond
Dave Allen . . . . .Miner
Bill Patton . . . . .Miner
Jimmy Wakely Trio (Jimmy Wakely, Cyrus Bond, Eddie Snyder)

87. RAIDERS OF SAN JOAQUIN

Copyrighted . . . . September 18, 1942
Released . . . . .May, 1943
Distributor . . . . .Universal
Length . . . . .59 Minutes
Director . . . . Lewis D. Collins
Associate Producer . . . . Oliver Drake
Screenplay . . . . Elmer Clifton, Morgan Cox
Based upon a Story . . . . Patricia Harper
Photography . . . . .William Sickner

Film Editor . . . . .Russell Schoengarth
Songs: "A Carefree Cowboy," "I'd Rather Be Footloose and Free," "The Hatches and the Morgans" by Oliver Drake
Cast
Johnny Mack Brown . . . . .Rocky Morgan
Tex Ritter . . . . Gil Blake
Fuzzy Knight . . . . .Eustace Clairmont
Jennifer Holt .Jane Carter
Henry Hall . . . . Bodine Carter
Joseph Bernard . . . . .Jim Blake
George Eldridge . . . . .Gus Sloan
Henry Roquemore . . . . Rogers
John Elliott . . . . .Morgan
Michael Vallon .Clark
Jack O'Shea .Detective
Jack Ingram . . . . Lear
Robert Thompson . . . . .Johnson
Carl Sepulveda . . . . Tanner
Scoop Martin . . . . .Tripp
Roy Brent . . . . .McQuarry

Johnny Mack and Tex Ritter watch as Fuzzy Knight tries out his "wings" in this scene from **Little Joe, the Wrangler** (1942, Universal). (WOY Collection.)

Budd Buster . . . . Deputy
Earle Hodgins
Slim Whitaker
Jimmy Wakely Trio

88. TENTING TONIGHT ON THE OLD CAMP GROUND

Copyrighted . . . . September 21, 1942
Released . . . . March, 1943
Distributor . . . . .Universal
Length . . . . .62 Minutes
Director . . . . Lewis D. Collins
Associate Producer . . . . Oliver Drake
Screenplay . . . . .Elizabeth Beecher
Based upon a Story . . . . Harry Fraser
Photography . . . . .William Sickner
Film Editor . . . . Charles Maynard
Musical Director . . . . .H. J. Salter
Songs: Jennifer Holt sings "Cielito Lindo" with the Jimmy Wakely Trio; Jimmy Wakely Trio

sings "Tenting Tonight on the Old Camp Ground" and "The Drinks Are on the House"; and Ritter sings "Ridin' Home."

Cast

Johnny Mack Brown . . . . .Wade Benson
Jennifer Holt . . . . Kay Randolph
Tex Ritter . . . . .Bob Courtney
Fuzzy Knight . . . . .Si Dugan
John Elliott . . . . .Talbot
Earle Hodgins . . . . Judge Higgins
Rex Lease . . . . Zeke Larkin
Lane Chandler . . . . .Duke Merrick
Alan Bridge . . . . Matt Warner
Dennis Moore . . . . Ed Randolph
Tom London . . . . .Pete
Bud Osborne . . . . Deputy Snell
Reed Howes . . . . .Smokey
Lynton Brent .Sheriff
George Plues . . . . .Stage Driver
Hank Worden . . . . Sleepy Martin
Ray Jones

Johnny Mack and Fuzzy Knight give Jennifer Holt some bad news as Florine McKinney comforts her in **Little Joe, the Wrangler** (1942, Universal). (Courtesy of Jerry Ohlinger's Movie Material Store.)

George Eldridge
Jimmy Wakely Trio (Jimmy Wakely, Scotty Harrel, Johnny Bond)

89. CHEYENNE ROUNDUP

Copyrighted . . . . October 8, 1942
Released . . . . April, 1943
Distributor . . . . .Universal
Length . . . . .59 Minutes
Director . . . . .Ray Taylor
Associate Producer . . . . Oliver Drake
Screenplay . . Elmer Clifton, Bernard McConville
Original Story . . . . Elmer Clifton, Bernard McConville
Photography . . . . .William Sickner
Film Editor .Otto Ludwig
Music Director . . . . H. J. Salter
Cast
Johnny Mack Brown . . . . .Gils & Buck Brandon
Tex Ritter . . . . .Steve Rawlins

Fuzzy Knight . . . . Cal Cawkins
Jennifer Holt . . . . .Ellen Randall
Harry Woods . . . . Blackie Dawson
Roy Barcroft . . . . .Slim Layton
Robert Barron . . . . Judge Hickinbottom
Budd Buster . . . . Bonanza
Gil Patric . . . . .Perkins
Ken Duncan . . . . Pony Express Rider
Roy Brent . . . . .Rider
Michael Vallon . . . . Miner
Lynton Brent . . . . .Jake
The Jimmy Wakely Trio (Jimmy Wakely, Cyrus Bond, Scotty Harrel)

90. THE OLD CHISHOLM TRAIL

Copyrighted . . . . October 12, 1942
Released . . . . January, 1943
Distributor . . . . .Universal
Length . . . . .61 Minutes
Director . . . . .Elmer Clifton

Tex Ritter gets the drop on Johnny Mack as Jennifer Holt looks on in **The Lone Star Trail** (1943, Universal). (Courtesy of Jerry Ohlinger's Movie Material Store.)

Associate Producer . . . . Oliver Drake
Screenplay .Elmer Clifton
Based upon a Story . . . . Harry Fraser
Photography . . . . .William Sickner
Songs: Oliver Drake, Jimmy Wakely, Milton Rosen

Cast

Johnny Mack Brown . . . . Dusty Gardner
Tex Ritter . . . . .Montana Smith
Fuzzy Knight .Polario
Jennifer Holt . . . . .Mary Lee
Mady Correll . . . . Belle Turner
Earle Hodgins . . . . .Chief Hopping Crow
Roy Barcroft . . . . .Ed
Edmund Cobb . . . . .Joe Rankin
Budd Buster . . . . .Hank
George Sherwood . . . . Mike Carey
Roy Butler . . . . Larry
Michael Vallon . . . . .Sheriff
Jimmy Wakely Trio (Jimmy Wakely, Scotty Harrell, Johnny Bond)

91. THE LONE STAR TRAIL

Copyrighted . . . . November 16, 1942
Released .September, 1943
Distributor . . . . .Universal
Length . . . . .58 Minutes
Director . . . . .Ray Taylor
Associate Producer . . . . Oliver Drake
Screenplay . . . . Oliver Drake
Based upon a Story . . . . .Victor Halperin
Photography . . . . .William Sickner
Film Editor . . . . .Ray Snyder
Songs: Oliver Drake, Milton Rosen, Jimmy Wakely

Cast

Johnny Mack Brown . . . . .Blaze Barker
Tex Ritter . . . . Fargo Steele
Fuzzy Knight . . . . .Angus McAngus
Jennifer Holt . . . . Joan Winters
George Eldredge . . . . Doug Ransom
Michael Vallon . . . . Jonathan Bentley

158

Budd Buster seems to hear something as Jimmy Wakely, Jennifer Holt, Tex Ritter, Scotty Harrel, Fuzzy Knight, Johnny Bond, and Johnny Mack Brown look on in this scene from **Raiders of San Joaquin** (1943, Universal). (Courtesy of Jerry Ohlinger's Movie Material Store.)

Harry Strange . . . . .Sheriff
Earle Hodgins . . . . Major Cyrus Jenkins
Jack Ingram . . . . .Dan Jason
Bob Mitchum . . . . Bob Slocum
Ethan Laidlaw . . . . .Steve Bannister
William Desmond . . . . .Bartender
Harry Roquemore . . . . .Bank Teller
Denver Dixon . . . . Townsman
Carl Mathews . . . . Townsman
Eddie Parker . . . . Lynch
Billy Engle . . . . .Stage Passenger
Bob Reeves . . . . Barfly
Tom Steele . . . . .Mitchum's Double
Jimmy Wakely Trio

92. THE GHOST RIDER

Copyrighted .April 2, 1943
Distributor . . . . Monogram
Length . . . . 52-58 Minutes
Director .Wallace W. Fox

Producer . . . . Scott R. Dunlap
Screenplay . . . . .Jess Bowers (Adele Buffington)
Photography . . . . .Harry Neumann
Film Editor . . . . Carl Pierson
Assistant Director . . . . William Strohbach
Production Manager . . . . Charles J. Bigelow
Sound Engineer . . . . Glen Glenn
Art Director . . . . .Ernie Hickson

Cast

Johnny Mack Brown . . Nevada Jack MacKenzie
Raymond Hatton . . . . .Sandy Hopkins
Beverly Boyd . . . . .Julie Wilson
Tom Seidel . . . . .Joe McNally
Bud Osborne . . . . .Lucky Howard
Milton Morante . . . . John Wilson
Harry Woods . . . . .Lash Edwards
Edmund Cobb . . . . .Zack Saddler
Charles King . . . . Steve Cook
Artie Ortego . . . . Roy Kern
George Denormand . . . . .Red
Jack Daley . . . . .Patrick McNally

A Lobby Card showing the principals of **Tenting Tonight on the Old Camp Ground**, Johnny Mack, Jennifer Holt, Fuzzy Knight and Tex Ritter. (1943, Universal). (WOY Collection.)

George Morrell

93. THE STRANGER FROM PECOS

Copyrighted . . . . May 10, 1943
Distributor . . . . Monogram
Length . . . . .56 Minutes
Director . . . . .Lambert Hillyer
Producer . . . . Scott R. Dunlap
Screenplay . . . . Jess Bowers (Adele Buffington)
Photography . . . . .Harry Neumann
Film Editor . . . . Carl Pierson
Music Director . . . . Edward Kay
Cast
Johnny Mack Brown . . Nevada Jack MacKenzie
Raymond Hatton . . . . .Sandy Hopkins
Kirby Grant . . . . Tom
Christine McIntyre . . . . .Ruth
Steve Clark . . . . .Clem
Sam Flint . . . . Ward
Roy Barcroft . . . . Sheriff

Robert Frazer .Burstow
Edmund Cobb . . . . .Burt
Charles King . . . . Harmond
Bud Osborne . . . . Gus
Artie Ortego . . . . .Ed
Tom London
Kermit Maynard
Milburn Morante
Lynton Brent
Carol Henry
George Morrell

94. SIX-GUN GOSPEL

Copyrighted . . . . July 13, 1943
Distributor . . . . Monogram
Length . . . . .55 Minutes
Director . . . . .Lambert Hillyer
Producer . . . . Scott R. Dunlap
Screenplay . . . Ed Earl Repp, Jess Bowers (Adele Buffington)

160

Johnny Mack disarms villain Tom London as Tex Ritter and a group of players look on in this scene from **Tenting Tonight on the Old Camp Ground** (1943, Universal). (Courtesy of Jerry Ohlinger's Movie Material Store.)

Photography . . . . .Harry Neumann
Film Editor . . . . Carl Pierson
Assistant Director . . . . William Strohbach
Production Manager . . . . C. J. Bigelow
Sound . . . . Glen Glenn
Musical Director . . . . Edward Kay

Cast

Johnny Mack Brown . . Nevada Jack MacKenzie
Raymond Hatton . . . . .Sandy Hopkins
Inna Gest . . . . .Jane Simms
Eddie Dew . . . . Dan
Roy Barcroft . . . . Durkin
Kenneth MacDonald . . . . Benton
Edmund Cobb . . . . .Waco
Milburn Morante . . . . .Zeke
Artie Ortego . . . . .Ed
Lynton Brent . . . . .Steve
Bud Osborne . . . . .Joe
Kernan Cripps . . . . .Simms
Jack Daley . . . . .Mr. Dailey
Mary MacLaren . . . . Mrs. Dailey

95. OUTLAWS OF STAMPEDE PASS

Copyrighted . . . . September 3, 1943
Distributor . . . . Monogram
Length . . . . 55 Minutes
Director . . . . .Wallace Fox
Producer . . . . Scott R. Dunlap
Screenplay . . . .Jess Bowers (Adele Buffington)
Based upon a Story . . . . . . .Johnston McCulley
Photography . . . . Marcel Le Picard
Film Editor . . . . Carl Pierson
Music Director . . . . Edward Kay
Assistant Director . . . . .Theodore Joos
Production Manager . . . . C. J. Bigelow
Sound . . . . Glen Glenn

Cast

Johnny Mack Brown . . Nevada Jack MacKenzie
Raymond Hatton . . . . .Sandy Hopkins
Ellen Hall .Mary Lewis
Harry Woods . . . . .Ben Crowley
Milburn Morante . . . . .Zeke

Fuzzy Knight restrains Tex Ritter and Jennifer Holt restrains Johnny Mack as a group of players look on (Hank Worden in the foreground) in this scene from **Tenting Tonight on the Old Camp Ground** (1943, Universal). (Courtesy of Jerry Ohlinger's Movie Material Store.)

Edmund Cobb . . . . Hank
Sam Flint . . . . Jeff Lewis
Jon Dawson . . . . Tom Evans
Charles King . . . . Steve Carse
Mauritz Hugo . . . . .Slick
Art Mix . . . . .Gus
Herman Hack . . . . .Ed
Artie Ortego . . . . .Joe
Eddie Burns . . . . Red
Bill Wolfe
Hal Prince
Dan White
Kansas Moehring
Tex Cooper
Cactus Mack

96. THE TEXAS KID

Copyrighted . . . . October 15, 1943
Distributor . . . . Monogram
Length . . . . .57 Minutes

Director .Lambert Hillyer
Producer . . . . Scott R. Dunlap
Screenplay . . . . .Jess Bowers (Adele Buffington)
Based upon a Story . . . . . . .Lynton Wright Brent
Photography . . . . .Harry Neumann
Film Editor . . . . Carl Pierson
Music Director . . . . Edward Kay
Cast
Johnny Mack Brown . . Nevada Jack MacKenzie
Raymond Hatton . . . . .Sandy Hopkins
Marshall Reed . . . . Texas Kid
Shirley Patterson . . . . .Nancy
Robert Fiske . . . . .Taylor
Edmund Cobb . . . . Scully
Lynton Brent . . . . .Jess
Bud Osborne . . . . .Steve
Kermit Maynard .Alex
John Judd . . . . .Ray
Cyrus Ring . . . . .Atwood
Stanley Price . . . . .Ed
Charles King

Judge Higgins (Earle Hodgins) seems to be having trouble hearing lawyer Fuzzy Knight as Tex Ritter and Johnny Mack and a group of players look on in **Tenting Tonight on the Old Camp Ground** (1943, Universal). (Courtesy of Jerry Ohlinger's Movie Material Store.)

George C. Lewis

97. CRAZY HOUSE

Copyrighted . . . . November 2, 1943
Distributor . . . . .Universal
Released . . . . October, 1943
Note: Starring Olsen and Johnson with Johnny Mack Brown only appearing for a moment in a cameo in the opening.

98. RAIDERS OF THE BORDER

Copyrighted . . . . .January 5, 1944
Distributor . . . . Monogram
Length . . . . 53-54 Minutes
Director . . . . John P. McCarthy
Producer . . . . Scott R. Dunlap
Screenplay . . . . .Jess Bowers (Adele Buffington)
Based upon a Story . . . . . . .Johnston McCulley
Photography . . . . .Harry Neumann

Film Editor . . . . Carl Pierson
Music Director . . . . Edward Kay
Songs: "Meadowland" from Soviet Army Song, "Cavalry of the Steppes" by Lev Knopper, Victor Gussev with English Lyrics by Harold Rome

Cast

Johnny Mack Brown . . Nevada Jack MacKenzie
Raymond Hatton . . . . .Sandy Hopkins
Christine McIntyre . . . . .Kate
Craig Woods . . . . .Joel
Robert Frazer .Edwards
Harry F. Price . . . . Dobbey
Jack Ingram . . . . .Trigger
Lynton Brent . . . . .Larn
Marshall Reed .Baker
Ben Corbett . . . . Duke
Steve Clark . . . . Colby
Lloyd Ingraham . . . . .Applegate
Ted Mapes

Fuzzy Knight, Johnny Mack and Tex Ritter face down villain Lane Chandler and his gang of crooked gamblers, while Jennifer Holt, Tom London and Sheriff Bud Osborne look on, in **Tenting Tonight on the Old Camp Ground** (1943, Universal). (Courtesy of Jerry Ohlinger's Movie Material Store.)

99. PARTNERS OF THE TRAIL

Copyrighted . . . . .February 19, 1944
Distributor . . . . Monogram
Length . . . . .57 Minutes
Director . . . . .Lambert Hillyer
Producer . . . . Scott R. Dunlap
Screenplay and Story . . . . .Frank H. Young
Photographer . . . . Harry Neumann
Film Editor . . . . .Carl Heim
Music Director . . . . Edward Kay
Cast
Johnny Mack Brown . . Nevada Jack MacKenzie
Raymond Hatton . . . . .Sandy Hopkins
Christine McIntyre . . . . .Kate
Craig Woods . . . . .Joel
Robert Frazer .Edwards
Harry F. Price . . . . Dobbey
Jack Ingram . . . . Trigger
Lynton Brent . . . . .Lem
Marshall Reed . . . . .Baker

Ben Corbett . . . . Duke
Steve Slark . . . . Cobly
Lloyd Ingraham . . . . .Applegate
Ted Mapes

100. LAW MEN

Copyrighted . . . . .April 1, 1944
Distributor . . . . Monogram
Length . . . . .57 Minutes
Director . . . . .Lambert Hillyer
Producer . . . . Scott R. Dunlap
Screenplay and Story . . . . Glenn Tyron
Photography . . . . .Harry Neumann
Film Editor . . . . John C. Fuller
Music Director . . . . Edward Kay
Cast
Johnny Mack Brown . . Nevada Jack MacKenzie
Raymond Hatton . . . . .Sandy Hopkins
Jan Wiley . . . . .Phyllis
Kirby Grant . . . . .Clyde Miller

Johnny Mack looks as if he is about to punch out villain Rex Lease as Jennifer Holt, Tex Ritter, Fuzzy Knight and townspeople look on in **Tenting Tonight on the Old Camp Ground** (1943, Universal). (Courtesy of Jerry Ohlinger's Movie Material Store.)

Robert Frazer .Bradford
Edmund Cobb . . . . .Slade
Art Fowler . . . . Gus
Harry F. Price .Haynes
Marshall Reed .Killifer
Isabel Withers . . . . Antie Mac
Ben Corbett . . . . .Simmons
Ted Mapes . . . . Curley
Steve Clark . . . . Wilson
Bud Osborne . . . . .Hardy
Jack Rockwell
George Morrell
Ray Jones

101. RANGE LAW

Copyrighted . . . . May 20, 1944
Distributor . . . . Monogram
Length . . . . .55 Minutes
Director .Lambert Hillyer
Producer . . . . .Charles J. Bigelow

Screenplay and Story . . . . .Frank H. Young
Photography . . . . .Harry Neumann
Film Editor .John C. Fuller
Music Director . . . . .Edward Kay

Cast
Johnny Mack Brown . . Nevada Jack MacKenzie
Raymond Hatton . . . . .Sandy Hopkins
Sarah Padden . . . . .Boots Annie
Ellen Hall . . . . Lucille Grey
Lloyd Ingraham . . . . .Judge
Marshall Reed . . . . Jim Bowen
Steve Clark . . . . Pop McGee
Jack Ingram . . . . Phil Randall
Hugh Prosser . . . . .Sheriff
Stanley Price . . . . Dawson
Art Fowler . . . . Swede Larson
Harry F. Price . . . . .Zeke
Ben Corbett . . . . .Joe
Bud Osborne . . . . .Davis
Tex Palmer

Tex Ritter, Johnny Mack and Fuzzy Knight fight off an outlaw attack in **Tenting Tonight on the Old Camp Ground** (1943, Universal). (Courtesy of Jerry Ohlinger's Movie Material Store.)

George Morrell
Horace B. Carpenter
Lynton Brent
Forrest Taylor

102. WEST OF THE RIO GRANDE

Copyrighted . . . . July 24, 1944
Distributor . . . . Monogram
Length . . . . .57 Minutes
Director .Lambert Hillyer
Producer . . . . .Charles J. Bigelow
Screenplay and Story . . . . .Betty Burbridge
Photography . . . . Arthur Martinelli
Film Editor . . . . .John C. Fuller
Music Director . . . . Edward Kay
Assistant Director . . . . .Theodore Joos
Sound Recorder . . . . .Glen Glenn
Cast
Johnny Mack Brown . . Nevada Jack MacKenzie
Raymond Hatton . . . . .Sandy Hopkins

Dennis Moore . . . . Ethan Boyd
Christine McIntyre . . . . .Alice Darcy
Lloyd Ingraham . . . . .Trooper
Kenneth MacDonald . . . . Martin Keene
Frank LaRue . . . . .Judge
Art Fowler . . . . Nate Todd
Hugh Prosser . . . . Lucky Cramer
Edmund Cobb .Curly
Steve Clark . . . . Doc Ely
Jack Rockwell . . . . Tom Boyd
Hal Price . . . . Pop Grimsby
John Merton . . . . Gunnerson
Bob Kortman
Bud Osborne
Pierce Lyden
Lynton Brent

103. LAND OF THE OUTLAWS

Copyrighted . . . . .August 26, 1944
Distributor . . . . Monogram

Johnny Mack and Tex Ritter comfort a dying player in the Universal feature, **Tenting Tonight on the Old Camp Ground** (1943). (Courtesy of Jerry Ohlinger's Movie Material Store.)

Length	55 Minutes
Director	Lambert Hillyer
Producer	Charles J. Bigelow
Screenplay and Story	Joseph O'Donnell
Photography	Harry Neumann
Film Editor	John C. Fuller
Music Director	Edward Kay
Assistant Director	Bobbie Ray
Sound Engineer	Glen Glenn

Cast

Johnny Mack Brown	Nevada Jack MacKenzie
Sandy Hopkins	Sandy Hopkins
Stephen Keyes	Frank Carson
Nan Holliday	Ellen
Hugh Prosser	Ed Hammond
Charles King	Bart Green
John Merton	Dan Broderick
Steve Clark	Sheriff
Art Fowler	Carter
Tom Quinn	Vic
Ray Elder	Clint
Chick Hannon	Joe
Bob Cason	Casey
Kansas Moehring	Jed
Ben Corbett	
George Morrell	

104. LAW OF THE VALLEY

Copyrighted	September 23, 1944
Distributor	Monogram
Length	52 Minutes
Director	Howard Bretherton
Producer	Charles J. Bigelow
Screenplay and Story	Joseph O'Donnell
Photography	Marcel Le Picard
Film Editor	Pierre Janet
Music Director	Edward Kay
Assistant Director	Theodore "Doc" Joos
Sound Engineer	Glen Glenn

Cast

Johnny Mack Brown	Nevada Jack MacKenzie

Tex Ritter gets the drop on Johnny Mack in **Cheyenne Roundup** (1943, Universal). (Courtesy of Jerry Ohlinger's Movie Material Store.)

Raymond Hatton . . . . .Sandy Hopkins
Lynne Carver .Ann
Edmund Cobb . . . . Stanton
Charles King . . . . .Miller
Kirk Barron . . . . .Tom Findley
Tom Quinn . . . . .Condon
Marshall Reed . . . . Al
Hal Price . . . . .Sheriff
George DeNormand . . . . .Red
Steve Clark . . . . Slim
George Morrell .Jenkins
Charles McMurphy

105. GHOST GUNS

Copyrighted . . . . October 15, 1944
Distributor . . . . Monogram
Length . . . . .60 Minutes
Director . . . . .Lambert Hillyer
Producer . . . . .Charles J. Bigelow
Screenplay . . . . .Frank H. Young

Based upon a Story . . . . Bennet Cohen
Photography . . . . Marcel Le Picard
Film Editor . . . . .Pierre Janet
Music Director . . . . Edward Kay
Assistant Director . . . . .Theodore Joos
Set Dressing .Vin Taylor
Sound Engineer . . . . Glen Glenn
Cast
Johnny Mack Brown . . Nevada Jack MacKenzie
Raymond Hatton . . . . .Sandy Hopkins
Evelyn Finley . . . . Ann Jordan
Sarah Padden . . . . Aunt Sally
Riley Hill . . . . Ted Connors
Ernie Adams . . . . .Doc Edwards
Jack Ingraham . . . . Waco
Tom Quinn . . . . .Stringer
Frank LaRue .Kelbro
John Merton .Matson
Bob Cason . . . . Henchman
Marshall Reed . . . . .Black Jack
Steve Clark

Johnny Mack introduces Roy Barcroft to heroine Jennifer Holt in **Cheyenne Roundup** (1943, Universal). (Courtesy of Jerry Ohlinger's Movie Material Store.)

George Morrell

106. THE NAVAJO TRAIL

Copyrighted	December 26, 1944
Distributor	Monogram
Length	60 Minutes
Director	Howard Bretherton
Producer	Charles J. Bigelow
Screenplay	Jess Bowers (Adele Buffington)
Based upon a Story	Frank H. Young
Photography	Marcel Le Picard
Film Editor	Arthur H. Bell
Assistant Director	Bobby Ray
Sound Mixer	Glen Glenn
Set Dresser	Vin Taylor

Cast

Johnny Mack Brown	Nevada Jack MacKenzie
Raymond Hatton	Sandy Hopkins
Jennifer Holt	Mary Trevor
Riley Hill	Paul

Jasper L. Palmer	Sergeant Trevor
Charles King	Red
Edmund Cobb	Farr
Ray Bennett	Slim Ramsey
Bud Osborne	Brad
Tom Quinn	Tober
Josh Carpenter	Steve
Jim Hood	Rusty
Earl Crawford	Joe
Mary McLaren	Stella
Edward Cassidy	

107. FOREVER YOURS

Copyrighted	December 22, 1944
Distributor	Monogram
Length	83 Minutes
Director	William Nigh
Producer	Jeffrey Bernerd
Original Screenplay	Neil Rau, George Sayre
Photography	Harry Neumann

Johnny Mack and Tex Ritter get together as Fuzzy Knight looks on in **Cheyenne Roundup** (1943, Universal). (Courtesy of Jerry Ohlinger's Movie Material Store.)

Film Editor .Ray Curtiss
Music Director . . . . Edward Kay
Songs: "Close Your Eyes" by Al Jaxton, Neil Rau; "You're the Answer" by Harry Brown, Robert Watson (sung by Gale Storm)

Cast

Gale Storm . . . . .Joan Randall
Sir Aubrey Smith . . . . Grandfather
Johnny Mack Brown . . . . .Tex
Frank Craven . . . . Uncle Charles
Conrad Nagle . . . . .Dr. Randall
Billy Wilkerson . . . . 1st Soldier
Mary Boland . . . . .Aunt Mary
Johnny Downs . . . . .Ricky
Catherine McLeod . . . . Martha
Selmer Jackson . . . . Williams
Matt Wills . . . . .Alabam
Russ Whitman . . . . 2nd Soldier
Leo Diamond and His Harmonaires

108. GUN SMOKE

Copyrighted . . . . .January 5, 1945
Distributor . . . . Monogram
Length . . . . .57 Minutes
Director . . . . Howard Bretherton
Producer . . . . .Charles J. Bigelow
Screenplay and Story . . . . .Frank H. Young
Photography . . . . Marcel Le Picard
Film Editor . . . . .J. M. Foley
Assistant Director . . . . Bobby Ray
Sound Engineer . . . . Glen Glenn
Set Dresser . . . . Vin Taylor

Cast

Johnny Mack Brown . . Nevada Jack MacKenzie
Raymond Hatton . . . . .Sandy Hopkins
Jennifer Holt . . . . Jane
Riley Hill . . . . .Joel Hinkley
Frank Ellis . . . . Duce
Ray Bennett . . . . Lucky
Marshall Reed . . . . .Cyclone

Judge Fuzzy Knight lays down the law to villains Roy Barcroft, a bad Johnny Mack and two other players in **Cheyenne Roundup** (1943, Universal). (Courtesy of Jerry Ohlinger's Movie Material Store.)

Steve Clark . . . . .Soda
Bob Cason . . . . Red
Elmer Napier . . . . .Cactus
Roy E. Butler . . . . .Sheriff
Wen Wright . . . . .Knuckles
Dimas Sotello . . . . Shag
Kansas Moehring . . . . .Whity
Louis Hart . . . . Pete
Chick Hannon

109. STRANGER FROM SANTA FE

Copyrighted . . . . .March 1, 1945
Distributor . . . . Monogram
Length .56 Minutes
Director .Lambert Hillyer
Producer . . . . .Charles J. Bigelow
Screenplay . . . . .Jess Bowers (Adele Buffington)
Story . . . . Charles N. Heckelmann
Photography . . . . .Harry Neumann
Music Director . . . . .Frank Sanucci

Production Manager . . . . Bobby Ray
Assistant Director . . . . .Eddie Davis
Recorder . . . . .Glen Glenn

Cast

Johnny Mack Brown . . Nevada Jack MacKenzie
Raymond Hatton . . . . .Sandy Hopkins
Beatrice Gray . . . . .Marcia Earley
Jo Ann Curtis . . . . .Beth Grimes
Jack Ingraham . . . . Ned Grimes
Bud Osborne . . . . .Clint
Jimmie Martin . . . . .Dan
Steve Clark . . . . Sheriff
Hal Price . . . . Hymer
John Merton . . . . .Cy Manning
Tom Quinn . . . . Bill
Dick Dickinson . . . . Justice of the Peace
Ray Elder
Eddie Parker
Louis Hart
Jack Rockwell

Johnny Mack and Jennifer Holt look angry as Tex Ritter and villains Harry Woods, Roy Barcroft and Robert Barron look on in **Cheyenne Roundup** (1943, Universal). (Courtesy of Jerry Ohlinger's Movie Material Store.)

110. FLAME OF THE WEST

Copyrighted . . . . .April 25, 1945
Distributor . . . . Monogram
Length . . . . 60-71 Minutes
Director . . . . .Lambert Hillyer
Producer . . . . Scott R. Dunlap
Screenplay . . . . .Adele Buffington
Based upon a Story . . . . .Bennett Foster
Photography . . . . .Harry Neumann
Film Editor . . . . .Danny Milner

Cast

Johnny Mack Brown . . . . John Poore
Raymond Hatton . . . . .Add
Joan Woodbury . . . . Poppy
Douglas Dumbrille . . . . Nightlander
Lynne Carver . . . . Abbie Compton
Harry Woods . . . . Wisdon
John Merton . . . . Compton
Riley Hill . . . . Midland
Steve Clark . . . . .Hendricks

Bud Osborne . . . . .Purcell
Jack Rockwell . . . . Knott
Raphael Bennett .Rocky
Tom Quinn . . . . .Ed
Jack Ingram . . . . .Slick
Pee Wee King and His Golden West Boys

111. THE LOST TRAIL

Copyrighted . . . . September 13, 1945
Distributor . . . . Monogram
Length . . . . .53 Minutes
Director . . . . .Lambert Hillyer
Producer . . . . .Charles J. Bigelow
Screenplay . . . . . Jess Bowers (Adele Buffington)
Photography . . . . Marcel Le Picard
Film Editor . . . . .Danny Milner

Cast

Johnny Mack Brown . . Nevada Jack MacKenzie
Raymond Hatton . . . . .Sandy Hopkins
Jennifer Holt . . . . .Jane Burns

In the finale, Johnny Mack holds Fuzzy Knight and Jennifer Holt as Tex Ritter looks on. Villains Harry Woods, Roy Barcroft and Robert Barron are tied up on the stagecoach in this scene from **Cheyenne Roundup** (1943, Universal). (Courtesy of Jerry Ohlinger's Movie Material Store.)

Riley Hill	.Ned Turner
Kenneth MacDonald	.John Corbett
Lynton Brent	.Hall
John Ince	Bailey
John Bridges	Dr. Brown
Eddie Parker	.Bill
Frank McCarroll	Joe
Dick Dickinson	.Ed
Milburn Morante	.Zeke
Frank LaRue	.Jones
Steve Clark	.Mason
George Morrell	
Carl Mathews	
Victor Cox	
Cal Shrum and his Rhythm Rangers	

112. FRONTIER FEUD

Copyrighted	October 25, 1945
Distributor	Monogram
Length	.54 Minutes

Director	.Lambert Hillyer
Producer	.Charles J. Bigelow
Screenplay	.Jess Bowers (Adele Buffington)
Based upon a Story	.Charles N. Heckelmann
Photography	.Harry Neumann
Film Editor	.Dan Milner

Cast

Johnny Mack Brown	.Nevada Jack MacKenzie
Raymond Hatton	.Sandy Hopkins
Dennis Moore	Joe
Christine McIntyre	.Blanche
Jack Ingram	.Don Graham
Edwin Parker	.Murphy
Frank Larue	Chalmers
Steve Clark	.Bill Corey
Jack Rockwell	.Sheriff Clancy
Mary MacLaren	Sarah Moran
Edmund Cobb	Moran
Lloyd Ingraham	.Si Peters
Charles King	

Tex Ritter has a serious talk with Jennifer Holt as Johnny Mack looks on in this scene from **Cheyenne Roundup** (1943, Universal). (Courtesy of Jerry Ohlinger's Movie Material Store.)

Stanley Price

113. BORDER BANDITS

Copyrighted . . . . .December 5, 1945
Distributor . . . . Monogram
Length . . . . .58 Minutes
Director . . . . .Lambert Hillyer
Producer . . . . Scott R. Dunlap
Screenplay . . . . .Frank H. Young
Photography . . . . William A. Sickner
Film Editor . . . . Carrol Lewis
Cast
Johnny Mack Brown . . Nevada Jack MacKenzie
Raymond Hatton . . . . .Sandy Hopkins
Riley Hill . . . . .Steve Holliday
Rosa Del Rosario . . . . Celia
John Merton . . . . Spike
Tom Quinn . . . . .Papper
Frank Larue . . . . .John Holliday
Steve Clark . . . . Doc Bowles

Charles Stevens . . . . .Jose
Lucio Villegas . . . . Nogales
Bud Osborne . . . . .Dutch
Pat R. McGee . . . . Cupid

114. DRIFTING ALONG

Copyrighted . . . . .January 26, 1946
Distributor . . . . Monogram
Length . . . . .60 Minutes
Director . . . . Derwin M. Abrahams
Producer . . . . Scott R. Dunlap
Screenplay and Story . . . . .Adele Buffington
Photography . . . . .Harry Neumann
Film Editor . . . . Carrol Lewis
Music Director . . . . Edward Kay
Songs: "Dusty Trails," "You Can Bet Your Boots and Saddles"
Cast
Johnny Mack Brown . . . . .Steve
Lynne Carver . . . . .Pat McBride

Johnny Mack looks tough at villain Harry Woods as Robert Barron looks on in **Cheyenne Roundup** (1943, Universal). (Courtesy of Jerry Ohlinger's Movie Material Store.)

Raymond Hatton . . . . .Pawnee
Douglas Fowley . . . . Jack Dailey
Smith Ballew . . . . Himself
Milburn Morante .Zeke
Thornton Edwards . . . . .Pedro
Steve Clark . . . . .Lou Woods
Marshall Reed . . . . .Slade
Jack Rockwell . . . . .Sheriff Devers
Lynton Brent . . . . .Joe
Terry Frost . . . . .Gus
Leonard St. Leo . . . . .Red
Ted Mapes . . . . Ed
Curt Barrett and the Trailsmen

115. THE HAUNTED MINE

Copyrighted . . . . .February 23, 1946
Distributor . . . . Monogram
Length . . . . .51 Minutes
Director . . . . Derwin M. Abrahams
Producer . . . . .Charles J. Bigelow

Screenplay . . . . .Frank H. Young
Based on a Story . . . . Elizabeth Burbridge
Photography . . . . .Harry Neumann
Film Editor . . . . Fred Maguire
Assistant Director . . . . .Theodore Joos
Cast
Johnny Mack Brown . . Nevada Jack MacKenzie
Raymond Hatton . . . . .Sandy Hopkins
Linda Johnson . . . . .Jenny Durant
Raphael Bennett . . . . .Old Hermit
Riley Hill . . . . Dan McLeod
Claire Whitney . . . . Mrs. Durant
John Merton . . . . Steve Twining
Marshall Reed . . . . Blackie
Terry Frost .Bill Mead
Bob Butt . . . . Kirk Tracy
Lynton Brent . . . . Skyball
Leonard St. Leo .Stirrup
Frank Larue .Matterson
Ray Jones

Johnny Mack is about to slug villain Harry Woods as henchman Roy Barcroft watches in **Cheyenne Roundup** (1943, Universal). (Courtesy of Jerry Ohlinger's Movie Material Store.)

116. UNDER ARIZONA SKIES

Copyrighted	April 2, 1946
Distributor	Monogram
Length	59 Minutes
Director	Lambert Hillyer
Producer	Scott R. Dunlap
Screenplay	J. Benton Cheney
Based upon a Story	John McCarthy
Photography	Harry Neumann
Film Editor	Fred Maguire
Music Director	Edward Kay
Production Manager	Charles J. Bigelow
Assistant Director	Eddie Davis
Recording Engineer	Frank McWhorter
Settings	Vin Taylor

Cast

Johnny Mack Brown	"Dusty" Smith
Raymond Hatton	Santa Fe Jones
Reno Blair (Brown)	Cindy
Riley Hill	Bill Simpson
Tristram Coffin	Blackie Evans
Reed Howes	Duke
Ted Adams	Carter
Raphael Bennett	Tom Sloan
Frank Larue	Jim Simpson
Steve Clark	Sam Stewart
Jack Rockwell	Sheriff Rigby
Bud Geary	Chuck
Ted Mapes	Red Connors
Kermit Maynard	Joe Forbes
Ray Jones	
Smith Ballew and Sons of the Sage	
Reno (the horse)	

117. THE GENTLEMAN FROM TEXAS

Copyrighted	June 5, 1946
Distributor	Monogram
Length	55 Minutes
Director	Lambert Hillyer
Producer	Scott R. Dunlap

Bad guy Johnny Mack looks tough at Fuzzy Knight as Budd Buster and villains, Roy Barcroft, Robert Barron and Harry Woods watch in **Cheyenne Roundup** (1943, Universal). (Courtesy of Jerry Ohlinger's Movie Material Store.)

Screenplay/ Original Story . . .J. Benton Cheney	
Photography . . . . .Harry Neumann	
Film Editor . . . . Fred Maguire	
Music Director . . . . Edward Kay	
Production Manager . . . . Charles J. Bigelow	
Assistant Director . . . . .Eddie Davis	
Sound Recorder . . . . .Frank McWhorter	
Settings . . . . Vin Taylor	

Cast

Johnny Mack Brown . . . . Johnny Macklin
Raymond Hatton . . . . .Jim Foster
Claudia Drake . . . . .Kitty Malone
Reno Blair (Brown) . . . . .Diane Foster
Christine McIntyre . . . . Flo Vickers
Tristram Coffin . . . . .Steve Corbin
Marshall Reed . . . . Duke Sprague
Terry Frost . . . . Ace Jenkins
Jack Rockwell . . . . .Pete
Steve Clark . . . . Jim Jamison
Ted Adams . . . . .Williams
Lynton Brent . . . . Slats Harper

Frank LaRue . . . . .Trevor
Tom Carter . . . . .Burke
Pierce Lyden
Wally West
Artie Ortego
Bill Wolfe
Curt Barrett and his Trailsmen

118. SHADOWS ON THE RANGE

Copyrighted . . . . .July 25, 1946	
Distributor . . . . Monogram	
Length . . . . .57 Minutes	
Director .Lambert Hillyer	
Producer . . . . Scott R. Dunlap	
Screenplay . . . . .Jess Bowers (Adele Buffington)	
Photography . . . . .James S. Brown	
Film Editor . . . . Fred Maguire	
Music Director . . . . Edward Kay	
Supervisor . . . . .Charles J. Bigelow	
Assistant Director . . . . .Eddie Davis	

Johnny Mack gives it to a villainous player in this scene from **Cheyenne Roundup** (1943, Universal). (Courtesy of Jerry Ohlinger's Movie Material Store.)

Sound Recorder . . . . L. John Myers
Settings . . . . Vin Taylor

Cast

Johnny Mack Brown . . . . .Steve Mason
Raymond Hatton . . . . Dusty
Jan Bryant .Ruth Denny
Marshall Reed . . . . .Butch
John Merton . . . . Paul Emery
Jack Perrin . . . . Ted Miller
Steve Clark . . . . .Sheriff Skinner
Terry Frost . . . . .Bill Cole
Cactus Mack . . . . Lefty
Pierce Lyden .Ed
Ted Adams . . . . Bart Brennan
Lane Bradford . . . . .Gus

119. TRIGGER FINGERS

Copyrighted . . . . .August 27, 1946
Distributor . . . . Monogram
Length .56 Minutes

Director . . . . .Lambert Hillyer
Producer . . . . .Charles J. Bigelow
Original Screenplay . . . . .Frank H. Young
Photography . . . . .Harry Neumann
Film Editor . . . . Fred Maguire
Music Director . . . . Edward Kay
Assistant Director . . . . .Eddie Davis
Sound Recorder . . . . .Franklin Hansen
Settings . . . . Vin Taylor

Cast

Johnny Mack Brown . . . . Sam Benton
Raymond Hatton . . . . .Pinto Peters
Jennifer Holt . . . . Jane Caldwell
Riley Hill . . . . Jimmy Peters
Steve Clark . . . ."Sloppy" Langford
Eddie Parker . . . ."Smoke" Turner
Pierce Lyden . . . . .Red
Ted Adams .Stub Allen
Cactus Mack . . . . Knuckles
Edward Cassidy . . . . .Sheriff Caldwell
Ray Jones

Johnny Mack faces down villain Harry Woods as co-villains Roy Barcroft and Robert Barron stand-by in **Cheyenne Roundup** (1943, Universal). (Courtesy of Jerry Ohlinger's Movie Material Store.)

George Morrell
Frank McCarroll

120. SILVER RANGE

Copyrighted . . . . October 14, 1946
Distributor . . . . Monogram
Length . . . . .53 Minutes
Director .Lambert Hillyer
Producer . . . . .Charles J. Bigelow
Original Screenplay . . . . .J. Benton Cheney
Photography . . . . .Harry Neumann
Film Editor . . . . Fred Maguire
Music Director . . . . Edward Kay
Assistant Director . . . . .Eddie Davis
Recording Engineer . . . . .Tom Lambert
Settings . . . . Vin Taylor
Cast
Johnny Mack Brown . . . . Johnny Bronton
Raymond Hatton . . . . Tucson Smith
Jan Bryant . . . . .Jeanne Willoughby

I. Stanford Jolley . . . . Sheriff Armstrong
Terry Frost . . . . .Red
Eddie Parker . . . . .Bart Nelson
Ted Adams . . . . .Jason Turner
Frank LaRue . . . . Steve Ferguson
Cactus Mack . . . . .Dave
Lane Bradford . . . . Browning
Dee Cooper . . . . Faro
Billy Dix . . . . Chuck
Bill Willmering . . . . Willoughby
George Morrell

121. RAIDERS OF THE SOUTH

Copyrighted . . . . .January 18, 1947
Distributor . . . . Monogram
Length . . . . .55 Minutes
Director .Lambert Hillyer
Producer . . . . Scott R. Dunlap
Screenplay and Story . . . . . . .J. Benton Cheney
Photography . . . . .Harry Neumann

Bad guy Johnny Mack has a talk with villain Harry Woods in the Universal feature, **Cheyenne Roundup** (1943). (Courtesy of Jerry Ohlinger's Movie Material Store.)

Film Editor . . . . Fred Magurie
Production Manager . . . . . . .Charles J. Bigelow
Assistant Director . . . . .Eddie Davis
Sound Technician . . . . Earl Sitar
Sound Recording . . . . .Paul Schmutz, Sr.
Set Dresser . . . . Vin Taylor

Cast

Johnny Mack Brown . . . . . . .Captain Brownell
Evelyn Brent . . . . .Belle Chambers
Raymond Hatton . . . . Shorty Kendall
Reno Blair (Brown) . . . . Lynne Chambers
Marshall Reed . . . . Larry Mason
John Hamilton . . . . General Lawson
John Merton . . . . .Preston Durant
Eddie Parker . . . . Jeb Warren
Pierce Lyden .Farley
Cactus Mack . . . . .Pete
Billy Dix . . . . .Preston
Dee Cooper . . . . .Wagon Boss
Frank LaRue
Ted Adams

George Morrell
Ray Jones
Artie Ortego
Curt Barrett and the Trailsmen

122. VALLEY OF FEAR

Copyrighted . . . . .February 15, 1947
Distributor . . . . Monogram
Length . . . . .54 Minutes
Director . . . . .Lambert Hillyer
Producer . . . . .Charles J. Bigelow
Original Screenplay . . . . .J. Benton Cheney
Photography . . . . .Harry Neumann
Film Editor . . . . Roy Livingston
Music Director . . . . Edward Kay
Assistant Director . . . . .Eddie Davis
Recording Engineer . . . . .Tom Lambert
Settings . . . . Vin Taylor

Cast

Johnny Mack Brown . . . . Johnny Williams

A mean looking Johnny Mack is telling a featured player what's what as Fuzzy Knight, Tex Ritter and Jennifer Holt look on in **Cheyenne Roundup** (1943, Universal). (Courtesy of Jerry Ohlinger's Movie Material Store.)

Raymond Hatton . . . . Rusty Peters
Christine McIntyre . . . . Joan Travers
Tristram Coffin . . . . .Henry Stevens
Edward Cassidy . . . . Les Travers
Eddie Parker . . . . Duke
Ted Adams . . . . .Frank Wilkins
Pierce Lyden . . . . .Sheriff Wheeler
Steve Darrell . . . . Tom Lansing
Cactus Mack . . . . Spence Mallory
Garry Garrett . . . . .Deputy
Robert O'Byrne . . . . Townsman
Dee Cooper
Jack Hendricks
Artie Ortego
Edward Piel, Sr.
Budd Buster

123. LAND OF THE LAWLESS

Copyrighted . . . . .March 27, 1947
Distributor . . . . Monogram

Length . . . . .59 Minutes
Director .Lambert Hillyer
Producer . . . . .Barney A. Sarecky
Original Screenplay . . . . .J. Benton Cheney
Photography . . . . William A. Sickner
Film Editor . . . . Robert Crandall
Music Director . . . . Edward Kay
Production Manager . . . . . . Charles A. Bigelow
Assistant Director . . . . .Eddie Davis
Sound Technician . . . . Frank McWhorter
Settings . . . . Vin Taylor
Song: "A Gal a Man Loves to Kiss" by Louis Herscher

Cast

Johnny Mack Brown . . . . Johnny
Raymond Hatton . . . . Bodie
Christine McIntyre . . . . Kansas City Kate
Tristram Coffin . . . . .Cameo
June Harrison . . . . Donna Webster
Marshall Reed .Yuma
I. Stanford Jolley . . . . .Cherokee

A Lobby Card showing Tex Ritter whipping a cowed Ed Cobb as Johnny Mack and Jennifer Holt look in in **The Old Chisholm Trail** (1943, Universal). (WOY Collection.)

Steve Clark . . . . .Jason
Edmund Cobb . . . . Hank
Roy Butler . . . . Doctor
Cactus Mack . . . . .Dave
Gary Garrett . . . . Clem
Carl Sepulveda
Victor Cox

124. TRAILING DANGER

Copyrighted . . . . .March 29, 1947
Distributor . . . . Monogram
Length . . . . .58 Minutes
Director .Lambert Hillyer
Producer . . . . .Barney A. Sarecky
Original Screenplay . . . . .J. Benton Cheney
Photography . . . . .Harry Neumann
Production Supervisor . . . . . Charles J. Bigelow
Assistant Director . . . . .Eddie Davis
Sound Technician . . . . .Tom Lambert
Set Dresser . . . . Vin Taylor

Cast

Johnny Mack Brown . . . . Johnny
Raymond Hatton .Waco
Peggy Wynne . . . . .Kay
Marshall Reed . . . . Jim Holden
Patrick Desmond . . . . Hal
Steve Darrell . . . . .George Bannister
Eddie Parker . . . . Riley
Bonnie Jean Hartley . . . . .Paradise Flo
Ernie Adams . . . . Pennypacker
Bud Osborne . . . . Mason
Cactus Mack . . . . Stage Driver
Kansas Moehring . . . . Sheriff
Gary Garrett . . . . .Bruce
Jack Hendricks . . . . Buck
Artie Ortego
Dee Cooper

125. THE LAW COMES TO GUNSIGHT

Copyrighted . . . . May 22, 1947

Jennifer Holt intercedes as Jack Ingram tries to get a cowed Johnny Mack to fight. Tex Ritter looks on in **The Lone Star Trail** (1943, Universal). (Courtesy of Merrill McCord.)

Distributor . . . . Monogram
Length . . . . 56-58 Minutes
Director . . . . .Lambert Hillyer
Producer . . . . .Barney A. Sarecky
Original Screenplay . . . . .J. Benton Cheney
Photography . . . . .Harry Neumann
Film Editor . . . . Fred Maguire
Music Director . . . . Edward Kay
Production Manager . . . . Charles J. Bigelow
Assistant Director . . . . .Eddie Davis
Sound Technician . . . . Frank McWhorter
Settings . . . . Vin Taylor

Cast

Johnny Mack Brown . . . . .Johnny McKay
Raymond Hatton . . . . .Reno
Reno Blair (Brown) . . . . .Judy Hartley
Lanny Rees . . . . Bud Hartley
Zon Murray . . . . .Drago
William H. Ruhl . . . . Brad Foster
Kermit Maynard . . . . Blacksmith
Ted Adams . . . . .Prescott

Gary Garrett . . . . Blackie
Lee Roberts . . . . .Pecos
Frank LaRue . . . . .Mayor Jim Blane
Ernie Adams . . . . .Simpson
Willard Willingham
Artie Ortego

126. CODE OF THE SADDLE

Copyrighted .July 5, 1947
Distributor . . . . Monogram
Length . . . . .53 Minutes
Director . . . . Thomas Carr
Producer . . . . .Barney A. Sarecky
Original Screenplay . . . . .Eliot Gibbons
Photography . . . . .Harry Neumann
Film Editor . . . . Fred Maguire
Production Manager . . . . Charles J. Bigelow
Assistant Director . . . . .Eddie Davis
Sound Technician . . . . Franklin Hanson
Sound Recorder . . . . .John Kean

Johnny Mack introduces himself to Christine McIntyre and Dennis Moore. Raymond Hatton looks on in **Frontier Feud** (1945, Monogram). (Courtesy of Jerry Ohlinger's Movie Material Store.)

Set Dresser . . . . Vin Taylor

Cast

Johnny Mack Brown . . . . Johnny Macklin
Raymond Hatton . . . . .Winks
Riley Hill . . . . Bill Stace
Kay Morley . . . . .Bess Benthan
William Norton Bailey . . . . Sheriff Wallace
Zon Murray . . . . Rubio
Ted Adams . . . . Buck Stace
Bud Osborne . . . . Bell
Kenne Duncan, Jr. . . . . Camus
Gary Garrett . . . . Randall
Curley Gibson . . . . Bart
Jack Hendricks . . . . Mike
Boyd Stockman . . . . Blackie
Bob McElroy . . . . Dade
Ray Jones . . . . .Jack
Chick Hannon . . . . Bud

127. FLASHING GUNS

Copyrighted . . . . .August 23, 1947

Distributor . . . . Monogram
Length . . . . .59 Minutes
Director .Lambert Hillyer
Producer . . . . .Barney A. Sarecky
Original Screenplay . . . . .Frank H. Young
Film Editor . . . . Fred Maguire
Music Director . . . . Edward J. Kay

Cast

Johnny Mack Brown . . . . .Johnny
Raymond Hatton . . . . .Shelby
Jan Bryant . . . . .Ann
Douglas Evans . . . . Longden
James E. Logan . . . . Ainsworth
Ted Adams . . . . .Ripley
Edmund Cobb . . . . .Sheriff
Norman Jolley . . . . .Foley
Ken Adams . . . . Dishpan
Gary Garrett . . . . Duke
Ray Jones . . . . .Stirrup
Jack O'Shea . . . . .Sagebrush
Steve Clark . . . . .Cannon
Frank LaRue . . . . .Judge

Johnny Mack has the drop on everyone in this saloon scene. Dennis Moore and Christine McIntyre are among the featured players in **Frontier Feud** (1945, Monogram). Courtesy of Jerry Ohlinger's Movie Material Store.)

Jack Rockwell . . . . Cassidy

128. PRAIRIE EXPRESS

Copyrighted . . . . October 25, 1947
Distributor . . . . Monogram
Length . . . . .55 Minutes
Director . . . . .Lambert Hillyer
Producer . . . . .Barney A. Sarecky
Original Screenplay . . . . .J. Benton Cheney,
Anthony Coldeway
Photography . . . . William A. Sickner
Film Editor . . . . Fred Maguire
Cast
Johnny Mack Brown . . . . .Johnny Hudson
Raymond Hatton . . . . Faro Jenkins
Robert Winkler . . . . .Dave Porter
Virginia Belmont . . . . .Peggy Porter
William H. Ruhl . . . . Gordon Gregg
Marshall Reed . . . . .Burke
Gary Garrett . . . . .Kent
Curley Gibson . . . . Langford

Ken Adams . . . . .Pete
I. Stanford Jolley . . . . .Sheriff
Hank Worden .Deputy
Carl Mathews . . . . Collins
Boyd Stockman . . . . Perry
Bob McElroy . . . . .Joe
Jack Hendricks . . . . Blaine
Artie Ortego . . . . Torgo
Ted Adams . . . . .Lem
Steve Clark . . . . .Jarrett
Frank LaRue
Steve Darrell
Jack Gibson

129. GUN TALK

Copyrighted . . . . .December 6, 1947
Distributor . . . . Monogram
Length . . . . .58 Minutes
Director . . . . .Lambert Hillyer
Producer . . . . .Barney A. Sarecky
Original Screenplay . . . . .J. Benton Cheney

Johnny Mack disarms Ed Cobb in **Frontier Feud** (1945, Monogram). (Courtesy of Jerry Ohlinger's Movie Material Store.)

Photography . . . . Harry Neumann
Film Editor . . . . Fred Maguire
Musical Director . . . . Edward Kay
Cast
Johnny Mack Brown . . . . Johnny McVey
Raymond Hatton . . . . Lucky Danvers
Christine McIntyre . . . . Daisy
Douglas Evans . . . . Rod Jackson
Geneva Gray . . . . June
Wheaton Chambers . . . . Herkimer Stone
Frank LaRue . . . . Simpson
Ted Adams . . . . Tim
Carl Mathews . . . . Pepper
Zon Murray . . . . Nolan
Cactus Mack . . . . Marshal Wetherby
Carol Henry . . . . Burke
Bill Hale . . . . Joe
Boyd Stockman . . . . Diggs
Ray Butler . . . . Bartender
Bob McElroy . . . . Pete

130. OVERLAND TRAILS

Copyrighted . . . . February 7, 1948
Distributor . . . . Monogram
Length . . . . .58 Minutes
Director . . . . Lambert Hillyer
Producer . . . . Barney A. Sarecky
Screenplay . . . . Jess Bowers (Adele Buffington)
Photography . . . . .Harry Neumann
Film Editor . . . . Johnny Fuller
Music Director . . . . Edward Kay
Production Manager . . . . Charles J. Bigelow
Assistant Director . . . . .Eddie Davis
Sound Technician . . . . Earl Sitar
Set Dresser . . . . Vin Taylor
Cast
Johnny Mack Brown . . . . Johnny Murdock
Raymond Hatton . . . . Dusty Hanover
Virginia Belmont . . . . Marcia Brandon
Bill Kennedy . . . . Carter Morgan
Virginia Carroll . . . . Mary Cramer
Holly Bane . . . . Rex Hillman

Jack Rockwell places a star on Johnny Mack as Dennis Moore, Raymond Hatton and assorted players watch in **Frontier Feud** (1945, Monogram). (Courtesy of Jerry Ohlinger's Movie Material Store.)

Ted Adams . . . . Cramer
Steve Darrell . . . . Marc Brandon
Sonny Rees . . . . .Bud
Carl Mathews . . . . .Tully
Milburn Morante . . . . Brooks
Bob Woodward . . . . Ed
Boyd Stockman . . . . .Joe
George Peters . . . . Paul
Pierce Lyden . . . . Martin
Roy Butler . . . . .Tobin
Post Park . . . . Old Miner
Marshall Reed
Artie Ortego
Tom London

131. CROSSED TRAILS

Copyrighted . . . . .April 11, 1948
Distributor . . . . Monogram
Length . . . . .57 Minutes
Director . . . . .Lambert Hillyer
Producer . . . . .Louis Gray

Screenplay . . . . Colt Remington (probably Adele
Buffington)
Photography . . . . .Harry Neumann
Film Editor . . . . Fred Maguire
Music Director . . . . Edward Kay

Cast

Johnny Mack Brown . . . . Johnny
Raymond Hatton . . . . Bodie
Lynne Carver . . . . .Maggie
Douglas Evans . . . . Hudson
Kathy Frye . . . . .Melissa
Zon Murray . . . . Curtin
Mary MacLaren . . . . Mrs. Laswell
Ted Adams . . . . .Laswell
Steve Clark . . . . Blake
Frank LaRue . . . . .Judge
Milburn Morante . . . . Anderson
Robert D. Woodward . . . . .Wright
Pierce Lyden . . . . Whitfield
Harry Hall . . . . Stoddard
Hugh Murray . . . . .Jury Foreman
Bud Osborne . . . . .Sheriff Cook

Raymond Hatton points a dagger at Dennis Moore as Johnny Mack and assorted players watch in this scene from **Frontier Feud** (1945, Monogram). (Courtesy of Jerry Ohlinger's Movie Material Store.)

Artie Ortego
Boyd Stockman

132. FRONTIER AGENT

Copyrighted	May 16, 1948
Distributor	Monogram
Length	57 Minutes
Director	Lambert Hillyer
Producer	Barney A. Sarecky
Original Screenplay	J. Benton Cheney
Photography	Harry Neumann
Film Editor	Fred Maguire
Music Director	Edward J. Kay
Production Manager	Charles J. Bigelow
Assistant Director	Eddie Davis
Sound Technician	Earl Sitar
Set Dresser	Vin Taylor

Cast

Johnny Mack Brown	Johnny McBrown
Raymond Hatton	Cappy
Reno Blair (Brown)	Sandra Kerrigan

Kenneth MacDonald	Wheelock
Dennis Moore	Larry
Riley Hill	Joe
Frank LaRue	Marshall
Ted Adams	Kerrigan
Virginia Carroll	Paula
William H. Ruhl	Carson
Kansas Moehring	Nevada
Bill Hale	Eddie
Lane Bradford	Slim
Bob Woodward	Straker
Boyd Stockman	Mugsy

133. TRIGGERMAN

Copyrighted	June 20, 1948
Distributor	Monogram
Length	61 Minutes
Director	Howard Bretherton
Producer	Barney A. Sarecky
Original Screenplay	Ronald Davidson
Photography	Harry Neumann

Jack Ingram has the drop on Johnny Mack as Ed LeSaint and assorted players get ready for action in this scene from **Frontier Feud** (1945, Monogram). (Courtesy of Jerry Ohlinger's Movie Material Store.)

Film Editor . . . . Johnny Fuller	**Producer** . . . . .Barney A. Sarecky
Music Director . . . . .Edward Kay	**Original Screenplay** . . . . .J. Benton Cheney
Assistant Director . . . . .Eddie Davis	**Photography** . . . . .Harry Neumann
Sound Technician . . . . .Buddy Meyers	**Film Editor** . . . . .Johnny Fuller
Sound Recorder . . . . .Fred Stahl	**Music Director** . . . . Edward Kay
Set Dresser . . . . Vin Taylor	

Cast

Johnny Mack Brown . . . . Johnny	**Johnny Mack Brown** . . . . .Johnny
Raymond Hatton . . . . .Rusty	**Raymond Hatton** . . . . Caboose
Virginia Carroll . . . . .Lois	**Mildred Coles** . . . . Helen
Bill Kennedy . . . . Kirby	**Marshall Reed** . . . . Lacy
Marshall Reed . . . . Moran	**James Horne** . . . . Terry
Forrest Matthews . . . . .Harris	**Snub Pollard** . . . . .Goofy
Bob Woodward . . . . .Davis	**Ted Adams** . . . . Frazer
Dee Cooper . . . . Joe	**Pierce Lyden** . . . . Gilmore

134. BACK TRAIL

Copyrighted . . . . July 18, 1948
Distributor . . . . Monogram
Length . . . . .54 Minutes
Director . . . . Christy Cabanne

135. THE FIGHTING RANGER

Copyrighted . . . . .August 15, 1948
Distributor . . . . Monogram
Length . . . . .57 Minutes
Director . . . . .Lambert Hillyer
Producer . . . . .Barney A. Sarecky

Johnny Mack shows his star to Sheriff Jack Rockwell in **Frontier Feud** (1945, Monogram). (Courtesy of Jerry Ohlinger's Movie Material Store.)

Original Screenplay . . . . .Ronald Davidson
Photography . . . . .Harry Neumann
Film Editor . . . . Carl Pierson
Music Director . . . . Edward Kay
Assistant Director . . . . .Eddie Davis
Sound Technician . . . . Louis Myers
Sound Recorder . . . . Harold McNiff
Set Dresser . . . . Vin Taylor

Cast

Johnny Mack Brown . . . . Johnny Brown
Raymond Hatton . . . . Banty
Christine Larson . . . . .Julia
Marshall Reed . . . . Hack
Eddie Parker . . . . Gill
Charles Hughes . . . . Dave
I. Stanford Jolley . . . . .Sinclair
Milburn Morante . . . . .Gus
Steve Clark . . . . Henderson
Bob Woodward . . . . .Bender
Peter Perkins . . . . .Adams

136. THE SHERIFF OF MEDICINE BOW

Copyrighted . . . . September 19, 1948
Distributor . . . . Monogram
Length . . . . .55 Minutes
Director . . . . .Lambert Hillyer
Producer . . . . .Barney A. Sarecky
Original Screenplay . . . . .J. Benton Cheney
Photography . . . . .Harry Neumann
Film Editor . . . . .Johnny Fuller
Music Director . . . . Edward Kay
Assistant Directors . .Eddie Davis & Harry Jones
Sound Technician . . . . .Tom Lambert
Set Dresser . . . . Vin Taylor

Cast

Johnny Mack Brown . . . . . Sheriff Johnny Mack
Raymond Hatton . . . . Banty
Max Terhune . . . . Alibi
Evelyn Finley .Nan
Bill Kennedy . . . . Stuart
George J. Lewis . . . . Buckeye
Frank LaRue .Carson

Johnny Mack brings villain Ed LeSaint to jail as Jack Rockwell, Dennis Moore and sidekick Raymond Hatton look on in **Frontier Feud** (1945, Monogram). (Courtesy of Jerry Ohlinger's Movie Material Store.)

Peter Perkins . . . . .Pardo
Carol Henry . . . . .Grogan
Bob Woodward . . . . Duke
Ted Adams

137. GUNNING FOR JUSTICE

Copyrighted . . . . November 7, 1948
Distributor . . . . Monogram
Length . . . . .55 Minutes
Director . . . . .Ray Taylor
Producer . . . . .Barney A. Sarecky
Screenplay . . . . J. Benton Cheney
Photography . . . . .Harry Neumann
Film Editor .John Fuller
Music Director . . . . Edward Kay
Assistant Directors . .Eddie Davis & Harry Jones
Sound Technician . . . . Earl Sitar
Set Dresser . . . . Vin Taylor
Cast

Johnny Mack Brown . . . . Johnny Mack
Raymond Hatton . . . . Banty

Max Terhune . . . . Alibi
Evelyn Finley . . . . .Winny
I. Stanford Jolley . . . . .Blake
House Peters, Jr. . . . . .Wheeler
Bill Potter . . . . Potter
Ted Adams . . . . .Tolliver
Bud Osborne . . . . Cook
Dan White . . . . Sheriff
Bob Woodward .Jarvis
Carol Henry . . . . .Petrie
Boyd Stockman . . . . Smokie
Dee Cooper . . . . .Luke
Artie Ortego

138. HIDDEN DANGER

Copyrighted . . . . .December 5, 1948
Distributor . . . . Monogram
Length . . . . .54 Minutes
Director . . . . .Ray Taylor
Producer . . . . .Barney A. Sarecky

Sidekick Raymond Hatton gets the drop on Jack Ingram as he holds Johnny Mack prisoner in **Frontier Feud** (1945, Monogram). (Courtesy of Jerry Ohlinger's Movie Material Store.)

Original Screenplay . . . .J. Benton Cheney, Eliot Gibbons
Photography . . . . .Harry Neumann
Film Editor . . . . .John C. Fuller
Music Director . . . . Edward Kay

Cast

Johnny Mack Brown	Johnny
Raymond Hatton	Banty
Max Terhune	Alibi
Christine Larson	Valerie
Myron Healey	Carson
Marshall Reed	Mason
Kenne Duncan	Benda
Edmund Cobb	Sheriff
Steve Clark	Russell
Milburn Morante	Clark
Carol Henry	Trigger
Bill Hale	Sanderson
Bob Woodward	Joe
Boyd Stockman	Loop
Bill Potter	Perry

139. LAW OF THE WEST

Copyrighted . . . . .February 20, 1949
Distributor . . . . Monogram
Length . . . . .54 Minutes
Director . . . . .Ray Taylor
Producer . . . . .Barney A. Sarecky
Original Screenplay . . . . .J. Benton Cheney
Photography . . . . .Harry Neumann
Film Editor . . . . .John C. Fuller
Music Director . . . . Edward Kay

Cast

Johnny Mack Brown	Johnny Mack
Max Terhune	Alibi
Bill Kennedy	Nixon
Gerry Pattison	Tennessee
Jack Ingram	Burke
Eddie Parker	Mike
Riley Hill	Charlie
Steve Clark	Lane
James Harrison	Sheriff
Bob Woodward	Spence

Johnny Mack has a discussion with Jack Ingram as heroine Christine McIntyre looks concerned in this scene from **Frontier Feud** (1945, Monogram). (Courtesy of Jerry Ohlinger's Movie Material Store.)

Marshall Reed . . . . Drago
Kenne Duncan . . . . Stevens
Bud Osborne . . . . .Brook
Frank Ellis

140. TRAIL'S END

Copyrighted . . . . .April 3, 1949
Distributor . . . . Monogram
Length . . . . .55 Minutes
Director .Lambert Hillyer
Producer . . . . .Barney A. Sarecky
Original Screenplay . . . . .J. Benton Cheney
Photography . . . . .Harry Neumann
Film Editor . . . . .John C. Fuller
Music Director . . . . Edward Kay
Cast
Johnny Mack Brown . . . . Johnny
Max Terhune . . . . Alibi
Kay Morley . . . . .Laurie
Douglas Evans . . . . .Porter
Zon Murray .Kettering

Myron Healey . . . . .Drake
Keith Richards . . . . .Bill
George Cheesebro . . . . .Stuart
William Norton Bailey . . . . Sheriff
Carol Henry . . . . .Rocky
Boyd Stockman .Idaho
Eddie Majors . . . . Luke

141. STAMPEDE

Released . . . . May 1, 1949
Distributor . . . . .Allied Artists
Length . . . . .78 Minutes
Director . . . . .Lesley Selander
Producers . .Scott R. Dunlap, John C. Champion, Blake Edwards
Screenplay . . John C. Champion, Blake Edwards
Based upon a Novel . . . . .E. B. Mann
Photography . . . . .Harry Neumann
Film Editor . . . . Richard Heermance
Songs: Edward Kay

Johnny Mack, Dennis Moore and Raymond Hatton take on Jack Ingram and his men in **Frontier Feud** (1945, Monogram). (Courtesy of Jerry Ohlinger's Movie Material Store.)

Cast

Rod Cameron . . . . .Mike
Gale Storm . . . . Connie
Don Castle . . . . Tim
Johnny Mack Brown . . . . .Sheriff Ball
Donald Curtis . . . . .Stanton
John Eldredge . . . . Cox
John Miljan . . . . Furman
Jonathan Hale . . . . Varick
James Harrison . . . . .Roper
Wes C. Christensen . . . . Slim
Duke York . . . . Maxie
Bob Woodward . . . . Whiskey
Steve Clark . . . . Dawson
Boyd Stockman . . . . .Fred
Ted Elliott . . . . Pete
Jack Parker . . . . .Jake
Chuck Roberson . . . . .Sandy
Tim Ryan . . . . Drunk
Kenne Duncan .Steve
Carol Henry . . . . .Ben
Artie Ortego . . . . Neal Hart

I. Stanford Jolley . . . . Link Spain
Marshall Reed . . . . Shires
Philo McCollough . . . . .Charlie
Adrian Wood . . . . .Sanderson

142. WEST OF ELDORADO

Copyrighted . . . . June 5, 1949
Distributor . . . . Monogram
Length . . . . .58 Minutes
Director . . . . .Ray Taylor
Producer . . . . .Barney A. Sarecky
Screenplay . . . . .Adele Buffington
Photography . . . . .Harry Neumann
Film Editor . . . . .John C. Fuller
Music Director . . . . Edward Kay

Cast

Johnny Mack Brown . . . . .Johnny
Max Terhune . . . . Alibi
Reno Browne . . . . Mary
Teddy Infuhr . . . . .Larry
Milburn Morante . . . . .Brimstone

Johnny Mack catches up with villain Ed LeSaint in **Frontier Feud** (1945, Monogram). (Courtesy of Jerry Ohlinger's Movie Material Store.)

Terry Frost . . . . Stone
Marshall Reed .Barstow
Boyd Stockman . . . . .Joe
Kenne Duncan .Steve
Bud Osborne . . . . .Jerry
William Norton Bailey . . . . Sheriff
Artie Ortego . . . . .Indian
Bill Porter . . . . .Bill
Bob Woodward

143. RANGE JUSTICE

Copyrighted . . . . .August 7, 1949
Distributor . . . . Monogram
Length . . . . .57 Minutes
Director . . . . .Ray Taylor
Producer . . . . Barney Sarecky
Original Screenplay . . . . .Ronald Davidson
Photography . . . . .Harry Neumann
Film Editor . . . . .John C. Fuller
Music Director . . . . Edward Kay

Cast

Johnny Mack Brown . . . . .Johnny
Max Terhune . . . . Alibi
Felice Ingersoll . . . . .Beth Hadley
Sarah Padden .Ma Curtis
Riley Hill . . . . .Glenn Hadley
Tristram Coffin .Dutton
Fred Kohler, Jr. .Stoner
Eddie Parker . . . . .Lacy
Kenne Duncan . . . . .Kirk
Bill Hale . . . . Bud
Myron Healey . . . . .Dade
Bill Potter . . . . Bill
Bob Woodward . . . . Bob
Bill Williams . . . . .Chuck

144. WESTERN RENEGADES

Copyrighted . . . . October 2, 1949
Distributor . . . . Monogram
Length . . . . .56 Minutes

Johnny Mack is surprised by Jack Ingram as villain Ed LeSaint and his gang are ready for action in this scene from **Frontier Feud** (1945, Monogram). Courtesy of Jerry Ohlinger's Movie Material Store.)

Director . . . . .Wallace Fox
Producer . . . . Eddie Davis
Screenplay . . . . .Adele Buffington
Photography . . . . .Harry Neumann
Film Editor . . . . John C. Fuller
Music Director . . . . Edward J. Kay
Cast
Johnny Mack Brown . . . . Johnny
Max Terhune . . . . Alibi
Riley Hill . . . . .Joe Gordon
Jane Adams . . . . Judy Gordon
Steve Clark . . . . Dusty
Marshal Bradford . . . . Paul Gordon
Hugh Prosser . . . . .Laren
Marshall Reed .Frank
Constance Worth . . . . Annie
James H. Harrison . . . . .Bill
Terry Frost . . . . .Carl
William H. Ruhl . . . . Curly
Myron Healey .Gus
Milburn Morante . . . . Jenkins

John Merton .Blacksmith
Dee Cooper . . . . .Cook
Chuck Roberson . . . . Jones
Bill Potter . . . . .Bob
Lane Bradford

145. WEST OF WYOMING

Copyrighted . . . . .February 19, 1950
Distributor . . . . Monogram
Length . . . . .57 Minutes
Director .Wallace W. Fox
Producer . . . . Eddie Davis
Screenplay . . . . .Adele Buffington
Photography . . . . .Harry Neumann
Film Editor . . . . .John C. Fuller
Cast
Johnny Mack Brown . . . . Johnny
Gail Davis . . . . .Jennifer
Myron Healey . . . . .Brody
Dennis Moore . . . . Dorsey

Johnny Mack stops a fight between Dennis Moore and Jack Ingram as Raymond Hatton and Terry Frost look on in **Frontier Feud** (1945, Monogram). (Courtesy of Jerry Ohlinger's Movie Material Store.)

Stanley Andrews . . . . Simon
Milburn Morante . . . . .Panhandle
Mary Gordon . . . . Nora
Carl Mathews . . . . .Ray
Paul Cramer . . . . Terry
John Merton . . . . Sheriff
Holly Bane (Mike Regan) . . . . Chuck
Steve Clark . . . . .Dalton
Frank McCarroll
Bud Osborne

146. OVER THE BORDER

Copyrighted . . . . .March 5, 1950
Distributor . . . . Monogram
Length . . . . .58 Minutes
Director/Producer . . . . Wallace Fox
Screenplay . . . . .J. Benton Cheney
Photography . . . . .Harry Neumann
Film Editor . . . . .John C. Fuller

Cast

Johnny Mack Brown . . . . Johnny Mack
Myron Healey .Jeff Grant
Marshall Reed . . . . .Bart Calhoun
Mike Regan . . . . .Duke Winslow
House Peters, Jr. . . . . Wade Shelton
Wendy Waldron . . . . .Tess Malloy
Pierre Watkin . . . . Rand Malloy
Hank Bell . . . . .Sheriff
George Denormand . . . . Tucker
Milburn Morante . . . . Mason
Frank Jaquet . . . . .Doc Foster
Buck Bailey . . . . .Ford
George Seward . . . . .Stage Driver
Carol Henry . . . . Stage Guard
Frank McCarroll . . . . .Carl
Bud Osborne . . . . Stableman
Herman Hack
Ray Jones
Artie Ortego
Bob Woodward

Johnny Mack ties up one of the villains in **Frontier Feud** (1945, Monogram). (Courtesy of Jerry Ohlinger's Movie Material Store.)

147. SIX GUN MESA

Copyrighted . . . . .April 30, 1950
Distributor . . . . Monogram
Length . . . . .61 Minutes
Director .Wallace Fox
Producer . . . . Eddie Davis
Screenplay . . . . .Adele Buffington
Photography . . . . Harry Neumann, ASC
Film Editor . . . . .John C. Fuller
Musical Director . . . . Edward Kay
Assistant Director . . . . Harry O. Jones
Sound Technician . . . . John Kean
Set Dresser . . . . Vin Taylor
Set Continuity . . . . .Grace Baughman

Cast

Johnny Mack Brown . . . . .Johnny
Milburn Morante . . . . .Whiskey
Gail Davis . . . . .Lynn
Steve Clark . . . . .Jones
Carl Mathews .Joe Land

Bud Osborne . . . . .Marshall
Leonard Penn . . . . Carson
George DeNormand . . . . Steve
Riley Hill . . . . .Dave Emmett
Marshall Reed . . . . Bradley
Stanley Blystone . . . . .Mullins
Frank Jaquet
Artie Ortego
Merrill McCormick
Holly Bane

148. LAW OF THE PANHANDLE

Copyrighted . . . . September 17, 1950
Distributor . . . . Monogram
Length . . . . .55 Minutes
Director .Lewis Collins
Producer . . . . Jerry Thomas
Screenplay . . . . Joseph Poland
Photography . . . . .Harry Neumann
Film Editor . . . . .William Austin

198

Johnny Mack and Raymond Hatton get the drop on two masked bandits in **Frontier Feud** (1945, Monogram). (Courtesy of Jerry Ohlinger's Movie Material Store.)

Cast

Johnny Mack Brown	Johnny Mack
Jane Adams	.Margie Kendall
Riley Hill	Tom Stocker
Marshall Reed	Rance
Myron Healey	Henry Faulkner
Ted Adams	Ezra Miller
Kermit Maynard	Luke Winslow
Bob Duncan	.Evans
Boyd Stockman	
George DeNormand	
Tex Palmer	
Ray Jones	

149. OUTLAW GOLD

Copyrighted	November 26, 1950
Distributor	Monogram
Length	.51 Minutes
Director	.Wallace Fox
Producer	Vincent M. Fennelly
Screenplay	.Jack Lewis

Photography	Gilbert Warrenton
Film Editor	Fred Maguire

Cast

Johnny Mack Brown	Dave Willis
Jane Adams	.Kathy
Myron Healey	Sonny Lang
Milburn Morante	.Sandy Barker
Marshall Reed	Jackson
Hugh Prosser	.Brigsley
Carol Henry	.Joe
Bud Osborne	Sheriff
George Denormand	.Whitley
Frank Jaquet	
Carl Mathews	
Ray Jones	
Steve Clark	
Bob Woodward	
Merrill McCormick	

150. SHORT GRASS

Copyrighted	December 24, 1950

Johnny Mack separates Dennis Moore and Jack Ingram as they appear ready to draw. Raymond Hatton looks on in **Frontier Feud** (1945, Monogram). (Courtesy of Jerry Ohlinger's Movie Material Store.)

Distributor .Allied Artists
Length . . . . .82 Minutes
Director . . . . .Lesley Selander
Producer . . . . Scott R. Dunlap
Screenplay . . . . .Tom Blackburn
From the Novel . . . . Tom Blackburn
Photography . . . . .Harry Neumann
Film Editor . . . . Otho Lovering
Songs . . . . Edward J. Kay

Cast

Rod Cameron . . . . .Steve
Cathy Downs . . . . .Sharon
Johnny Mack Brown . . . . Keown
Raymond Walburn . . . . .McKenna
Alan Hale, Jr. . . . . .Chris
Morris Ankrum . . . . Hal Fenton
Jonathan Hale . . . . Bissell
Harry Woods . . . . Dreen
Marion Dwyer . . . . Jennie
Riley Hill . . . . .Randee
Jeff York . . . . Curly
Stanley Andrews . . . . Pete

Jack Ingram . . . . .Jack
Myron Healey . . . . .Les
Tris Coffin . . . . John Devore
Rory Mallinson . . . . Jim Westfall
Felipe Turich . . . . Manuel
George J. Lewis . . . . Diego
Lee Tung Fong . . . . Lin
Kermit Maynard

151. COLORADO AMBUSH

Copyrighted . . . . .January 14, 1951
Distributor . . . . Monogram
Length . . . . .51 Minutes
Director . . . . .Lewis Collins
Producer . . . . Vincent M. Fennelly
Screenplay . . . . .Myron Healey
Photography . . . . Gilbert Warrenton
Film Editor . . . . Fred Maguire

Cast

Johnny Mack Brown . . . . Johnny
Myron Healey . . . . Chet Murdock

Johnny Mack restrains Dennis Moore from fighting with villain Ed LeSaint in **Frontier Feud** (1945, Monogram). (Courtesy of Jerry Ohlinger's Movie Material Store.)

Lois Hall . . . . Janet Williams
Tommy Farrell . . . . Terry Williams
Christine McIntyre . . . . Mae Star
Lee Roberts . . . . Gus
Marshall Bradford . . . . B. Williams
Lyle Talbot . . . . Sheriff Ed Lowery

152. MAN FROM SONORA

Copyrighted . . . . .March 11, 1951
Distributor . . . . Monogram
Length . . . . .54 Minutes
Director . . . . .Lewis Collins
Producer . . . . Vincent M. Fennelly
Screenplay . . . . .Maurice Tombragel
Photography . . . . Gilbert Warrenton
Film Editor . . . . .Fred McGuire
Assistant Director . . . . .Melville Shyer
Musical Director . . . . Edward Kay
Sound Recording . . . . .John Carter
Art Director . . . . Fred Preble

Settings . . . . .Harry Reif
Set Continuity . . . . Polly Craus

Cast

Johnny Mack Brown . . . . . Johnny Mack Brown
Phyllis Coates . . . . Cinthy Allison
Lyle Talbot . . . . .Sheriff
House Peters, Jr. . . . . .Ed Hooper
Lee Roberts . . . . Duke
John Merton . . . . Pete
Stanley Price . . . . .Spence
Dennis Moore . . . . .Carrol
Ray Jones
Pierce Lyden
Sam Flint
George DeNormand

153. BLAZING BULLETS

Copyrighted . . . . May 6, 1951
Distributor . . . . Monogram
Length . . . . .51 Minutes

Johnny Mack covers Jack Ingram while Dennis Moore, Raymond Hatton and Sheriff Jack Rockwell watch in **Frontier Feud** (1945, Monogram). (Courtesy of Jerry Ohlinger's Movie Material Store.)

Director . . . . .Wallace Fox
Producer . . . . Vincent M. Fennelly
Screenplay . . . . George Daniels
Photography . . . . Gilbert Warrenton
Film Editor . . . . Fred Maguire
Assistant Director . . . . .Melville Shyer
Musical Director . . . . .Ozzie Caswell
Sound Recording . . . . .John R. Carter
Art Director . . . . Fred Preble
Settings . . . . .Harry Reif
Set Continuity . . . . Polly Craus

Cast

Johnny Mack Brown . . . . . Johnny Mack Brown
Lois Hall . . . . Carol Hawkins
House Peters, Jr. . . . . Bill Grant
Stanley Price .Hawkins
Dennis Moore . . . . Crowley
Edmund Cobb .Sheriff
Milburn Morante . . . . Andy
Forrest Taylor . . . . .John Roberts
Edward Cassidy

George DeNormand
Carl Mathews

154. MONTANA DESPERADO

Copyrighted . . . . June 24, 1951
Distributor . . . . Monogram
Length . . . . .51 Minutes
Director . . . . .Wallace Fox
Producer . . . . Vincent M. Fennelly
Screenplay .Dan Ullman
Photography . . . . Gilbert Warrenton
Film Editor . . . . Fred Maguire

Cast

Johnny Mack Brown . . . . Dave Borden
Virginia Herrick . . . . Sally Wilson
Myron Healey . . . . .Ron Logan
Marshall Reed . . . . .Hal Jackson
Steve Clark . . . . .The Sheriff
Edmund Cobb . . . . Jim Berry
Lee Roberts . . . . Jackson

Johnny Mack and Raymond Hatton capture villains Steve Clark and Douglas Evans in **Crossed Trails** (1948, Monogram). (Courtesy of Jerry Ohlinger's Movie Material Store.)

Carl Mathews
Ben Corbett

155. OKLAHOMA JUSTICE

Copyrighted . . . . .August 19, 1951
Distributor . . . . Monogram
Length . . . . .56 Minutes
Director .Lewis Collins
Producer . . . . Vincent M. Fennelly
Screenplay . . . . Joseph O'Donnell
Photography . . . . Ernest Miller, ASC
Film Editor . . . . Sam Fields
Assistant Director . . . . .Melville Shyer
Sound Recorder . . . . .Charles Cooper
Script Director . . . . .Mary Chaffee
Settings . . . . .Harry Reif
Art Director . . . . David Milton
Musical Director . . . . Raoul Kraushaar
Cast
Johnny Mack Brown . . . . . Johnny Mack Brown

James Ellison . . . . .Clancy
Phyllis Coates . . . . .Goldie
Barbara Woodell . . . . Ma Posey
Kenne Duncan .Sheriff
Lane Bradford . . . . Deuce
Marshall Reed . . . . Blackie
Zon Murray . . . . Tad
Stanley Price . . . . .Bartender
I. Stanford Jolley . . . . .Fleming
Bruce Edwards . . . . .Jim Redding
Richard Avonde
Carl Mathews
Edward Cassidy
Lyle Talbot
George DeNormand

156. WHISTLING HILLS

Copyrighted . . . . October 7, 1951
Distributor . . . . Monogram
Length . . . . .58 Minutes

Johnny Mack talks with villain Douglas Evans while Kathy Frye and Raymond Hatton listen in **Crossed Trails** (1948, Monogram). (Courtesy of Jerry Ohlinger's Movie Material Store.)

Director . . . . Derwin Abrahams
Producer . . . . Vincent M. Fennelly
Screenplay . . . . Fred Myton
From a Story . . . . Jack Lewis
Photography . . . . Ernest Miller
Film Editor . . . . Sammy Fields
Cast
Johnny Mack Brown . . . . Johnny
James Ellison . . . . Dave Holland
Noel Neill . . . . Beth Fairchild
Lee Roberts . . . . Slade
I. Stanford Jolley . . . . Chet Norman
Marshall Reed . . . . Claine
Lane Bradford . . . . .Cassidy
Pamela Duncan . . . . .Cora
Bud Osborne . . . . Pete
Pierce Lyden
Frank Ellis
Ray Jones
Merrill McCormick

157. TEXAS LAWMEN
(aka **Lone Star Lawmen**)

Copyrighted . . . . .December 2, 1951
Distributor . . . . Monogram
Length . . . . .53 Minutes
Director . . . . .Lewis Collins
Producer . . . . Vincent M. Fennelly
Screenplay . . . . .Joseph Poland
Based upon a Story . . . . .Myron Healey
Photography . . . . Ernest Miller
Film Editor . . . . Sammy Fields
Cast
Johnny Mack Brown . . . . Johnny
James Ellison . . . . Sheriff Tod
I. Stanford Jolley . . . . .Bart Morrow
Lee Roberts . . . . Steve Morrow
Lane Bradford . . . . .Mason
Marshall Reed .Potter
John Hart
Lyle Talbot

Kathy Fyre shows off her new dress to Lynne Carver as Johnny Mack and Raymond Hatton study the situation in **Crossed Trails** (1948, Monogram). (Courtesy of Jerry Ohlinger's Movie Material Store.)

Pierce Lyden
Stanley Price
Terry Frost

158. TEXAS CITY

Copyrighted . . . . .January 27, 1952
Distributor . . . . Monogram
Length . . . . .54 Minutes
Director . . . . .Lewis Collins
Producer . . . . Vincent M. Fennelly
Screenplay . . . . Joseph Poland
Photography . . . . Ernest Miller
Film Editor . . . . Sam Fields
Cast
Johnny Mack Brown . . . . Johnny
Jimmy Ellison . . . . .Jim Kirby
Lois Hall . . . . .Lois
Lorna Thayer . . . . .Aunt Harriet
Lane Bradford . . . . .Hank
Marshall J. Reed . . . . Varnell

Terry L. Frost . . . . .Crac
Pierce Lyden .Markham
Lennie (Bud) Osborne . . . . Birk
John Hart . . . . First Sergeant
Stanley Price . . . . Second Sergeant
Lyle Talbot . . . . .Hamilton

159. MAN FROM THE BLACK HILLS

Copyrighted . . . . .March 30, 1952
Distributor . . . . Monogram
Length . . . . .57 Minutes
Director . . . . Thomas Carr
Producer . . . . Vincent M. Fennelly
Screenplay . . . . Joseph O'Donnell
Photography . . . . Ernest Miller
Film Editor . . . . Sam Fields
Cast
Johnny Mack Brown . . . . Johnny
James Ellison . . . . .Jim Fallon
Randy Brooks . . . . .Jimmy Fallon

Johnny Mack gives testimony about Raymond Hatton's long barrelled pistol in **Crossed Trails** (1948, Monogram). (Courtesy of Jerry Ohlinger's Movie Material Store.)

Lane Bradford . . . . .Sheriff Moran
I. Stanford Jolley . . . . Pete Ingram
Robert Bray .Ed Roper
Stanley Price . . . . Shelby
Denver Pyle . . . . .Hartley
Ray Bennett . . . . .Hugh Delany
Joel Allen . . . . Bates
Stanley Andrews . . . . .Pop Fallon
Florence Lake . . . . .Martha

160. DEAD MAN'S TRAIL

Copyrighted . . . . June 22, 1952
Distributor . . . . Monogram
Length . . . . .59 Minutes
Director . . . . .Lewis Collins
Producer . . . . Vincent M. Fennelly
Screenplay . . . . Joseph Poland
Photography . . . . Ernest Miller
Film Editor . . . . Sam Fields
Assistant Director . . . . .Melville Shyer

Dialogue Director . . . . Stanley Price
Script Supervisor . . . . Eleanor Donahoe
Sound Recorder . . . . Frank Webster
Wardrobe . . . . Eugene Martin

Cast

Johnny Mack Brown . . . . . Johnny Mack Brown
James Ellison . . . . .Dan
Barbara Allen . . . . Mrs. Winslow
Lane Bradford . . . . Brad
I. Stanford Jolley . . . . .Sheriff
Terry Frost . . . . .Kelvin
Gregg Barton . . . . Yeager
Dale Van Sickel . . . . .Walt
Richard Avonde . . . . .Stewart
Stanley Price . . . . Blake

161. CANYON AMBUSH

Copyrighted . . . . October 12, 1952
Distributor . . . . Monogram
Length . . . . .53 Minutes

Kathy Fyre shows Johnny Mack that she can handle a gun in this scene from **Crossed Trails** (1948, Monogram). (Courtesy of Jerry Ohlinger's Movie Materials Store.)

Director . . . . .Lewis Collins
Producer . . . . Vincent M. Fennelly
Screenplay . . . . Joseph Poland
Photography . . . . Ernest Miller, ASC
Film Editor . . . . Sam Fields
Assistant Director . . . . .Melville Shyer
Sound Recorder . . . . .John Kean
Dialogue Director . . . . Stanley Price
Script Supervisor . . . . Emilie Ehrlich
Cast
Johnny Mack Brown . . . . . Johnny Mack Brown
Phyllis Coates . . . . Marian Gaylord
Lee Roberts . . . . .Sheriff Bob Conway
Denver Pyle . . . . Tom Carlton
Dennis Moore . . . . .Henry Lockwood
Hugh Prosser . . . . George Millarde
Marshall Reed . . . . .Macklin
Pierce Lyden . . . . .Brackett
Stanley Price . . . . Hodge
Frank Ellis
Bill Koontz

Russ Whiteman
Carol Henry
George DeNormand

162. THE MARSHAL'S DAUGHTER

Copyrighted . . . . May 21, 1953
Distributor . . . . United Artists
Length . . . . .71 Minutes
Director .William Berke
Producer . . . . Ken Murray
Screenplay .Bob Duncan
Photography . . . . .Jack McKenzie
Songs: Marjorie, Thrasher, Jimmy Wakely, Jack Rivers, Stan Jones, Ken Murray
Cast
Laurie Anders . . . . Laurie Dawson
Hoot Gibson . . . . .Ben Dawson
Ken Murray . . . . Sliding Bill Murray
Harry Lauter . . . . Russ Mason
Bob (Robert) Bray . . . . Anderson

Johnny Mack, Lynne Carver and Kathy Fyre appear to be interested in something in this scene from **Crossed Trails** (1948, Monogram). (Courtesy of Jerry Ohlinger's Movie Material Store.)

Bob Duncan	Trigger Gans
Forrest Taylor	Uncle Jed
Tom London	Sheriff Flynn
Bruce Norman	Little Boy
Cecile Elliott	Miss Tiddleford
Betty Lou Waters	Miss Bolton
Francis Ford	Grandpa
Julian Lipton	Brad
Ted Jordan	Angie
Lee Phelps	Sheriff Barnes
Harry Harvey	Bartender
Danny Duncan	Drunk
Bob Gross	Frenchie

Guest Stars

Preston Foster
Johnny Mack Brown
Jimmy Wakely
Buddy Baer

163. THE BOUNTY KILLER

Released	1965
Distributor	Embassy
Length	92 Minutes, Technicolor, Techniscope
Director	Spencer Gordon Bennet
Producer	Alex Gordon
Screenplay	W. R. Alexander, Leo Gordon
Photography	Frederick West
Film Editor	Ronald Sinclair

Cast

Dan Duryea	Willie Duggan
Rod Cameron	Jimmy Liam
Audrey Dalton	Carole
Richard Arlen	Ridgeway
Buster Crabbe	Mike Clayman
Fuzzy Knight	Luther
Johnny Mack Brown	Sheriff Green
Peter Duryea	Youth
Bob Steele	Red
Eddie Quillen	Pianist

Here is a photo of a Hollywood Football Team. (Courtesy of John Arnold.) See how many stars you can identify?

Norman Willis	Hank Willis
Edmund Cobb	Townsman
Duane Amont	Ben Liam
Grady Sutton	Minister
Emory Parnell	Sam
Daniel J. White	Marshal Davis
I. Stanford Jolley	Sheriff Jones
John Reach	Jeb
Red Morgan	Seldon
Delores Delano	Waitress
Dudley Ross	Indian
Ronn Delano	Joe
Tom Kennedy	Waiter

164. REQUIEM FOR A GUNFIGHTER

Released	1965
Distributor	Embassy
Length	91 Minutes, Technicolor, Techniscope
Director	Spencer Gordon Bennet
Producer	Alex Gordon
Screenplay	R. Alexander
Based upon a Story	Evans W. Cornell, Gary J. Tedesco
Photography	Frederick E. West
Film Editor	Charles H. Powell

Cast

Rod Cameron	Dave McCloud
Stephen McNally	Red Zimmer
Chet Douglas	Larry Young
Mike Mazurki	Ivy Bliss
Tim McCoy	Judge Irving Short
Johnny Mack Brown	Enkoff
Chris Hughes	Billy Parker
Olive Sturgess	Bonnie Young
Lane Chandler	Bryan Comer
Bob Steele	Max
Raymond Hatton	Hoops
Dick Jones	Fletcher
Rand Brooks	Gentry
Dale Van Sickel	Kelly
Doris Spiegel	

Johnny Mack seems to be taking an interest in heroine Reno Browne as Max Terhune looks amused in **West of Eldorado** (1949, Monogram). (Courtesy of Bobby Copeland.)

Zon Murray
Frank Lackteen
Ronn Delanor
Edmund Cobb
Margo Williams
Dick Alexander
Fred Carson
Red Morgan

165. APACHE UPRISING

Copyrighted . . . . .December 29, 1965
Distributor . . . . .Paramount
Length . . . . 90 Minutes, Technicolor
Director . . . . .R. G. Springsteen
Producer . . . . .A. C. Lyles
Screenplay . . . . Harry Sanford, Max Lamb
Based upon a Novel . . "Way Station" by Harry Sanford, Max Steeber
Photography . . . . .Wallace Kelley
Film Editor . . . . .John Schreyer
Songs . . . . .Jimmie Hashell

Cast

Rory Calhoun . . . . .Jim Walker
Corinne Calvet . . . . .Janice MacKenzie
John Russell . . . . .Vance Buckner
Lon Chaney, Jr. . . . . .Charlie Russell
Gene Evans . . . . .Jess Cooney
Richard Arlen . . . . .Captain Gannon
Robert H. Harris . . . . Hoyt Taylor
Arthur Hunnicutt . . . . Bill Gibson
Deforest Kelly . . . . .Toby Jack Saunders
George Chandler . . . . Jack Asher
Jean Parker . . . . .Mrs. Hawkes
Johnny Mack Brown . . . . .Sheriff Ben Hall
Donald Barry . . . . .Henry Belden
Abel Fernandez . . . . Young Apache
Robert Carricart . . . . Chico Lopez
Paul Daniel . . . . .Old Antone

References:

ADAMS, Les and RAINEY, Buck. *Shoot-Em Ups*. New York: Arlington House, 1978.

HARDY, Phil. *The Western*. New York: William Morrow and Co., 1983.

_____. The Hollywood Reporter. Hollywood, California, August 12, 1939: December 11, 1940; July 8, 1941; May 23, 1943.

MENDALL, Ronald L. and PHARES, Timothy B. *Who's Who in Football*. New York: Arlington House, 1974.

MILLER, Don. *Hollywood Corral*. New York: Popular Library, 1976.

_____. The New York Times. "Sports": January 2, 1926; "Obituary": November 16, 1974: "Film Reviews": May 6, 1931.

_____. *The New York Times Film Reviews*. New York: Arno Press, 1971.

PARRISH, James Robert. *Great Western Stars*. New York: Ace Books, 1976.

SMITH, Richard B., III. Unpublished Filmography of Johnny Mack Brown.

_____. Variety: Tuesday, November 7, 1933; Wednesday, September 29, 1937; Tuesday, September 20, 1932.

WEISS, Ken, and GOODGOLD, Ed. *To Be Continued...* New York: Crown Publishers, 1972.

Johnny Mack Brown and Nell O'Day were co-starred in many Universal westerns in the late 30s. (Courtesy of Bobby Copeland.)